The Beaverkill
The History of a River and Its People

2ND EDITION, REVISED AND UPDATED

Oct. 2019

To President Carter
With best wishes
Ed Van Put

The Beaverkill

The History of a River and Its People

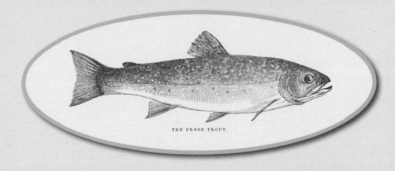

THE BROOK TROUT.

2ND EDITION, REVISED AND UPDATED

Ed Van Put

STACKPOLE
BOOKS

For my mother, Agnes Van Put,
in celebration of her 100th birthday.

Published by
STACKPOLE BOOKS
5067 Ritter Road
Mechanicsburg, PA 17055
www.stackpolebooks.com

Printed in the United States of America

10 9 8 7 6 5 4 3 2 1

Second edition

Photo on p. ii by Richard Franklin
Photos by the author except where noted

Library of Congress Cataloging-in-Publication Data

Names: Van Put, Ed, author.
Title: The Beaverkill : the history of a river and its people / Ed Van Put.
Description: 2nd edition, revised and updated. | Mechanicsburg, PA :
   Stackpole Books, 2016. | Includes bibliographical references and index.
Identifiers: LCCN 2015035677 | ISBN 9780811715461
Subjects: LCSH: Trout fishing—New York (State)—Beaver Kill (Ulster
   County-Delaware County) | Beaver Kill (Ulster County-Delaware County, N.Y.)
Classification: LCC SH688.U6 V36 2016 | DDC 799.17/570974734—dc23 LC record
available at http://lccn.loc.gov/2015035677

Contents

Acknowledgments

A great deal of the information gathered for this book was obtained from the weekly newspapers published in the small hamlets of the Catskills and the larger communities along its borders. Newspapers were found in regional libraries, either in their original form, bound into yearly volumes, or on microfilm. In a few instances, volumes were available through newspapers that are still publishing or individuals who owned collections.

Further research was collected through an invaluable service known as interlibrary loan. Rare books, antiquated periodicals, and newspaper microfilm became available close at hand, through local libraries.

Early on, I had the good fortune to meet Catskill historian Alf Evers at the Kingston Area Library, and while our encounters were brief, his advice on research was extremely helpful. He once stated that a good librarian could be of great assistance, and I was fortunate in finding several. I owe a special debt of gratitude to the librarians of Livingston Manor, Walton, and Delhi.

The collecting of material for this book spanned a period of thirty years, and I continue to enjoy great satisfaction when new information is uncovered. I am indebted to my wife, Judy, for getting involved with my project; searching old newspapers and periodicals is tedious, difficult, time-consuming work. There are no shortcuts. It takes countless hours, at times with no useful data gathered, only the satisfaction of knowing your research was thorough.

I extend my gratitude to the following individuals who made my work easier by giving advice and direction, or who allowed access to their photographs, libraries, files, records, and collections: Julie Allen, Dr. Paul D'Amico, the Anglers' Club of New York, Archives of the Archdiocese of New York, Rev. Edward Bader of St. Aloysius Parish in Livingston Manor, the Balsam Lake Club, Irene Barnhart, Jim Elliott, Evelyn Gerow, Joe Purcell, Judie Darbee Smith, Charlotte Steenrod, Delbert Van Etten, Joan and Lee Wulff, and the Historical Societies of Greene and Sullivan Counties. I appreciate the suggestion of Jay Nichols, acquisitions editor, Stackpole Books, to include fly patterns in this edition and his fine photographs of the flies I tied.

Photographs, especially old photographs, are difficult to obtain, and I am grateful to Anisha Arouza, Jean Boyd, Emerson Bouton, Doug Bury, Mary Dette Clark, Jim Elliott, Timothy Foote, Richard Franklin, Francis W. Davis, Bill Goetz, Bob and Alice Jacobson, Barbara Jaffe, Roger Lynker, Dan Myers, Jack Niflot, Ray Pomeroy, Shelly Rusten, Patricia M. Sherwood, Agnes Van Put, Judy Van Put, and Matt Vinceguerra for their contributions.

I also owe a special thank you to Joe Horak, who over the years allowed me to use the copy machines at his law office in Livingston Manor, and to my son Lee for the many hours he spent on technical assistance with the artwork and for his photography.

Author's Note

In this edition of *The Beaverkill*, I expanded my research on the origin of the rainbow trout introduced into the Delaware River and its watershed, which includes the Beaverkill. In recent years, the subject of which strain of rainbows were first introduced in New York State has been taken up by angling authors and fisheries professionals from other states. Their view is that the first rainbow trout sent to Seth Green at the Caledonia hatchery in 1875 came from the McCloud River in northern California and were from California's San Leandro hatchery, but this is incorrect, as the San Leandro hatchery was not even constructed until 1878.

Additionally, I have spent an inordinate number of hours revisiting the records of the New York State Fish Commission and researching the records of the California Fish Commission, the history of California's hatcheries, and California newspapers during this time period. All written evidence suggests that the rainbow trout sent to Caledonia in 1875 by Dr. Newell, president of the Acclimatization Society of California, to Seth Green were from San Pedro Creek, where the Society maintained their ponds and hatching house. San Pedro Creek is a small, spring-fed stream in the San Francisco Bay Area that contained resident steelhead/rainbow trout and flowed directly into the Pacific Ocean.

Seth Green did not receive McCloud River rainbow eggs until 1878, when they came from the newly constructed San Leandro hatchery. Those trout did not reproduce until 1881, and by that date, the offspring of the rainbows received in 1875 had been stocked in the Beaverkill and Delaware River watershed. McCloud River rainbow trout were not stocked in New York State until 1883.

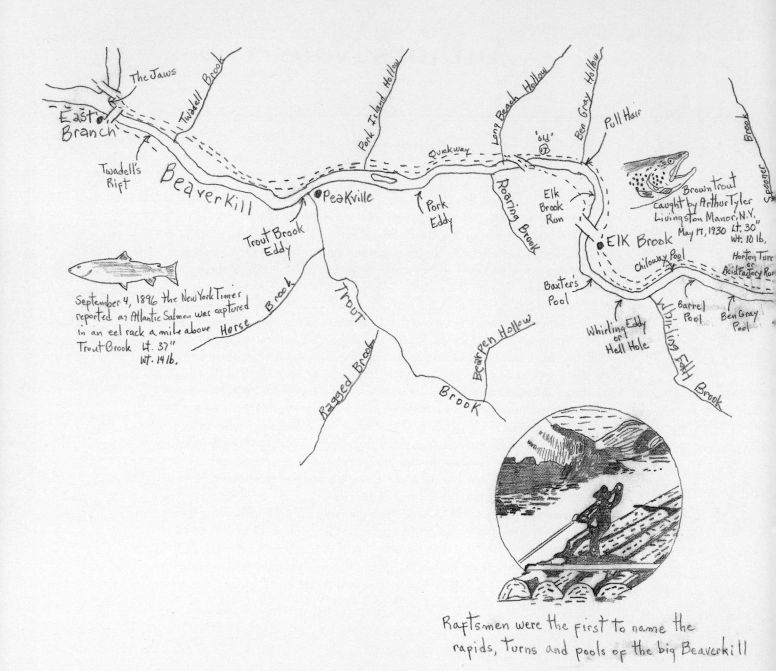

The Jaws

Twadell Brook

East Branch

Twadell's Rift

Beaverkill

Pork Island Hollow

Quickway

Long Beach Hollow

'old' 17

Ben Gray Hollow

Pull Hair

Peakville

Pork Eddy

Roaring Brook

Elk Brook Run

Brown trout caught by Arthur Tyler Livingston Manor, N.Y. May 17, 1930 Lt. 30" Wt. 10 lb.

Spooner Brook

Trout Brook Eddy

Elk Brook

Horton Turn or Acid Factory Run

September 4, 1896 the New York Times reported an Atlantic Salmon was captured in an eel rack a mile above Trout Brook Lt. 37" Wt. 14 lb.

Horse Brook

Trout Brook

Ragged Brook

Bearpen Hollow

Chilousy Pool

Baxter's Pool

Whirling Eddy or Hell Hole

Whirling Fish Brook

Barrel Pool

Ben Gray Pool

Raftsmen were the first to name the rapids, turns and pools of the big Beaverkill

Maps of the Watershed

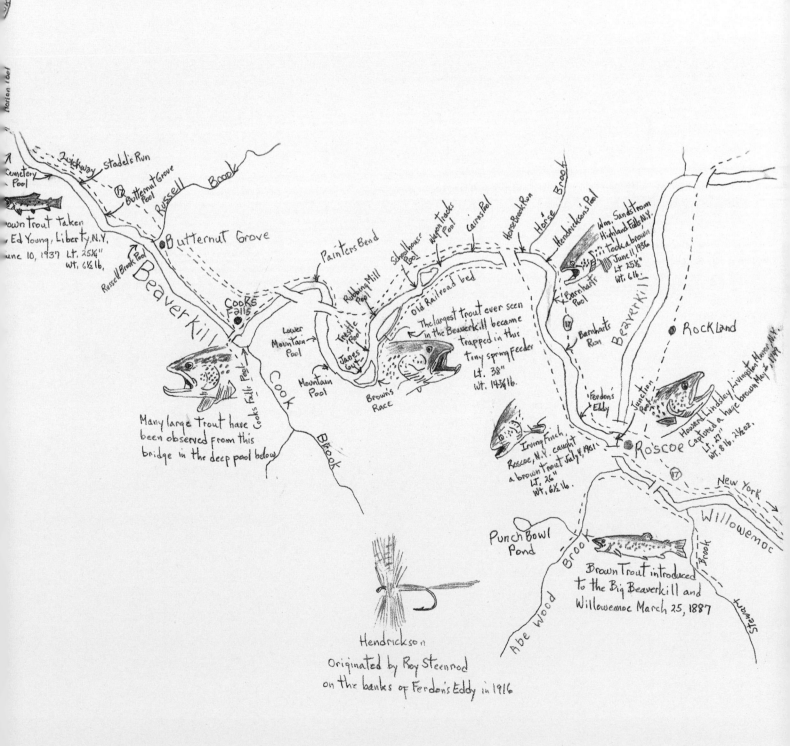

Brown trout taken by Ed Young, Liberty, N.Y. June 10, 1937 Lt. 25¼" Wt. 6½ lb.

Many large trout have been observed from this bridge in the deep pool below

The largest trout ever seen in the Beaverkill became trapped in this tiny spring feeder Lt. 38" Wt. 14¾ lb.

Wm. Sandstrom Highland Falls, N.Y. took a brown June 11, 1936 Lt. 25½" Wt. 6 lb.

Irving Finch, Roscoe, N.Y. caught a brown trout July 8, 1961 Lt. 26" Wt. 6½ lb.

Howard Lindsley Livingston Manor, N.Y. captured a huge brown May 8, 1959 Lt. 27" Wt. 8 lb. 2½ oz.

Brown Trout introduced to the Big Beaverkill and Willowemoc March 25, 1887

Hendrickson
Originated by Roy Steenrod
on the banks of Ferdon's Eddy in 1916

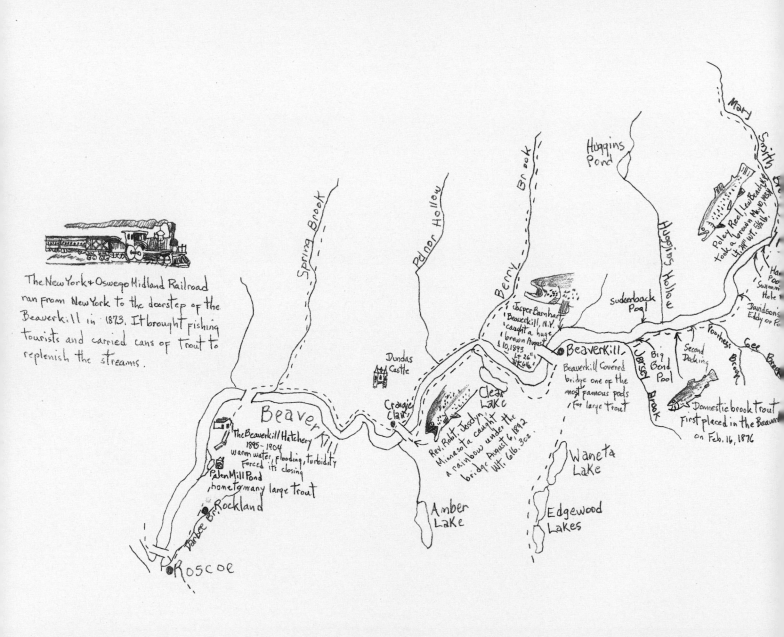

The New York & Oswego Midland Railroad ran from New York to the doorstep of the Beaverkill in 1873. It brought fishing tourists and carried cans of trout to replenish the streams.

Spring Brook

Palnor Hollow

Brook

Huggins Pond

Huggins Hollow

Mary Smiths

Poley Reel, Lew Beaudry took a brown May or pres. 4'2¼" wt. 5½lb.

Berry

Jasper Barnhart Beaverkill, N.Y. caught a huge brown August 10, 1893 Lt 26" Wt 6lb

Sudderback Pool

Second Decking

Toothess Brook

Gee

Davidson's Eddy or Po

Dundas Castle

Craigie Clair

Clear Lake

Rev. Robt. Josselyn Minnesota caught a rainbow under the bridge August 6, 1892 Wt. 6lb. 3oz.

Beaverkill Beaverkill Covered bridge one of the most famous pools for large trout

Jersey Brook

Big Bend Pool

Domestic brook trout First placed in the Beaverk on Feb. 16, 1876

Beaverkill

The Beaverkill Hatchery 1895–1904 warm water, flooding, turbidity Forced its closing

Palen Mill Pond home to many large trout

Danse Br.

Rockland

Waneta Lake

Amber Lake

Edgewood Lakes

Roscoe

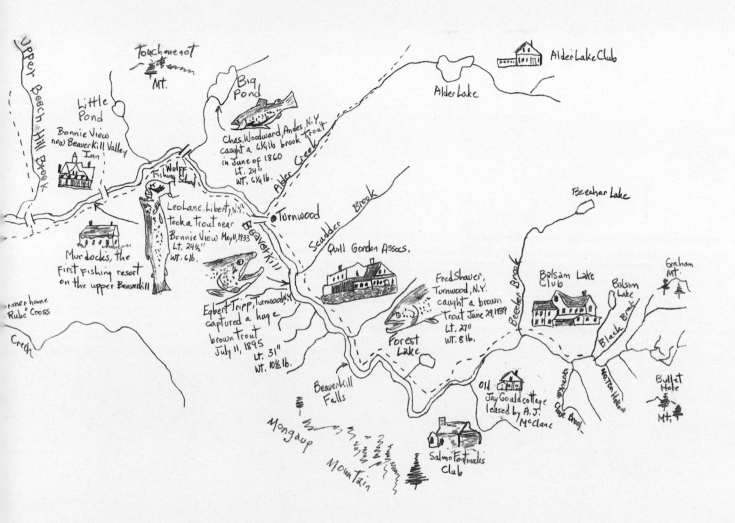

Upper Beech Hill Brook

Touchmenot Mt.

Little Pond

Bonnie View now Beaverkill Valley Inn

Wolff Fishing School

Big Pond

Chas. Woodward, Andes, N.Y. caught a 6¼ lb brook trout in June of 1860 Lt. 24", Wt. 6¼ lb.

Alder Creek

Alder Lake

Alder Lake Club

Leo Lane, Liberty, N.Y. took a trout near Bonnie View May 11, 1933 Lt. 24½", Wt. 6 lb.

Turnwood

Scudder Brook

Beecher Lake

Murdocks, the First Fishing resort on the upper Beaverkill

Beaverkill

Quill Gordon Assocs.

Fred Shaver, Turnwood, N.Y. caught a brown Trout June 29, 1939 Lt. 27", Wt. 8 lb.

Beecher Brook

Balsam Lake Club

Graham Mt.

Balsam Lake

former home "Rube" Cross

Egbert Tripp, Turnwood, N.Y. captured a huge brown trout July 11, 1895 Lt. 31", Wt. 10½ lb.

Forest Lake

Black Brook

Creek

Beaverkill Falls

Mongaup Mountain

Old Jay Gould cottage leased by A. J. McClane

Clear Brook

Mattenhollow

Bullet Hole Mt.

Salmo Fontinalis Club

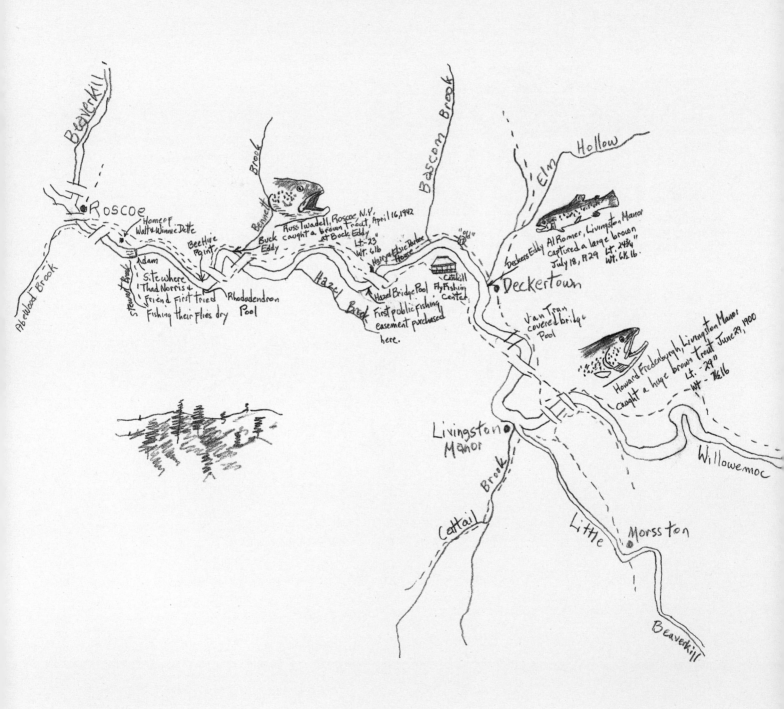

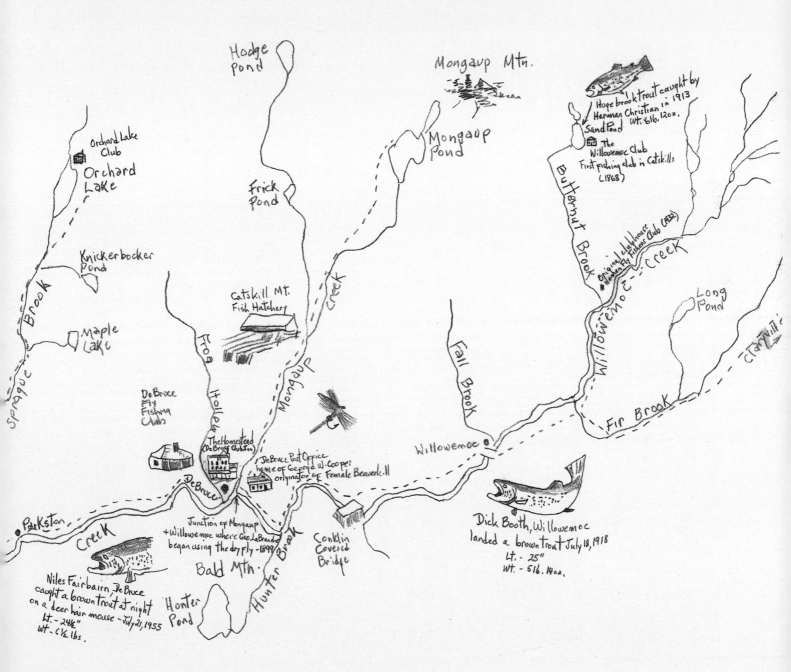

Hodge Pond

Mongaup Mtn.

Hoge brook trout caught by
Herman Christian in 1913
Wt. 6 lb. 12 oz.

Sand Pond

The
Willowemoc Club
First fishing club in Catskills
(1868)

Mongaup Pond

Orchard Lake Club

Orchard Lake

Frick Pond

Original clubhouse
Willowemoc Flyfishers Club (1870)

Butternut Brook

Knickerbocker Pond

Catskill Mt. Fish Hatchery

Willowemoc Creek

Long Pond

Sprague Brook

Maple Lake

Frog Hollow

Mongaup Creek

Fall Brook

Fir Brook

Claryville

DeBruce Fly Fishing Club

The Homestead (DeBruce Club Inn)

DeBruce Post Office
home of George W. Cooper
originator of Female Beaverkill

Willowemoc

DeBruce

Parkston

Creek

Junction of Mongaup
+ Willowemoc where Geo. LaBranche
began using the dry fly - 1899

Conklin Covered Bridge

Dick Booth, Willowemoc
landed a brown trout July 18, 1918
Lt. - 25"
Wt. - 5 lb. 14 oz.

Bald Mtn.

Hunter Pond

Hunter Brook

Niles Fairbairn, DeBruce
caught a brown trout at night
on a deer hair mouse - July 21, 1955
Lt. - 24½"
Wt. - 6½ lbs.

America's Stream

To a great many fly fishers, the Beaverkill is the standard by which all other trout streams are judged. It is first and oldest in reputation. Heralded as the cradle of fly fishing in America, the Beaverkill is known all over the world, wherever men and women fly fish for trout. Even before sporting periodicals and angling books began recording the history of American fly fishing, the Beaverkill's fame was well established. Steeped in tradition and lore, the stream was the favorite of many of our earliest and most gifted anglers.

Down through the decades, countless men have learned the art of fly fishing along its banks, and bonded with the Beaverkill. Many became regulars, forming a brotherhood that not only fished its waters but also acted as guardians, preserving its fisheries and protecting the stream from would-be despoilers. Angling writers, too, have enjoyed an intimate relationship with the stream, and its reputation has been furthered not by one but by every generation of our best-known and most talented fishing journalists. The Beaverkill, with its storied pools such as Barnhart's, Hendrickson's, and Cairns, is as familiar to fly fishermen as Brahms, Bach, and Beethoven are to music lovers. And just as football fans view the Dallas Cowboys as "America's team," trout-fishing enthusiasts look upon the Beaverkill as "America's stream."

Perhaps some streams have more natural beauty—in some the trout grow larger and are more abundant—but the Beaverkill is revered by fly fishermen, in much the same manner as Cooperstown is revered by baseball fans. To wade and cast a fly in waters where fly-fishing immortals have before them can be likened to taking the mound at Fenway or roaming center field at Yankee Stadium.

Fly fishers come from across the land, as if on a pilgrimage, to walk the well-worn streamside paths, and to fish and

The source of the Beaverkill is found at an elevation of approximately three thousand feet between Graham and Doubletop mountains in the Catskills.

stand in the pools and shadows of the legendary anglers. Corey Ford, in a fine article titled, appropriately, "The Best-Loved Trout Stream of Them All," expressed these thoughts as well as anyone:

> Watch your back cast; the ghosts of a hundred departed anglers are standing behind you. That pool you are entering was once the favorite fishing hole of John Taintor Foote. Ted Townsend used to perch atop that very rock on which you are standing now. Perhaps Theodore Gordon dropped his first Quill over that small dark eddy where you have just cast your fly . . .
>
> A trout stream is more than the fish in it. A great trout stream like the Beaverkill is a legend, a fly book filled with memories, a part of the lives of all the devoted anglers, living or dead, who ever held a taut line in its current.

The source of the Beaverkill is found deep in the forest of the Catskills, far from any road, in a narrow, rocky ravine between the mountains Graham and Doubletop. The elevation is 2,900 feet, and even though there is very little soil, beech, birch, and maple dominate the landscape; their roots reach down, through, and over an indefinite number of gray-colored rocks that clog the narrow pass. Though all of the rocks are of varying grayish hues, some are obvious in that they wear robes of bright green moss, marking a barely discernable stream flow. Water as clear as the finest crystal seeps under these mossy rocks, nourishing their velvety emerald clusters—this is where the celebrated Beaverkill is born, and its growth begins.

At first the water appears motionless, lying in a series of diminutive shallow pools. But gravity forces it along, forming a tiny rill that takes on the appearance of a pristine mountain spring. The spring runs only a few hundred feet before flowing into an ancient beaver meadow, where pools and riffles are formed, and the cold, clean, well-oxygenated water becomes the home of native brook trout.

Traveling down through the forest, the stream receives additional water from every hollow and glen, from other springs and tributary feeders. The waters flow in a general westerly direction, and by the time the Beaverkill reaches Alder Creek, a dozen miles later, it widens, and the mountain stream has become a little river. It continues westerly until reaching the base of Touchmenot Mountain, where it turns southwesterly and flows, uninterrupted, an additional 14 miles to where its waters join Willowemoc Creek.

This uniting with the Willowemoc doubles the Beaverkill's size, turning it into a large river. Its pools are large and deep, its riffle areas lengthy; before meeting the East Branch of the Delaware River, the Beaverkill widens to over 200 feet. The stream's gradient changes dramatically over the last 15 miles, from a drop of 56 feet per mile to approximately 19 feet per mile. The lower Beaverkill becomes so wide that even the tallest, most mature trees are unable to adequately shade it from bright sunlight, which warms its waters. Water temperatures at times rise above those preferred by trout, and in years of drought, flows are greatly reduced. The first 5 miles of the river have only one small cold-water tributary.

The Beaverkill trout fishery is largely dependent on upstream environmental conditions—notably, the clean, cold water that flows through and over semipermeable soils on steep forested slopes, abundant summer precipitation, and gradient sufficient to keep the water moving and oxygenated. Countless springs, numerous lakes and ponds, and more than a hundred tributaries contribute to the flow of the Beaverkill. The drainage area covers approximately 292 square miles and includes 86 classified trout streams that, in addition to providing cold water, serve as spawning grounds for mature trout and nursery habitat for trout fry.

The Beaverkill Valley is narrow and steep-sided throughout its length; floodplains are relatively narrow, and mountain slopes often come right down to the water's edge. Flat- or bottomland is scarce. Mountainsides are densely forested with beech, birch, maple, and, as is often the case in northern hardwood forests, hemlock.

The streambed of the Beaverkill and its tributaries is composed of sand, gravel, fragmented rock, boulders, and bedrock. Some of the best trout habitat is formed where the stream flows over or against bedrock. Water cascading over solid rock creates plunge pools that are deep, fairly stable, and picturesque. This bedrock is of sedimentary origin, and geologists believe that the mountainous region known as the Catskills was formed from the eroding soils of much larger mountains, located in what is now New England and southeastern New York.

Hundreds of millions of years ago, streams flowing from these mountains carried soil, sand, and gravel into a vast

An ancient beaver meadow located near the source of the Beaverkill and the home to abundant numbers of brook trout.

A small beaver dam across the headwaters of the Beaverkill. The stream derived its name from the numerous beaver colonies settlers found along the upper river. Judy Van Put

inland sea, which covered western New York, Pennsylvania, and parts of the Mississippi Valley. This eroding material deposited into a great sinking delta, or alluvial fan. Eventually, as the mountains were worn low, deposits into the delta halted, and rock strata were formed. The strata, piled layer upon layer, accumulated to a thickness of several thousand feet. About 225 million years ago, the delta was uplifted far above sea level to form a plateau. In time, the plateau took on a mountainous form as it was dissected into deep valleys by weathering, stream erosion, and the breakdown of the flat-lying rocks.

A further event in creating the physiography of the Catskills occurred approximately twenty thousand to fifty thousand years ago, when the mountains were completely covered by glaciers. The glaciers reworked the soil, scattering rocks of all sizes and shapes through it. When the ice moved over the landscape, it scraped off the loose soil, sandstone, and rocks, and carried everything in, on, and under the ice. As the ice melted, glacial drift piled up at the ice borders was either carried away by streams coming off the melting ice or spread out as a sheet of till. This glacial till covers much of the region and is composed of an unsorted mixture of clay, sand, silt, and rock fragments of various sizes.

The present form of the mountains is mainly due to the continuing actions of the many streams, which cut narrow valleys into the landscape. All Catskill streams are basically unstable; the glacial till that is found in the area forms fragile banks and forever-changing streambeds. Understandably, banks composed of clay, sand, and unsorted gravel form a loose, erodible soil and collapse quite readily. Streams are steep-gradient, and runoff from rains and melting snow is rapid. Streams rise quickly and overflow their banks often. Flooding is a common occurrence, and erosion is evident on all streams.

2

"The People at the Rising of the Sun"

ollowing deglaciation, an arctic-alpine flora first covered the region. In time, animals such as mammoths and caribou found their way into the area, and approximately thirteen thousand years ago, Paleo-Indians, the first humans to inhabit the Catskills, roamed the valleys in search of these large animals, armed with little more than spears. These Indians grew no crops; their existence depended on gathering whatever wild foods were available, hunting, and fishing.

In time, milder climate allowed the arctic-alpine flora to be replaced by a boreal forest of red spruce, balsam fir, paper birch, and mountain ash. From the south, a northern hardwood forest of beech, birch, maple, and hemlock ascended the mountain slopes and slowly took over, in varying degrees, the boreal forest. (Although hemlock is not a hardwood, it is often associated with this type of forest.)

This largely deciduous forest was similar to the woodlands of the Catskills today. It provided excellent habitat for deer, bear, and a variety of small mammals and birds, especially wild pigeons. Abundant wildlife and seasonal runs of shad formed a food supply for Archaic Indians, who lived in the region until approximately three thousand years ago. At that time, these Indians were replaced by the Woodland Indians, who used bows and arrows instead of spears and, in addition to hunting and fishing, grew crops of corn, beans, and pumpkins along the lowlands bordering the larger streams and rivers.

These were the Indians that Belgian, Dutch, and English settlers encountered when they came to the region. To the English they were known as Delawares, from the name of their principal river; to the French they were Loups, meaning "Wolves"; to other Indian tribes or nations they were known as Wapanachki, or "The People at the Rising of the Sun"—Eastlanders.[1] They, however, preferred to call themselves Lenape or Lenni-Lenape (*Lay nee Lay-na pay*), equivalent to "Real Men" or "Original People."[2] The Lenni-Lenape were said to be honored with the title of "Grandfather" by the nearly forty tribes that descended from them. Being of Algonquian stock, they spoke that language; according to their tradition and oral history handed down by their ancestors, they came from the west many centuries ago.[3]

When the first Europeans visited the waters of the nearby Hudson, the Lenni-Lenape inhabited the land extending from the Catskill Mountains south to the Potomac, occupying all of the region watered by the Delaware, Hudson, Potomac, and Susquehanna Rivers. They were composed of three principal tribes: the Unami, or "Turtle"; the Unalachto, or "Turkey"; and the Minsi, or "Wolf." Minsi also means "People of the Stony Country" or "Mountaineers," and these Indians of the Minsi, or Wolf, tribe were the ones who chose to live along the rivers of the Catskills.[4]

Tribes were often subdivided into groups, which took their names from the places where they lived. Families whose dwellings and cultivated fields were near a river or stream often bore the name of that waterway: for example, the Esopus, Navisings (Neversink), Papagonk (East Branch Delaware), and the Whelenaughwemack, which is what the Indians called the Beaverkill.[5]

The Lenni-Lenape were river Indians who depended on agriculture, hunting, and fishing. While they pursued game, trapped, and traveled watercourses throughout the Catskills, they did not settle in the narrow valleys of the higher elevations. The Lenni-Lenape preferred to live in semipermanent

4

villages along the lower, larger stream or river sections, where travel by canoe was possible and fields could be cultivated in the floodplains. Because of the narrowness of the valley, there were few sites along the Beaverkill that met the needs of the Indians. They were, however, reported to have lived along the flats at what today is called Rockland; at the mouth of Russell Brook (Cooks Falls); and at the mouth of the Beaverkill (the hamlet of East Branch).

It was shad, not trout, that attracted the Indians to the waters of the Beaverkill. Each spring, these anadromous fish traveled hundreds of miles upstream to spawn, just as they do today. Great schools of shad ran up the branches of the Delaware and the Beaverkill and provided an abundant food supply for the Lenni-Lenape. By piling stones from the stream bottom, Indians constructed walls from bank to bank in the shape of a large V, with a narrow opening in the middle. Here, the fish could be forced or driven into a net and speared or taken by pinching, a method in which a split stick was used to pin the fish to the stream bottom. The Indians also made brushwood mats, which they moved along like seines to drive shad and other fish into shallow areas. There the fish were taken by hand or with dip nets. Shad

were cured by drying in the sun or over fires; they were ground and packed in skins for later use; and some were even used as fertilizer.

An interesting method used by the Indians to capture trout involved the bark from the root of the walnut tree. The bark was crushed to a pulp to obtain the juices. This extract was then poured in the riffles at the head of a pool, and when it mixed with the water and was ingested, it drugged and stupefied the trout, causing them to come to the surface, where they were easily collected. Apparently, the use of poison was a popular method in harvesting fish from rivers and streams, especially during periods of low flows. Woodland Indians were known to use the root of a plant called devil's shoestring (*Virburnum alnifolium*), although turnip root and poke berry were also used. Devil's shoestring was a common plant growing on the sandy ridges bordering many eastern streams. Several large posts were driven into the streambed, their tops extending just above the water's surface. The roots that had been gathered were then pulverized with a wooden maul on the tops of the posts. As the mashed roots fell into the water, they exuded their toxins, and the affected fish weakly finned on the surface, gasping for air. Women and

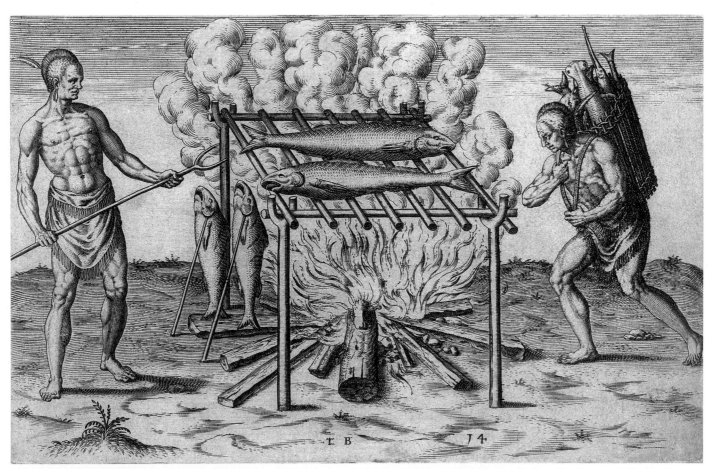

Early Indian method of cooking fish. By piling stones from the stream bottom, Indians constructed walls from bank to bank in the shape of a large V, with a narrow opening in the middle. Here shad, trout, and common suckers were driven into a net or speared for use as food. *Fish, Fishing and Fisheries of Pennsylvania*, 1893

children braved the irritating effect the substance had on their skin and waded downstream to gather the fish.[6]

Riverside settlements were usually small and rarely permanent; when the soil became less productive after years of use, or when nature did not keep up with the needs of the Indians, they moved to other areas where fish and wildlife were plentiful. Of the various groups of Lenni-Lenape that inhabited the area, the Esopus, who resided near present-day Kingston and lower Rondout Creek, were the most numerous. They were of the Minsi, or Wolf, tribe and claimed almost the entire Catskill region stretching from the Hudson to the Delaware as their hunting grounds.

Contact with the Esopus by European traders probably occurred as early as 1609, when Henry Hudson sailed the *Half Moon* up the Hudson River.[7] Over the next few years, explorers and fur traders visited the region, and in 1614 they started small settlements at Fort Nassau (Albany) and Manhattan Island (New York). In 1650 a settlement began at Catskill, and in 1652 another was started along the flats of Esopus Creek at Esopus (Kingston).[8]

In the years that followed, these principal settlements of New York depended greatly on trade with the Indians of the Catskills, and Kingston was the hub for these exchanges: "At this point the three valleys of the Esopus, Rondout and Wallkill converge. Down all these valleys came Indians in the spring with furs and skins to meet the Albany traders."[9]

Furs, especially the highly prized beaver pelts, were traded for brass kettles, steel knives, blankets, firearms, and other items never before seen by the Esopus. Eager for manufactured goods, the Indians quickly decimated the beaver population. They hunted and trapped the animal until it could no longer be found in the Catskills. Even though unlawful, traders often gave the Indians alcohol to get the better of them in a trade. The resulting intoxication caused some of the first conflicts between the Esopus and the early Dutch settlers.

As the number of settlers increased, greater pressure was placed on the Indians to sell or convey their land. The Dutch wished to grow their own crops on the tilled fields used by the Indians, whom they referred to as Kaalebakkers, or "Barebacks." To the Indians, land had no value; the custom of owning or having dominion over the land through words on paper was incomprehensible. The Esopus had no written language, and in their world the land could not be reduced to a private possession. Though not always understood by the Indians, land purchases by the Dutch began in 1652. At that time, European and Indian began living alongside one another—two cultures with vastly different values and philosophies that did not, and could not, live peacefully side by side.

> When there was an abundance with the Indian, they feasted; when scarcity, they starved. They were improvident. When they were in need they saw no reason why they should not help themselves from the stores of provisions of the whites. This the whites resisted. Red men were willing to share their abundance when there was aplenty. If his family were hungry, why should not a red man kill the fat porker of his white neighbor, which he found feasting upon acorns in the forest? If that white man neighbor were out of food, would the Indian not throw into his white brother's door half of the deer which he had killed on his last hunt?[10]

It was not long before the friction between the two races grew and turned to war. In 1659, and again in 1663, armed conflicts were fought, and the Indians suffered many more casualties than the settlers. In addition, hundreds more died from epidemics of smallpox, measles, and other diseases not known to the Esopus. Slowly, steadily, the settlers drove the remaining Indians off the desirable, tillable river bottomlands and forced them into the more inhospitable mountainous areas of the Catskills where they had previously only hunted and fished. Here they lived in huts or shelters built for temporary occupancy.

Some Indians settled along the Papagonk (East Branch) and its tributaries, such as the Whelenaughwemack (Beaverkill), or alongside lakes and ponds. Some went farther west and lived along the Susquehanna River, and still others migrated into Ohio, Indiana, Missouri, and Kansas. Those who stayed wandered about the Catskills, clinging to a way of life they had known for generations.

The last of the Indian lands, their ancient hunting and fishing grounds, would also be taken, incredibly, by a single land transaction with a merchant-trader from Kingston. When New York was under Dutch control, the government at times would grant land in the colony without the formality of buying the land from the Indians. However, when the English took possession of the Dutch holdings in 1665, they insisted on first extinguishing the aboriginal title. It was customary to apply to the governor for leave to purchase; if this was granted, the next step was to secure a deed from the Indians. After a survey, the attorney general was then directed to prepare a draft of a patent, which then went before the governor for approval. In a few cases, grants of land were made directly by the Crown.

On March 22, 1707, Johannes Hardenbergh purchased an immense parcel of land—almost two million acres—from Nanisinos, "an Indian of the Esopus Indians, and rightful owner and proprietor of several parts of land in the County of Ulster."[11] On April 20, 1708, Queen Anne granted a patent to Hardenbergh and six others for the land he had acquired from the Indians. This land included virtually all of the Catskill Mountains, as well as the remaining lands owned by the Esopus. This immense forest of mountains and valleys remained a wilderness as long as it was not divided. When surveyors tried to measure the land, they were met by Indians who were unfriendly and antagonistic, who tried to turn them back, stole their instruments, and hampered the completion of the survey. For years, the boundaries of the Hardenbergh Patent were disputed by the Esopus.

In 1726 Hardenbergh persuaded a group of Indians to sign a statement saying that he had paid them for their rights to the land inside the patent. Twenty years later, in 1746, he again rounded up Indian claimants, and for the sum of three hundred pounds acquired the signatures or marks of more than thirty Indians on a new deed for the lands he believed were already a part of the patent. This deed included the phrase "together with all Creeks, Rivers, Brooks, Waters, Ponds, Meadows, Reed Lands, Swamps, Woods, Underwoods, Fishing, Fowling and all the benefits, profits and emoluments."[12]

As early as 1743 there were a few scattered settlers living among the Indians; they lived along the Papagonk (East Branch), north of the Beaverkill, and in the nearby Lackawack and Neversink valleys. For the most part, the lands of the patent and the Catskills remained unchanged, and the Indians continued to live in the mountains very much as they had in the past. Their population, however, was decreasing, and by the start of the Revolutionary War, the number of Indians living in and about the region was small. On June 1, 1774, Lieutenant Governor Cadwallader Colden wrote the Earl of Dartmouth:

> The Indians who formerly possessed that part of the Province which lies below Albany are now reduced to a small number, and are in general, so scattered and dispersed, and so addicted to wandering, that no certain account can be obtained of them. They are remnants of the tribes; Montocks and others of Long Island—Wappingers of Dutchess County—Esopus, Papagunk, etc., in Ulster County, and a few Skachticokes. These tribes have generally been denominated River Indians, and consist of about three hundred Fighting Men. They speak a language radically the same, and are understood by the Delawares, being originally of the same race.[13]

Near the end of the war, new roads and trails into the region were being constructed, and additional settlers created increasing problems for the Indians. By the conclusion of the Revolutionary War in 1783, only a thin scattering of Indian people was left. The Lenni-Lenape retreated to the west, the same direction from which their ancestors had come so many centuries ago. They left behind their names for rivers, streams, mountains, and localities, but not much else. Theirs was a society that lived in harmony with the natural world. The differences between the Indians and the Europeans who came into their world are best explained by Dr. William A. Ritchie, state archaeologist, in an article titled "The Indian in His Environment." Dr. Ritchie indicates that the average Western man "suffers a cultural compulsive to 'improve' everything," therefore striving to attain a "technological domination of his environment." The Indian, on the other hand, happily adjusted himself harmoniously into the scheme of nature, learning the ecological relationships surrounding him: "It is probable that the Indian knew and loved the world of his environment in a way that few white men, reared in the competitive, exploitive and possessive traditions of Western civilization, can ever comprehend."[14]

The Lenni-Lenape left the environment of the region very much as they found it. The first major human disturbances to the wilderness of the Catskills began with the people who came after them.

3

Whelenaughwemack, Pioneers, and Rafting Days

In 1751 the Hardenbergh Patent was surveyed and divided among its shareholders into fifty-two "Great Lots." While some of these lands were further subdivided and sold, the Catskills remained a wild, rugged, unbroken forest. Colonists built their homes and farms on the fringe of the mountains, and even though within sight of them every day, they made no attempt to penetrate the Catskills. The narrow valleys, rocky soils, and steep mountainsides did not favor tillage of the soil, and there were no minerals. Remarkably, Kingston, which was less than twenty miles away, was nearly 150 years old before settlers began to enter the mountainous region. There was little attempt to settle the Beaverkill Valley until after the Revolutionary War. Permanent settlers did not arrive until shortly after the Declaration of Peace in 1783.

By 1785 a trail had been measured and cut from Lackawack (in the Rondout valley), through the forest, and across the headwaters of the Beaverkill, to "Pawpacton" on the East Branch. It had marked and numbered "mile trees," 1 through 35, and was known as "the common road." It crossed the Beaverkill, Shin Creek, Willowemoc Creek, and the Neversink. The present-day Beech Hill Road, located upstream of Lew Beach, is said to be a portion of this original route. Undoubtedly, hunters and trappers also traveled it and found their way into the Beaverkill and Willowemoc valleys.

Settlers came mostly from Connecticut, and many were veterans of the Revolution. According to local legend, they were told of good flatlands located along the "Great Beaverkill" by scouts who had been in the Catskills keeping an eye on the remaining Indians who, it was feared, would aid the English. These pioneers at times traveled Indian trails and, not surprisingly, settled in some of the very areas that had been sites of Indian settlements. In 1789 Jehial Stewart constructed a temporary shelter of bark and poles near the forks of the Great Beaverkill and the Whelenaughwemack.[15] Farther downstream, John Cook built a cabin at the mouth of Russell Brook, where the Indians formerly had a cornfield.[16] And in 1791 settlement also began at the mouth of the Whelenaughwemack (Beaverkill at East Branch).[17]

Originally the river known today as the lower Beaverkill, below Junction Pool, was called the Whelenaughwemack; the upper Beaverkill was known as the Great Beaverkill. "Whelenaughwemack" is derived from the name used by the Lenni-Lenape, who lived at the mouth of the river, a noted rendezvous of the Indians before, during, and after the Revolutionary War. Since then, "Whelenaughwemack" evolved into "Welawemacks" and eventually, "Willowemoc."

When the first settlers came to the region, they learned the meaning of the name directly from the Indians: "It is 'the kettle that washes itself clean,' and the stream was so called because of the spring freshets, which carry off all the driftwood, etc., from its banks."[18]

On the heels of these pioneers came many more "Yankees." These men were knowledgeable woodsmen and expert with an ax; they quickly went to work clearing the land and constructing log cabins from the trees they had felled. Wildlife in the region was plentiful, and while hunting tales of wolves and panthers became a part of pioneer history, it was deer, bear, partridge, squirrels, and especially wild pigeons that found their way to the dinner table. Shad, too, became an important food supply each spring. Just as the Indians before them had done, neighbors joined together when the fish arrived, made collective efforts to capture them, and shared the catch with one another.

Until fields could be cultivated for livestock, the wild grasses found in abandoned beaver meadows were cut and used as fodder. A few of the settlers living along the "big flats," upstream of the Forks, traveled to the Susquehanna River and traded with the Indians for seed corn for planting.[19] (Today, two hundred years later, these same fields that were used by the Indians are still planted with corn, which is sold to passing motorists from roadside stands in Rockland.)

Those living along the river flats were fortunate: their land was level and mostly cleared. Away from the floodplain, hillsides were steep and stony, with outcroppings of rocks, which made deep plowing impossible. The high mountains and narrow valleys caused morning and evening shadows to be long; frosts could occur late in the spring and early in the fall. Farming the land was not easy, and many looked to the forest for survival.

When the first white settlers followed the Indian trails into the mountains, they found the forest of the Beaverkill region to be a predominately northern hardwood forest. Many of the first settlers took advantage of the immense forest and rapidly descending streams and became, by turns, lumbermen or raftsmen, farmers, and hunters.

"Rafting" became the first and principal industry of the pioneer settlers. Rafts were constructed from logs or rough-sawed planks and floated to Philadelphia, two hundred miles downstream, on the lower Delaware River. The Delaware and its headwater streams, like the Beaverkill, provided cheap, uninterrupted transportation for lumber from the remote forests of the Catskills. Rafting on the Beaverkill began in 1798; the first men to really know the river were those who risked their lives floating and steering rafts of lumber down its waters. Each spring, after ice-out, they braved the chilling flows of a swollen river and steered their crudely made rafts through rapids, around fast and dangerous twists and turns, and past perilous boulders. For men who had spent their youth as soldiers of the Revolution, witnessing the dangers and excitement of war, rafting held a special appeal.

Most settlers were directly involved in rafting, either piloting rafts, working as oarsmen, or hauling logs to the stream; others simply sold the lumber, but it touched the lives of all who lived in the valley. When the rafting industry began, sawmills, eager to supply the lumber, sprang up on almost every stream. In time, there were more than thirty mills located above the Forks of the Beaverkill and Willowemoc. These early mills were all powered by waterwheels and were generally quite small; the number of men employed at sawing logs was usually fewer than ten. In the beginning, they used only soft woods, such as hemlock, pine, spruce, and basswood.

While the steersman keeps his eyes on the river, raft passengers pose for the camera. Note the full flow of the river and how the logs are lashed into the form of the raft. Delilah Babcock

Logs were hauled to the river with oxen or horses and piled along the bank. Raftsmen waited for the ice to go out of the river and then floated the logs to Philadelphia. *One Hundred Years' Progress of the United States*, 1870

In 1860 the steam engine and circular saw began replacing the small waterwheel mills. Steam mills were larger and could handle more board feet of timber; this, in turn, increased the number of rafts that were floated each spring.

Four types of timber made up the rafts: toggle timber, square timber, sawed timber, and ordinary logs. Nearly 80 percent of all rafts were made of hemlock, the bulk of which was used for wharves and pilings along the Philadelphia riverfront. The sale of timber gave settlers a cash crop, while at the same time it helped in clearing the land for cultivation. The economic impact on the community was extensive—so much so that often notes were given and taken that read: "Thirty days after a general rafting freshet I promise to pay _____ or bearer."[20]

Farmers and their oxen spent the winter in the woods, cutting and hauling logs to the river. After the ice went out in the spring, the stream bank, or docking bank, swarmed with activity. Everyone hastily constructed "colts," which measured, on the average, twenty-two feet by eighty feet. These were tied up in every sizable pool or eddy along the Beaverkill while the men waited for a "fresh," or rising river.

The forward oar is used to turn the head of the raft; the rear oar is used for steering the raft. *The Quaker*, October 1899

When rains raised the flow, hundreds of rafts were started, almost simultaneously. Colts were floated downstream, by one to three men, to the confluence of the East Branch of the Delaware. Here they were lashed together to form a raft, which was generally forty to fifty feet wide and one hundred fifty to two hundred feet long. If the raft was not broken up by the river, the trip to Philadelphia, in clear weather and with a good fresh, took four to five and a half days.

Raftsmen were a hardy lot; they were generally fearless, rough, tough, daring men. More than a few lost their lives in their attempts to challenge the river when it was at its wildest; some "kept their courage up by putting their liquor down."[21] Through perseverance and bravery, the ever-exciting adventure down the river culminated with a sense of victory, when tidewater and Philadelphia were reached safely.

After receiving payment for their timber, the men started their long and sometimes adventurous journey home. With their coils of rope, augers, and assorted tools, the raftsmen became famous figures on the stagecoaches between Philadelphia and New York City. From New York City they took a night boat to Newburgh and then a stagecoach to Monticello. Some, wishing to save the stage fare, walked the sixty or seventy miles from Newburgh or Kingston, and others walked the entire distance, all the way back from Philadelphia to the Beaverkill!

To make the Beaverkill safer for raftsmen, the falls at Butternut Grove (Cooks Falls), which were considered a navigational hazard, were dynamited. Two years later, in 1875, over three thousand rafts passed down the Delaware River. A record keeper at Lackawaxen counted 3,140 by the 4th of May. The number of rafts floated each year increased steadily, peaking in the late 1870s or early 1880s, when hundreds of thousands of feet of hemlock logs found their way downriver.

Railroads, and more importantly, the lack of salable hemlock, caused the decline of the rafting industry. In 1888 the last raft went down the Willowemoc, and in 1904 veteran raftsman L. D. Francisco ran a pair of rafts to Easton, Pennsylvania. Later that year, the last raft of any kind went down the Beaverkill from Spooner's Eddy to Callicoon.

Though gone, the rafting industry will never be forgotten. The spirit of the men who challenged the river with their courage is remembered in the names of pools along the Beaverkill. These rivermen were the first to identify the pools and rapids that formed their experiences. A dangerous and dreaded area was at the mouth of the Beaverkill, where it was joined by the East Branch of the Delaware. The swirling currents made it one of the most difficult places to keep a raft from smashing against rocks, and so this hazardous junction, with its crooked channel, was known as the Jaws of Death.[22]

Others with self-descriptive names include Whirling Eddy, Hell Hole, Brown's Race, and Pull Hair. Pools such as Ferdon's Eddy, Cairns, and Ben Gray's pay tribute to Beaverkill landowners who were also raftsmen. Even today, when local residents speak of the bygone days when timber was floated downriver to market, they do so with admiration. If their family lineage includes one who actually participated in these early river adventures, there is more than a hint of boastful pride.

4

Steamboats, Stagecoaches, and Trout-Fishing Tourists

When settlement in the region began, men either walked or rode on horseback; most trails were too narrow to allow travel with a team. As more people found their way into the area, Indian trails and bridle paths became wagon roads, yet remained difficult to travel. They were rough-cut, nothing more than a swath with the trees cut down; stumps, boulders, and other obstructions were left in the roadway. Since wagons had no springs, people traveled only by necessity.

By the early 1800s roads began to improve, and more comfortable stagecoach travel came into existence, at least on nearby turnpikes. Turnpikes opened up the Beaverkill to tourists, who traveled up the Hudson by steamboat to Newburgh and Kingston, and then came overland by stagecoach. While some were attracted by the scenery and wildness of the uncultivated mountains, many more came seeking trout, which it was said the region had in abundance.

The Ulster and Delaware Turnpike was constructed north of the Beaverkill; in 1802 it ran from Kingston into neighboring Delaware County. To the south, the Newburgh and Cochecton Turnpike opened in 1808, allowing travel from Newburgh across Sullivan County to the Delaware River. It was over this route that many raftsmen traveled on their way back to the Beaverkill. These same raftsmen carried the word out to the civilized world that the Beaverkill offered trout fishing of the first order. Soon, on their return trips, they were sharing steamboats to Newburgh and stagecoaches to Monticello with fishing tourists, who had learned of the Beaverkill and Willowemoc in the tackle shops of Philadelphia and New York.

Many of the first anglers headed for the Darbee House, which was located on a knoll overlooking the famous junction of the Beaverkill and Willowemoc Creek. Samuel and Hannah Darbee constructed the first hotel in Westfield Flats (now Roscoe) between 1805 and 1810. Upon the accidental death of Samuel, this "publick house," known to sportsmen for many years, became simply Mrs. Darbee's. Meals, for which Mrs. Darbee's was celebrated, cost "a shilling, or one and eight pence, if toddy was ordered."[23]

Inside the hotel were seven immense stone fireplaces, a ballroom, and many fine paintings by artists who had boarded there while trouting. Outside, drawn and cut in outline on the side of the building, were large trout, taken from the Beaverkill:

> Eminent doctors, artists and men of letters came for the excellent nearby trout fishing, relaxation, and charms of the wild countryside.
>
> Mrs. Darbee told of a party of men stopping there, who expressed a wish before retiring for the night, that they might see wolves. Arising in the night, which was bright with moonlight, Mrs. Darbee looked down on the flat toward the Beaverkill bridge, and saw wolves playing like lambs. The guests were awakened, and their wish had materialized.[24]

Prior to 1820 or 1825 there is very little written history of the Catskill region, especially as it relates to trout fishing. This is primarily because the Catskills, including the Beaverkill, had barely been settled, and those few newspapers available rarely reported on activities other than politics. In addition, historical data regarding trout fishing in America before 1830 is rare.

The *American Turf Register and Sporting Magazine*, the first of its kind in the United States, made its debut in 1829; by this date the Beaverkill was already well-known to trout fishermen. Though the magazine featured fishing articles of predominantly English origin, the reputations of the Beaverkill and Mrs. Darbee's appeared on its pages in an article titled "Fly And Bay Fishing," written by William T. Porter, editor of the *Spirit of the Times*. Porter was an avid trout fisherman who was familiar with the Beaverkill and the trout streams of Sullivan County:

> Two or three parties, made up principally of "old hands," have lately made a descent upon the rivers of Sullivan and Montgomery counties, in this state, and with immense success. The Williewemauk, Calikoon, and Beaver-kill, are three of the finest trout streams in this country; they are comparatively unknown to city anglers, and are less fished than any others of like pretensions within our knowledge. The trout are large, very numerous, and of the most delicious flavour . . . Make your headquarters at Mrs. Darbys, [*sic*] and you will be sure to find excellent accommodations, and capital fishing. You will reach the Williewemauk, seven miles further on, where Mrs. Purvis will take every care of you. At the present residence of these two "ancient and most quiet" ladies, you may spend a few weeks as delightfully a heart could wish.[25]

By 1839 Porter had purchased the *American Turf Register and Sporting Magazine*, and began publishing more articles on American trout fishing, often written by himself, that not only directed trout fishers where to go, but also gave tips on what flies to use when they got there.

During the 1830s trout fishing was becoming a popular pastime; to exemplify this fact, one need only look at the many tackle stores in New York dealing in rods, reels, flies, and other fishing paraphernalia. Fishing enthusiasts frequented Abraham Brower's on Water Street, Charles Taylor's on Maiden Lane and Broadway, and Lewis's at New and Wall Streets. On Fulton Street alone were the shops of T. W. Harsfield, J. B. Crook's, Thomas Conroy's, John Brown's Anglers Depot, and the famous Pritchard Brothers.

In 1831 the *Spirit of the Times* began publication in New York and was the first weekly all-around sporting journal. With the emergence of publications that featured articles and advertisements on trout fishing, the sport began to have a greater following. With an increasing interest in trout fishing, the Beaverkill and country inns such as the Darbee House began receiving publicity that increased the number of trout-fishing tourists.

Trout Fishing. When settlement in the region began, most trails or roads were too narrow to travel with a team; men either walked or rode on horseback. *One Hundred Years' Progress of the United States,* 1870

The Darbee House, the first hotel and fishing resort along the Beaverkill, constructed around 1805–1810. Eminent doctors, artists, and pioneer trout fishermen often stayed here. Jim Elliott

Henry Inman

One noted trout fisherman who did know about the Beaverkill, the Callicoon, and the Willowemoc Creek was Henry Inman (1801–1846). Inman achieved great fame as an artist; however, he was equally admired as one of America's earliest and most accomplished fly fishermen. He fished when the sport was in its infancy, when streams were in their original unspoiled state and inhabited by an abundance of trout that future trout fishers could only imagine. During the 1830s and '40s Henry Inman enjoyed many days at the Darbee House and fished the Beaverkill, Willowemoc, and surrounding waters.

Although he was born in Utica, New York, Inman spent most of his life in New York City, where his family relocated in 1812. As a child he studied art under John Wesley Jarvis, a well-known portrait painter. He assisted Jarvis for seven years, and then opened his own shop on Vesey Street in lower Manhattan when he was twenty-two years old.

Henry Inman belonged to the first generation of American-trained artists and, while he worked in landscapes, miniature, and genre, he was primarily a painter of life-sized portraits.

During the 1830s he was considered New York's finest portrait painter, and his list of patrons included many famous men and women such as President Martin Van Buren, De-Witt Clinton, John J. Audubon, Nathaniel Hawthorne, and Clara Barton.

It was believed that Inman's "social qualities were of the richest order,"[26] and that his personality and skill as a conversationalist aided him with those he painted; he made them more at ease and captured a sitter's natural expression. In this he excelled, and while his paintings may have improved the appearance of those who posed, there was always a likeness that he captured better than others who painted portraits.

Henry Inman's devotion to trout fishing was well known to the New Yorkers of his day. On his many visits to the Darbee House he found solace from the turmoil of the city, and he found great joy in the natural beauty of a trout stream. In an article published in the *Atlantic Souvenir*, he wrote:

Who that has enjoyed the pleasures of wandering free and far among scenes of rural beauty; has not learned to loathe more deeply the irksome bondage of a city life. Give me the blue and lofty mountain shutting out another world behind it—the sequestered valley where I may quietly muse among overhanging rocks, soothed by the murmurs of the bubbling stream.[27]

Inman was also a member of a famous New York piscatorial club that gathered at Ward's Hostelery. This coterie included Henry William Herbert (Frank Forester), William T. Porter, Richard Fosdick, and William Brough, who was retired from the stage and was a disciple of the rod and gun. The small group was united by a bond of friendship that formed a brotherhood, and it was said that to know one was to know them all. Inman's studio on Vesey Street was one block south of Barclay Street and Broadway, which was the location of the office of William T. Porter and the *Spirit of the Times*. The *Spirit* published some of the brightest names in American literature, many of whom were of the first generation of outdoor writers.

Porter also moved in the same literary circles as "Knickerbocker" writers Nathaniel P. Willis, Charles Fenno Hoffman, George P. Morris, and Fitz-Greene Hallock. Sportsmen and literary men of celebrity could not pass by the *Spirit's* office without paying homage to the "Tall Son of York." Porter's office was dubbed "The Sanctum," and contained a high desk where he wrote while standing; along the wall was a series of wooden shelves containing a thousand or so sporting volumes neatly bound and systematically arranged. Other furnishings included a massive armchair, a small table, a used bureau,

Henry Inman, one of America's best-known portrait painters and a pioneer trout fisherman. Inman spent many days fishing the Beaverkill and Willowemoc in the 1830s and '40s. Print collection, Miriam and Ira D. Wallach Division of Art, New York Public Library, Astor, Lenox and Tilden Foundations

fishing tackle, and a "superb collection of artificial flies." It was here that Porter was visited by many of the first sportsmen of our country, and for some time Henry Inman made almost daily visits to the *Spirit* office to converse for an hour or so with Porter.

Porter was an enthusiastic fisherman, and during the 1830s and '40s he wrote frequently of the wonderful trout fishing found in Sullivan County along the Beaverkill, the Willowemoc, and the Callicoon Creek. He and Inman were the best of friends, and the two often escaped city life to share fly-fishing adventures along the Beaverkill and in the wilds of Sullivan County.

Henry Inman was also a lifelong friend of Henry William Herbert, who became well known as a sporting writer under the name of Frank Forester. Herbert wrote numerous articles and books on fishing and hunting; however, he was more of a hunter than a fisherman, though he joined Inman on occasion on some of Inman's many journeys to Sullivan County and the Beaverkill. The men were known to frequent a restaurant known as Windust's, one of the earliest "Eating-Houses" in old New York. Edward Windust opened his establishment in 1824 on Park Row, only a few steps from the famous Park Theatre. Windust's was known for its fine dinners, as well as for being a rendezvous for actors, actresses, newspapermen, artists, writers, musicians, and prominent members of New York society.

Edward Windust was said to be an excellent host, and his place was filled between the acts and after the show with "the wit and talent" of the city. The walls were covered with artifacts of the stage: actors' portraits, old playbills, press revues, and stage mementos. The place was a veritable actor's museum of New York. On one side of the restaurant were stalls that could seat six comfortably, and it was here that the piscatorial club held their "all-game dinners."

Richard Fosdick originated the affairs, which were limited to six, and each guest had to contribute fish or game that he had killed himself. Edward Windust personally prepared the feast, ". . . the like of which have never been set before kings, were discussed by the elect alone, the vulgar herd of frequenters being uncompromisingly denied access to a 'parlor,' whose very walls were redolent with ancient and fish like smells."[28]

When Henry Inman stayed at the Darbee House and fished the Beaverkill, there were, on the side of the building drawn in outline, the actual tracings of large native brook trout that were taken from the nearby Beaverkill and Willowemoc. One such silhouette was placed there by Inman in late June of 1841. He drew the outline of the magnificent trout, which weighed three pounds, three ounces, on the plain surface of a window shutter. Years later it was still remembered that the drawing was placed there by the "distinguished artist" and "how enthusiastic he was when he held up the prize to the admiring crowd previous to 'taking its likeness.'"[29]

It is difficult today to imagine what trout fishing was like for those anglers who first cast their lines into the lakes, ponds, and streams of the Catskills, before trout populations were depleted by overfishing, or were altered by the introduction of domestic fish, or whose stream habitat was altered or destroyed. Documented accounts are rare, and when they are found they usually reveal a fishery dramatically different from today's.

One of Inman's close friends gives some insight into the trout fishing of this era, and the particulars of the large native brook trout Inman drew on the side of the Darbee House. Richard T. Fosdick recorded information on several trips that he and Inman made together in the early 1840s:

1841. June 21.—Inman, Warner, Dawley and I left for Chester Darbie's [sic][30] in Sullivan Co. Took 7 o'clock train at Jersey City and arrived at Hankin's Station at 1:30. Hired two wagons to take us across mountains over the most infernal road ever invented. Arrived at Darbie's [sic] about ten at night; took rest next morning and spent the day fixing tackle. Tried sundown fishing, but with no success. In morning was fishing by 5 o'clock and kept busy until 8. Upon show of hands we counted ninety-eight of as pretty fish as man could wish to see; seven about 1 lb. each and the balance averaging a half. Next day same success, and so on for six days. In figuring up we found the number of fish caught to be 548; the largest was a beauty, weighing 3 lbs. 3 oz. Inman was so delighted that he sketched the trout on the woodwork of Darbie's [sic] porch.[31]

A few weeks later, Inman, Warner, and Fosdick returned to the Darbee House, and in addition to their stream fishing, they spent a couple of days and nights camping and fishing at Russell Pond. The pond is located in Delaware County, approximately ten miles northwest of the junction of the Beaverkill and Willowemoc Creek, and is at the headwaters of a Beaverkill tributary called Russell Brook:

1841. July—Inman, Warner and I at Chester Darbie's, [sic] Sullivan Co. Three day's fishing brought 271 trout. Camped out by Mother Russell's Pond two nights. Splendid time. Inman caught 69; Warner, 65; and I, 66. Pretty even fishing, as there was not 3 lbs. difference in the catches; some weighing 1¼ lb. down to ¼ lb. The united weight was 107½ lbs.[32]

A couple of years later, Richard Fosdick recorded another trip made with Henry Inman to the Beaverkill and Misner's Pond (Tennanah Lake), known for many years for its large native brook trout:

1843. August—Sam Warner, Dr. Jim Quackenboss, Henry Inman, John Farren, Dr. Bill King, Henry Muir and myself start for Sullivan County to fish the Beaverkill and Willowhemack Rivers. A lively party, ready for any thing. First day caught 103 trout and kept increasing to the end of the week. Camped out one night on the mountains to fish Misenor's [sic] Pond. Great catch of fish; more than was wanted; 792 trout in all, 38 weighing 2 lbs. and over each, the average of balance being over a pound.[33]

Henry Inman was a popular New Yorker; his celebrity as the city's leading portraitist led to contacts with many of its prominent citizens. He was cultivated, possessed great wit and humor, and was an eloquent conversationalist. This personality endeared him to many, and he had a wide circle of friends and acquaintances in the intellectual life of New York. Most everyone connected with art and literature knew Inman and of his love of trout fishing. He knew and socialized with many of the famous men then living in the city, such as Washington Irving, Asher B. Durand, and William Cullen Bryant. Inman suffered from poor health for many years, and annually he had debilitating bouts of asthma. By the time he reached forty years of age his illness worsened, and Inman would be sick for days with constant fevers; as his health declined it caused him to cease work and go into depression. His income was greatly reduced from previous years and, on January 3, 1843, he wrote:

Fine prospect of starving to death this year. Not a soul comes near me for pictures. Ambition in Art is gone. Give me a fortune, and I would fish and shoot for the rest of my life, without touching a brush again.[34]

With his health improving somewhat in 1844, he decided to go abroad to seek commissions painting portraits and landscapes. His traveling to Europe was considered a special event, and his good friend, William T. Porter of the *Spirit of the Times*, wrote a humorous article to celebrate the occasion:

This poet, wit, and painter—as ardent a disciple of old Izaak Walton as ever threw a fly, and who never wet a line out of season, is about to sail for Europe, having recovered, we are delighted to add, his usual health. . .

Personally, and purely from selfish impulses, we hate to hear of his going abroad at all! Who shall now put us up to the trick of hornswoggling a salmon trout of forty pounds? Who will teach us the art and mystery of fabricating a fly that will induce a sockdolager [an old term for very large trout] to "rise" at its first pirouette, though lying over a spring hole in ten feet of water?[35]

Inman returned to New York on April 16, 1845, and his health soon worsened; he had bad attacks of asthma throughout the year, and his income was reduced to the point where he was barely meeting expenses. In December, his condition became critical, and in January he died of heart disease at his home on Murray Street: "His death, which occurred January 17, 1846, called forth an unusually deep expression of public feeling; the press, throughout the country, teemed with the warmest eulogies of his social character, and his artistic abilities."[36]

Speckled Trout. A fine display of rather plump native brook trout, which inhabited streams, lakes, and ponds until the introduction of brown and rainbow trout. *The American Agriculturist*, June 1881

Seven or eight hundred people attended Inman's funeral. Relatives, friends, and dignitaries from New York and other cities formed a long procession of mourners who followed the artist's casket, on foot, two miles through the winter evening. Pallbearers included Richard Fosdick, the artist Asher B. Durand, and several members of the National Academy of Design. Inman was interred at Greenwood Cemetery; immediately after his funeral a meeting of his friends was held, and it was decided to hold an exhibition of his work to benefit his family. The exhibition was held at the American Art-Union, and was open to the public; one hundred twenty-six paintings were exhibited, and all proceeds were given to Inman's widow and five children.

"HENRY INMAN is no more!" wrote William T. Porter in the *Spirit of the Times*. The terse statement exudes the sorrow Porter must have felt over the death of his dear friend. He wrote:

Next to his devotion to his friends and his art, was Inman's fondness for Field Sports. In trout fishing, especially he excelled . . . And a more ardent, accomplished, or delightful disciple, good old Izaak Walton never had.[37]

One of the paintings presented at the Inman Memorial Exhibition was a landscape titled *Trout Fishing in Sullivan County, New York*. The painting had been on display in New York at the sixteenth annual exhibition of the National Academy of Design on May 3, 1841, and it also appeared at the third Boston Artists' Association showing in 1844, and again at the annual exhibition of the Pennsylvania Academy of the Fine Arts in Philadelphia in 1847.

At these events *Trout Fishing in Sullivan County, New York* was well received and was thought to be the artist's most celebrated landscape. In time, the painting disappeared and was only known from an engraving published in *New York Illustrated Magazine of Literature and Art* in 1847.

Fortunately, in 1983 the painting resurfaced and was purchased by the Munson-Williams-Proctor Arts Institute, Museum of Art. The museum, located in Utica, New York, Inman's birthplace, has acquired an extraordinary collection of American art, including paintings by many of our most famous artists. When the Museum of Art purchased the painting, the price was greater than was spent on any other American work, perhaps deservedly, as the acquisition gives the public an opportunity to view not only a work of art, but an important historical work as well; angling scenes, especially of Inman's era, are quite rare.

It is most likely that the scene painted by Inman is where the Beaverkill and Willowemoc Creek join, one of the most celebrated pools in angling history. The site is but a short walk from the old Darbee House, where Inman spent so many days fishing in Sullivan County. In a catalogue titled *The Art of Henry Inman*, William H. Gerdts,

Trout Fishing in Sullivan County, New York, Henry Inman c. 1841. Considered Inman's finest landscape and most autobiographical, the painting is said to document Henry Inman's enthusiasm for trout fishing. Munson-Williams-Proctor Arts Institute, Museum of Art, Utica, New York

professor of art history at The City University of New York, wrote of the painting: "It was in its time the most renowned landscape effort, and is probably also the most autobiographical, for it documents the artist's piscatorial enthusiasms, for which he was almost as well known as for his artistry."

Henry Inman left behind many fine paintings; some are found in New York's City Hall and in Washington, D.C., others in museums from Boston to San Francisco. They are reminders of his wonderful talent as an artist. Sullivan County was a special place to Henry Inman, and he enjoyed the scenic beauty of the countryside and the challenge of its trout fishing. It is his *Trout Fishing in Sullivan County, New York* that goes beyond artistic achievement and serves as a lasting monument, reminding contemporary fly fishers that Henry Inman was here, that he loved their sport, and that he, too, walked the stream banks, waded the riffling waters, and cast his fly in those difficult places a wary trout would likely rise. And while the famous artist applied his skills with the fly more than 160 years ago, we remember that he was one of the first; and his memory is yet retained in a beautiful landscape he painted of a special pool formed by two streams he had a deep affection toward.

While Mrs. Darbee's attracted many of the earliest anglers who found their way to the Beaverkill, farther upstream Murdock's, another pioneer fishing resort, was building an equally impressive reputation. James and Hannah Murdock owned a section of the stream above Shin Creek (Lew Beach), and there were few veteran anglers in New York who did not visit their delightful fishing retreat. The Murdocks had provided lodging to the first trout fishermen who found their way up the valley to explore the primitive, unbroken wilderness of the upper Beaverkill.

James Murdock had come to the Beaverkill Valley in 1835, when it truly was a wilderness. That same year a wealthy New York gentleman had constructed a beautiful Gothic cottage near the banks of the Beaverkill for an invalid relative. It was Murdock's duty to care for the man, and as part of the exchange he was given the privilege of entertaining a limited number of anglers.

After the owner died, Murdock purchased the property and operated what early trout fishermen viewed as "the" place to stay when fishing the upper Beaverkill. Guests at the pioneer resort enjoyed walks, picnics to Beaverkill Falls, trout fishing, moonlight rides, and Hannah Murdock's cooking.

Formerly Murdock's, one of the earliest and famous resorts on the upper Beaverkill. Owned and operated by James and Hannah Murdock.

Early angler fishing lower Shin Creek Falls; the stream is noted for its beauty and significant population of wild brown and brook trout.

In the years that followed, the renown of Murdock's and Mrs. Darbee's grew, along with the fame of the Beaverkill. Amid a mountainous landscape, the stream, with its pure, icy waters that abounded in trout, attracted increasing numbers of fishing tourists. But travel in and out of the region remained difficult, particularly in spring and early summer, when rains turned Sullivan and Ulster County roadways into a mass of soft mud and fording streams became impossible.

5

The Troutist

At first, at least in the Catskills, the native brook trout were referred to simply as "trout," and an angler who pursued them among the mountain streams was, at times, known as a "troutist."

Fitz–James Fitch

One of the first to fish the Beaverkill was a Catskill native by the name of Fitz-James Fitch, who was born in Delhi, Delaware County, in 1817. Being a pioneer troutist, he sampled the Beaverkill when it was special: when its trout were naïve and inexperienced and possibly as numerous and unsuspecting as they would ever be again.

Early in his professional career, he became the county judge of Greene County; he held that position for several years before leaving the mountains and opening a law office in New York. "Judge" Fitch, as he was known throughout his life, was popular in the fly-fishing circles of his day. A highly regarded fisherman and distance caster, he was recognized by his peers as being "courtly, precise, considerate, and observant of all the little amenities of social life; he was withal a loyal friend and charming companion."[38]

Judge Fitch first came to the Beaverkill in 1838, accompanied by William Adams of New York and John Smedburgh of Prattsville. They made the journey with a team of three-year-old horses that belonged to Smedburgh. The trio repeated the trip every year, with the same pair of horses, for twenty-one years! They always started out on or near the 24th of May and would stay ten days, always at Murdock's. They were gentlemen of the old school: ". . . none of them was ever known to utter a profane or coarse word, to fish on Sunday, to travel in or out on Sunday, and although abundantly supplied they were never known to offer a single drop of liquor to any one, even a guest."[39]

After spending but ten years in New York, the Judge's health began to fail, and his physician advised him to return to the mountains. He spent the following summer fishing along the Neversink, living in a little streamside shanty. The Judge was so rejuvenated by the experience that he decided to spend the greater part of every summer along the Catskill streams, fishing Rondout Creek, Dry Brook, Mill Brook, the Neversink, and the Beaverkill with regularity.

Judge Fitch was an excellent trout fisherman, and he kept accurate accounts of his fishing experiences for fifty consecutive years. He recorded every trout he caught, even those he returned to the stream. He began keeping records in 1845, the year he caught the fewest—ninety-one; his best year was 1863, when he caught 1,089. After the first five years, all of the trout were caught on a fly. Two years before

Judge Fitz-James Fitch, a pioneer Beaverkill fly fisherman. From 1845 to 1894 the Judge recorded catching and (mostly) releasing 28,478 trout! *Catskill Rivers,* Austin M. Francis, Nick Lyons Books, New York, 1983

his death in Prattsville in 1896, it was reported that the judge had caught a remarkable 28,478 trout! This feat probably has not been duplicated, and it places Fitz-James Fitch right up there with the best of the Catskill anglers.

While it may appear that the Judge was a victim of "fishing for count," he knew there was more to fishing than catching fish, and said so:

> There are many things besides catching fish that give pleasure to the fisher; vigorous, healthful exercise in the open air and usually in the midst of beautiful scenery. He should keep his eyes open and see everything worthy of admiration—the waterfall, the landscape, the towering mountain and the pretty, tiny flower at his feet.[40]

The Judge took his amazing numbers of trout on wet flies, a fact that should not be lost to those fly fishermen today who bypass their use in favor of dry flies and nymphs. Like most early Catskill anglers, he generally used a cast of three flies, of which his favorites were the Gray Hackle, Coachman, and Beaverkill.

The Beaverkill, one of the first popular trout flies tied in America, was named by Judge Fitch to honor his favorite stream. The pattern stems from an unknown fly of English origin that the Judge found in his fly book and used with great success. He took the fly to Harry Pritchard, a well-known New York fly tier, and requested three dozen more like it. The fly was first tied by Pritchard in 1846[41] or 1850.[42]

Fitz-James Fitch made other notable contributions to American fly fishing. From 1864 on, he was a capable rod maker and invented a rod grip known as the Fitch grip. Under the pen name of Fitz, he frequently contributed articles on fly fishing and rod making to fishing journals such as *The American Angler*. His invention of the creel, with the familiar shoulder strap and waistband, was much welcomed by anglers of his day. Previously, they had struggled with cumbersome baskets, which were carried laboriously by a single strap over the shoulder and rocked back and forth with the casting motion. Fitch came up with the idea for the creel in the summer of 1859, while staying at Murdock's and fishing the Beaverkill.

Though he invented the means with which to carry one's catch away from the stream, Judge Fitch, nevertheless, was an early proponent of catch and release. He wrote about releasing trout in the 1880s, a time when the idea was not practiced by many: "I look with great pleasure and pride upon my trout scores . . . but I look with more pleasure and pride upon the figures which tell me of the number of those trout that were put back in the stream."[43]

One of the most interesting gifts Judge Fitch gave to fly fishing was the record-keeping of his early experiences. From him we are able to glean an idea of the population and size of the trout he and other pioneer anglers found in the Beaverkill. Those anglers who first cast their lines into the flowing waters of the Beaverkill encountered only one species of trout: the brook trout, *Salvelinus fontinalis*. While they prefer cold, clean, well-oxygenated waters and thrive in streams, their natural habitat includes lakes and ponds. *Salvelinus* means "char"; *fontinalis*, "living in cold springs"; and as their name implies, brook trout prefer to live where water temperatures are the coolest.

At least one angler, as reported in an area newspaper, found a way to use the brook trout's scientific name to improve his casting stroke:

> An eccentric fisherman once thought the last portion of the name sounded so pleasantly, and had such a musical rhythm, that he used to steady himself when throwing the fly, by gently murmuring in a slightly ascending and descending scale, fon-ti-na-lis.[44]

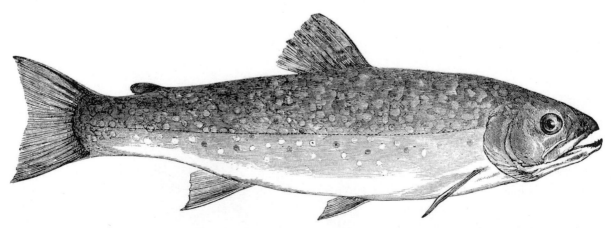

THE BROOK TROUT.

At the time of settlement there were only native brook trout in the Catskill region. They were referred to simply as "trout," and anglers who pursued them among the mountain streams were known at times as "troutists." *The American Angler's Book,* 1864

A beautiful wild brook trout in excellent condition caught in the Beaverkill upstream of the waters of the Balsam Lake Club.

Early fishermen found brook trout to be plentiful, from the headwaters all the way downstream to the junction of the Willowemoc Creek. Below this point, because of warming water temperatures, the stream offered limited trout fishing. The farther upstream one traveled, the more abundant trout became; brook trout were most numerous upstream of the hamlet of Beaverkill.

Though their population was great, the brook trout of our forefathers' day was a predominantly small fish. And it was many years before fishermen spoke of, or wrote about, lengths of trout; in these pioneer days of trout fishing they measured their success by the pound—not of individual fish, but of the total catch! Anglers who first waded the waters of the Beaverkill carried baskets that, when filled, contained an approximate weight of the accumulated fish. The most popular sizes held fifteen, eighteen, and twenty-four pounds. The lack of size was of small concern to those who delighted in stream fishing; they found attributes in the brook trout that were unequaled by other fish:

The lines of grace and beauty, so gratifying to the poet and the artist, culminate in absolute perfection in the trout. The perfect symmetry, the harmonious blending of colors, the graceful motions of this exquisite of the brook, give it a value of great price, to all who look at it with appreciative eyes. Look at its large round eyes, orbs of light that nev-set; its snow white belly; look at its sides clad in mail of rainbow hue dotted with pink stars in sky blue tints.[45]

As noted previously, Fitz-James Fitch fished the stream when it yet contained its "original" strain of brook trout, and he kept a diary of his angling experiences. Writing about the Beaverkill in the 1840s and '50s, Fitch recalled "when one hundred 'saving' trout per day, weighing from fifteen to twenty pounds, was considered but the average sport." To obtain some idea of how large these trout were, on the average, we can use the maximum weight of 20 pounds, or 320 ounces, and realize that the average weight of the fish is 3.2 ounces. The conversion length of a trout weighing 3.2 ounces is approximately 8½ inches.

More accurately, perhaps, Fitch writes of a day when the sport was "exceptionally good" toward the end of May in 1859. He recorded: "I had scored, as memoranda made at the time shows, 121 trout, having thrown back perhaps half that number of 'small fry.' The weight of those saved was twenty-five and a half pounds."[46] On this exceptional day, the total weight in ounces is 408, with the average weight of 121 fish being 3.4 ounces, or a brook trout again measuring approximately 8½ inches. An 8½-inch brook trout is not a large fish, but it is respectable; it should be remembered that this was the average of 121 trout.

Then, as now, habitat often dictates how large a fish will grow, and brook trout between twelve and fifteen inches were taken in the deeper pools. In-stream dams, constructed by sawmills or tanneries, often created some of the largest and best pools, from which would come the biggest trout in the Beaverkill—brook trout that measured fifteen to twenty inches, with weights of from one to three pounds. These were rare; generally any trout caught that weighed a pound or more made the newspapers, and not just locally but in other parts of the Catskills as well.

How rare a trout this size was can be seen from an article on the weights of native trout by James S. Van Cleef, a protégé of Judge Fitch's. Van Cleef also provides insight into the existing population of brook trout in the Beaverkill, prior to the introduction of hatchery trout:

I took in one year, about 1859, three trout, two of which weighed 1 lb. each, and one 1lb. 5 oz. About that time I commenced fishing with a fly exclusively, and have taken quite a large number of trout weighing 15 oz., but none tipped the scales at 1 lb. Judge Fitch, after fishing the Beaverkill with a fly for about forty years, told me that he had never taken a trout in that stream with a fly that would tip the scales at 1 lb.[47]

Native brook trout larger than three pounds were unusual, and those taken were almost always caught in ponds and lakes. So rare were they, in fact, that for many years P. T. Barnum offered a cash prize of one hundred dollars for any brook trout weighing four pounds, delivered alive and uninjured to the aquarium department of his New York museum, "the trout to be warranted to live one week in a stream of fresh water."[48]

One such trout was delivered to Barnum in the 1850s. Fishing-resort owner James Murdock received a "great price" for a five-pound, two-ounce brook trout he captured in the pond known today as Big Pond, located near Turnwood. Another even larger fish, and the largest brook trout ever reported from the Beaverkill Valley, also came out of Big Pond. In June 1860 Charles Woodward of Andes caught a magnificent 24-inch trout weighing 6¼ pounds.[49] Appropriately enough, when the region was first surveyed in 1809, the pond was known as Trout Pond; it later became Big Trout Pond and, finally, Big Pond.

In time, fishing writers and newspaper editors referred to the native trout as "speckled trout" or, more fondly and more often, "speckled beauties." Whichever name was used, the fact remained that the fish was greatly admired and always held in high esteem:

The speckled trout, that prince of the pure, cold, spring water brook or pond, like the sportsman who follows him, is in a class by himself. He is the aristocrat of fishes. Brainy and valiant, he is a delight from his capture to his place on the table.[50]

The brook trout's place at the table was indeed a delight, and trout fishermen took an epicurean approach as to when trout should be eaten. Most held to the theory that there was a "season" when brook trout were "fit to eat." One indication of this was to measure the condition of the fish—they were

Brook trout between twelve and fifteen inches in length were at times taken above and below mill dams, but generally Beaverkill brook trout did not exceed ten inches along most of the stream.

Big Pond produced the two largest brook trout to come out of the Beaverkill Valley. In the 1850s James Murdock took a trout weighing 5 pounds and 2 ounces, and in 1860 Charles Woodward caught a brook trout measuring 24 inches that weighed 6¼ pounds.

edible when their heads were so small as to be disproportionate to the size of their bodies. Pioneer troutist Fitz-James Fitch remarked: "It is not until the first of May, or thereabouts, that trout are fit to eat, and not until June that they are in perfect condition."[51] It was generally believed that brook trout were only "in season" in May and June, and were never eaten in late summer, fall, winter, or early spring.

There were anglers who believed that the "season" for brook trout began with spring floods, but others did not adhere to this thought: "No man with a palate sufficiently delicate to distinguish between a 'redwing' and a 'canvas back' will ever in our latitude covet a brook trout before the middle of May."[52] Thaddeus Norris, another pioneer trout fisherman, claimed that as the fall spawning approaches, brook trout "fall off" in "flesh and flavor," which they do not regain until late spring: "In the streams of the forest however, they are seldom in season before the 10th of May."[53]

It was said that brook trout in the spring were weak, lean, and unwholesome, and were still recovering from fall spawning; and that until they restored their strength sufficiently to frequent the riffles of the streams they inhabited, they were not totally healthy or flavorful. Some anglers believed that the trout were infested with parasites during the winter, which kept the trout in a weakened condition until warm weather appeared and the fish could rub the parasites from their body into the gravel. Those who ate trout in winter or early spring dined on "an unhealthy" fish, and the "offensive parasites." Others believed that brook trout fed heavily on caddis larvae in the early spring: "the caddis fly enwraps itself in twigs and leaves, and as the trout swallows house and all, its flesh takes on a state of decayed vegetation."[54]

Epicures of the past also insisted that the proper method to preserve the delicate flavor of brook trout necessitated dispatching the fish immediately. This was followed by placing the trout in damp moss, and away from the sun and heat. The fish should be placed in a basket or creel so that they do not touch each other, and kept cool by frequent wetting; being kept in this manner secures the "full delicacy of the trout."

In the years ahead, Catskill fishermen would be introduced to other species of trout, which they would accept and value as game fish; but it is doubtful that any generation of anglers ever held the same affection and warm attachment as did those who knew and loved the "speckled beauties."

6

James Spencer Van Cleef— A Beaverkill (and Sand Pond) Reminiscence

Countless men have fished the Beaverkill—novice and expert, from near and far, for recreation and sport. Some made infrequent trips, while others became regulars. A few who fished in the era of the speckled beauties left behind a record of their experiences; this is fortunate, since it is from these men that we are able to learn about the Beaverkill in its earliest years.

One man who contributed significantly to the history and preservation of the Beaverkill watershed was James Spencer Van Cleef (1831–1901). Van Cleef was a prominent attorney who lived and practiced law in the not-too-distant city of Poughkeepsie. For more than twenty-five years he contributed articles and letters to *Forest and Stream*, writing "out of his rich experience and abundant knowledge of angling and anglers."[55] His readers looked forward to his articles,

James Spencer Van Cleef was an early Beaverkill trout fisherman/conservationist. He was concerned with the importance of keeping the watersheds forested, and is credited with preserving large portions of the Beaverkill and other Catskill streams. *The Courier*, Poughkeepsie, New York, December 20, 1901

which he usually closed with his familiar "J.S.V.C." Van Cleef wrote fondly of the bygone days of the Beaverkill, its trout, and its people.

He first visited the stream in 1857, when he was twenty-six years old. The following year he joined the trio of Judge Fitch, William Adams, and John Smedburgh and stayed at Murdock's, where the veteran anglers took the young man under their wing and taught him the "gentle art."

An enthusiastic angler, he enjoyed the friendship of, and shared the stream with, many of the more prominent trout fishermen of his generation, including Thaddeus Norris, Fred Mather, John Burroughs, and Harry Pritchard. He wrote of being at Murdock's on one occasion when most of the guests apparently did not recognize Harry Pritchard. In addition to being a longtime, well-known professional fly tier, Pritchard had a reputation as an excellent tournament caster and was an ex-"champion fly-caster of the world."[56] The roll cast as we know it today was, for many years, known as the Pritchard cast. Harry and his brother Thomas operated a fly shop and tackle store on Fulton Street in New York that was a popular rendezvous for anglers. Wrote Van Cleef:

> There was a large number of anglers at Murdock's when Pritchard put in an appearance, none of whom seemed to know him, and all of whom were disposed to enjoy a little fun at his expense on account of his hesitancy in speech, but when Harry Pritchard proposed to fish upstream instead of down, there was a huge guffaw.

At the time, the Beaverkill had suffered from one or two severe freshets, and the ordinary angler was rarely able to take more than 6 or 8 lbs. of trout. Pritchard, in his early life, had been employed to catch fish on an estate in Ireland, and had there learned the merits of fishing upstream. Pritchard carried, on this occasion, a creel which would contain 15 or 18 lbs. of trout, and every night when he came in, his creel was full of large trout.[57]

In another reminiscence, Van Cleef recalled the religious attitude of the early settlers of the Beaverkill Valley and how their customs were shared by the trout fishermen of his era. Natives never fished on the Sabbath, and if a visiting angler defied this rule he was ordered to leave the stream and never return. The gentlemen anglers who visited the Beaverkill recognized the inhabitants' welcome invitation to fish on their private property and, in return, respected the Sabbath as a day of rest and quiet.

The harmony that existed between visiting anglers and local people culminated each Sunday as they came together for religious services, as depicted in the following story:

Two miles below Murdock's, there was a little hamlet (Lew Beach) consisting principally of a church, an old graveyard, a grocery, blacksmith shop and cobbler's shop. At this point a small stream joined the Beaverkill from the east, with the charming name of Shin Creek, and those who fished this stream with its ragged edges and narrow gorges and came in with sore ankles, have always recognized this name, which was adopted by the Post Office Department as exceedingly appropriate. The church at this place was built in the forties or early fifties by the joint contributions of several denominations, and when some minister did not happen to be on the stream to take charge of the service, it was usually conducted by a Methodist minister, who preached some six or eight miles elsewhere in the morning, and then afterward walked to Shin Creek to conduct the service there in the afternoon . . .

The anglers in those days esteemed it a privilege as well as a pleasure to contribute from year to year, something for the purpose of keeping this church in proper paint and repair, and also to quietly add to the collection taken on every Sabbath day for the benefit of the minister . . .

On the Sabbath day every one attended the services in this little church, rain or shine, often riding ten miles or more from up the stream, for this was the only church between the head of the Beaverkill and a place ten miles below it. It was always full. There was a person then living in the neighborhood by the name of Hotchkiss, long since gone to his rest, and by common consent he led the music. He always came in his shirt sleeves when the day was warm, and when the hymns were given out he usually stood at the front seat, threw his foot over the back, and after listening to his music fork started the tune, which on almost every Sabbath was either "China" or "Mear" and sometimes both. I have heard the best church music in the country, but I have never heard anything which seemed to bring every person who joined in these services nearer to the Heavenly Throne of God than these simple

services in this little church in which every one joined, many of them with tears in their eyes . . . And these services and teachings bore rich fruit. The Sabbath was always observed as a day of holiness and rest, and what is more, these services made their visible impress upon the daily lives of all who lived upon the stream.[58]

One can see that James Spencer Van Cleef enjoyed a special relationship with the Beaverkill and its people, and he wrote warmly and intimately of his personal experiences.

Sand Pond

Van Cleef also wrote often about the preservation of streams, trout habitat, and conserving natural resources. In 1868, he purchased Sand Pond and the 143 acres surrounding it. The pond, located deep in the forest at the headwaters of Willowemoc Creek, was noted for its exceptionally large brook trout, and was thus the frequent target of illegal netters. Following his purchase, Van Cleef took out an advertisement in the local newspapers, announcing his purchase of "the pond generally known as Sand or East Pond" and forbidding trespassing and fishing in the pond under the penalty of the law. Newspapers at the time reported on the event, stating that a "company of sportsmen from the City of Poughkeepsie" planned to create a trout preserve at Sand Pond for their own private use during the summer.[59]

Sand Pond was eminent among Catskill trout ponds because of its sizable brook trout; brook trout weighing between two and three pounds were not uncommon. It was reported that a party of anglers from Ellenville once caught a number of trout and graded them according to size—the first thirty averaged 2½ pounds! Brook trout measuring between twelve inches and sixteen inches were common, and in 1872, club records revealed that the average size taken weighed 1 pound; the largest, 2¼ pounds.

Van Cleef and his friends constructed a lodge overlooking the 14½-acre lake, and it was here that the first organized trout-fishing club in the Catskills was founded in 1868. Having obtained leases on four miles of the Willowemoc Creek, they decided to call their group the Willewemoc Club (note the different spellings). In 1870, the club purchased Sand Pond from Van Cleef and renamed it Lake Willewemoc. Membership was limited to twenty, and the first president was Cornelius Van Brunt, who, like Van Cleef, was from Poughkeepsie.

In addition to his interest in trout fishing, Cornelius Van Brunt was known as a naturalist who made significant contributions to botanical science. After retiring from business in 1869, he devoted his time to fishing and studying nature, becoming knowledgeable about plant life and making many scientific contributions to the Poughkeepsie Academy of Science and Vassar Brothers Institute. Van Brunt was also a member of the New York Academy of Science, American

Museum of Natural History, American Forestry Association, and the New York Horticultural Society.

By 1886 he became interested in photography and began photographing plants and flowers, developing the ability to take close-up pictures by experimenting for years with lenses, plates, and developers. Van Brunt is credited with enlarging photographs of "minute parts of flowers" that, in some cases, were better than the best scientific illustrated drawings.

He, with the assistance of his wife, gave illustrated lectures on botany, photography, and wildflowers that created great interest in preserving native plants and protecting natural woodlands. Van Brunt lectured in and around New York City, and at the American Museum of Natural History, Brooklyn Institute, and New York Botanical Garden, where his lectures were said to be the most successful of any presented. This earned him the title of honorary floral photographer of the Botanical Garden. He and his wife, Adelaide, had a passion for wildflowers, and they spent a portion of every year at Balsam Lake, Sand Pond, and other locations in the Catskills. Their work in the field of botany is: ". . . commemorated in the beautiful *Polemonium Van Bruntiae. . .*"[60] Commonly known as Jacob's-ladder, this plant was recognized as a new species in 1870 and named after Adelaide Van Brunt, who with her husband, made "excellent collections from the Catskill Mountains of New York."[61] It is said that New York State has some of the largest populations of the plant in the world; and while the plant is rare, it is well protected, with many of the sites being in isolated wetlands.

Though of good size, the trout in Sand Pond were never very plentiful, mostly because of limited spawning opportunity. Writing about Sand Pond a couple of years after the club took ownership, Cornelius Van Brunt described the lake as having an even depth of only five feet, with a heavy growth of aquatic vegetation. He also wrote that the only stream entering the lake was almost inaccessible, and that the trout were accustomed to spawning along the shoreline "without much regard to the character of the bottom, and a very few by great effort went upstream. The result in the past has been that the greater part of the eggs were destroyed, and the young when hatched had no refuge."[62]

Club members immediately set about to "help the fish." They constructed a "spawning race" (artificial spawning bed) and then raised the lake level to cover it. They also cleaned the stream of siltation, debris, and barriers and made it easier for trout to enter to spawn. This example of habitat improvement and the club's foresight is remarkable, considering the work was accomplished in the 1870s!

Members also recognized that the brook trout of Sand Pond were special and took great care to preserve the quality of the fishery. They not only limited their sport to fly fishing but also put into practice a unique form of catch and release. A guest of Van Cleef's who fished the lake describes the custom:

Cornelius Van Brunt was the first president of the Willewemoc Club, the first organized private trout-fishing club in the Catskills.
Bulletin of the Torrey Botanical Society, December 1903

The hook was carefully extracted and they were consigned to a wired creel, which was fastened to the stern of the boat. Taken ashore, the fish were transferred to a spring near the landing, where they were closely watched, and if one showed symptoms of any mortal hurt, he was forthwith dispatched for table use. The rest were put back into the pond, except such as might be needed on the "festal board." And thus the fish are caught over and over again affording abundant sport with no destructive waste.[63]

These were indeed knowledgeable anglers who understood their fisheries resources and acted wisely in their preservation. Incredibly, the Willewemoc Club membership employed most of the primary techniques of modern fisheries management. They restricted the method of angling, reduced creel limits, practiced catch and release, and increased spawning and productivity through habitat improvement.

James S. Van Cleef continued purchasing vast tracts of wild forest lands surrounding the headwaters of the Willewemoc and Beaverkill. He and other members of the Willewemoc Club acquired thousands of acres, including Balsam Lake, Thomas Lake, and a portion of the upper Beaverkill.

In 1883 they founded the Balsam Lake Club, and after they constructed a lodge, or clubhouse, their trips to and from Sand Pond became less frequent. Finally, in 1889, the Willewemoc Club members abandoned their interests in Sand Pond and settled permanently at Balsam Lake.

As a lasting tribute, founding member George W. Van Siclen dedicated the reprinting of an English classic to the Willewemoc Club. Van Siclen was considered a scholarly angler, and in 1875 he brought out *An American Edition of the Treatyse of Fysshynge wyth an Angle*, by Dame Juliana Berner. In his dedication, he reminisced wistfully of the little lake deep in the forest and of the companionship he enjoyed along the Willowemoc:

> The present Willewemoc Club is not composed of Indians; nor is its club-house an Abbey, but a house of hemlock boards, with comfortable rooms; floors uncarpeted, except by the bedside; and a broad piazza, furnished with easy chairs, and overlooking a beautiful lake, full of trout; with an appanage of acres of woodland, and four miles of a fine trout stream.
>
> There I shall go when the apple trees are in blossom. And to please the congenial spirits of the modern monks who form that club, and the brethren of the angle through our land, is this little book reprinted.[64]

George Van Siclen had fond memories of Sand Pond, and one day he most assuredly cherished occurred in 1877, when he caught three trout on one cast. Using a Black Gnat, Cowdung, and Coachman, Van Siclen hooked and successfully landed three brook trout, measuring 10 inches, 12¼ inches, and 16 inches respectively—38¼ inches of trout!

For more than forty years, James Spencer Van Cleef fished the Beaverkill and Willowemoc, and during that span he was important in the preservation of both the trout resources and the history of these two famous streams. In time, Van Cleef came to believe that the only way to preserve trout waters, or to restore streams to their former productivity, was through the control of private clubs or associations. He was a dedicated conservationist at a time when there were but a few. He deplored the practice of destroying the forest lands, which he strongly believed were crucial to the protection of watersheds. On occasion, he even delivered his message to the Fisheries Society and read papers before the society on the decadence of trout streams. During these years he was a member of the State Association for the Protection of Fish and Game, and was retained as counsel for the Senate Committee on Fish and Game. Van Cleef was recognized across the state as a conservation leader, and in 1895 he wrote the general fish and game laws for New York State.

7

"Scarcely Less Famous Than the Beaverkill"

Not everyone who came to the Beaverkill fished the stream. Early anglers also found their way to the extreme headwaters and discovered Balsam Lake—a fairly shallow, cold-water lake of approximately twenty acres that teemed with brook trout. In the early days of Catskill trout-fishing history, Balsam Lake was "scarcely less famous than the Beaverkill."[65] What the lake's brook trout lacked in size, they made up in numbers; catches by fishing parties numbered in the hundreds, and sometimes even the thousands.

During this period, the public roamed freely over the land, hunting, trapping, and fishing the many lakes, ponds, and streams, very much as the Indians had done. Even though the almost two million acres of the Hardenbergh Patent had been divided into fifty-two "Great Lots" and then subdivided, the Catskills remained sparsely settled. Most of the land was still owned by a relatively few absentee landlords, the majority of whom had never even seen their holdings. These tracts were vast areas of wild, mountainous, unbroken forest, and as such, it was difficult, if not impossible, to prohibit their use by the public.

From the time Balsam Lake was discovered, it had been a favorite haunt of outdoorsmen. Not only did the lake have a bountiful supply of trout, but the area surrounding it was populated by a large number of deer, many of which found their way to markets. Sleds of venison went weekly from the backwoods to the settlement of Kingston.

By the 1840s reports on the fishing at Balsam Lake appeared frequently in the weekly newspapers in and about the Catskills. They generally described the rugged countryside, the difficulty of travel, and the phenomenal number of trout caught and kept by fishing parties. The first visitors to these waters far from any roads experienced great hardship. They traveled the last several miles on foot, through a wilderness, over steep mountains, with no trails to guide them.

One story illustrating the perils and primitive nature of such a trip appeared in the *Rondout Courier* in the winter of 1853. Titled "The Balsam Lake Fishermen," the story chronicled the toils and sufferings of a party of anglers and revealed that "one need not travel very far to get into perilous ways and make hairbreadth escapes."[66] Lured by the traditional stories of Balsam Lake, five Rondout sportsmen traveled some forty miles by sleigh, and then up the Dry Brook valley another fourteen miles to the last clearing; at this point their sleigh was abandoned and they started on foot for Balsam Lake:

> The route was over three dreaded mountain ridges, trackless, precipitous, clothed in dense forest, and with snow some three feet deep on the heights, and a trifle less in the gorges, ravines and valleys. To add to their toil, a crust had formed on the snow some two feet deep and on this was a dry powdered snow of a foot, and the wayfarers broke through the crust at every step. Four hours of wearisome effort brought them to Balsam Lake, an inconsiderable pond lying hemmed in by the feet of three or four mountains. Here a fire was built, and holes cut in the ice. The trout were abundant, biting on anything, a bit of white rag answering as well as the best bait, and, so eager were the fish, when one was drawn out others jumped out of the water in unsuccessful pursuit of the line.[67]

A "traditional" shanty at the lake had disappeared, and winter camping in the woods was deemed not an option; and so the party began the arduous trek back down the mountains. They left at four in the afternoon, and with nightfall overtaking them as they struggled over the second mountain, the scream of a mountain lion was heard in the distance. Traveling in the dark, with a cold wind blowing, it was impossible to retrace the tracks they had made earlier in the day. The men trudged through the chilling night, breaking a new trail through the crusting snow "along precipices, and up and down declivities." One by one the men tired, lying in the snow utterly exhausted and looking "upon an inevitable death as not so very terrible." Being near the Dry Brook valley they fired a gun, and a nearby settler found the men and aided them to safety. The trip had taken seven hours of "wearing exertion" and "frightful mental anxiety."

The majority of those who made raids on Balsam Lake came from within the Catskills or from the larger communities just outside its borders, such as Kingston, Rondout, and Ellenville. Quite often their goal was not merely to have a good time and catch fish but to collect and take home a supply of trout that would serve as food in the months ahead.

An article that appeared in the *Prattsville Advocate* in 1847 reported on the typical success of a party of five: "On returning to the house and summing up the sport of the two days, we found we had taken thirteen hundred and six fine trout, most of which we pickled for home consumption."[68]

Hunters and fishermen made camp for days, even weeks, along the lake's shoreline. Upon arriving, they made rafts to fish from or fashioned canoes by hollowing out large trees. They slept on beds of hemlock boughs, in crude shanties, or under open skies. Bonfires, ostensibly made to provide light and warmth, also illuminated the woods, keeping away "panthers," or mountain lions, and other wild animals:

> Soon after we started our watch fires, we retired for the night; but our rest was soon broken by a shriek from the midst of the forest, which greatly alarmed us; for we soon became aware of the near approach to our camp of some of the wild beasts that infect these woods.[69]

Men from towns and cities hired guides who were acquainted with forest life. They came to Balsam Lake to live

Balsam Lake is a fairly shallow cold-water lake located at the extreme headwaters of the Beaverkill. Members of the Willewemoc Club eventually formed the Balsam Lake Club, which is still in existence as a private fishing club.

Camping in the Forest. Balsam Lake was a rendezvous for men of different backgrounds; gentlemen-sportsmen hired or mingled with men acquainted with forest life and market hunters. *Harper's New Monthly Magazine,* February 1860

in the style of backwoodsmen and once there, they were often joined by men who *were* backwoodsmen. Gentlemen-sportsmen met and mingled with tough characters—dead-shot, mountaineer market hunters. The lake was a rendezvous for men of vastly different backgrounds and social standings; yet, in the confines of the forest, they joined company and shared campfires. Their love for the outdoors brought them together; they sang songs and feasted on hindquarters of venison and delicious trout. As the fires burned low, the men exchanged woods lore and told tales of bears, wolves, and panthers.

8

The Little Club
of Houseless Anglers
and Wagon Fishermen

During the 1840s and '50s the reputation of the Beaverkill continued to grow, attracting trout fishermen and the attention of America's earliest angling writers. John J. Brown, a New York tackle dealer, is often credited with the authorship of the first useful American angling book. His pocket-sized manual was popular with the angling public and went through several editions.

First published in 1845, and titled *The American Angler's Guide*, the book included chapters on fish, tackle, bait, and angling. Brown attempted to persuade his readers to try their hand at fly fishing, claiming that the sport was not difficult, and to prove his point, he wrote of his personal experiences with the rugged raftsmen of the Delaware River:

> The scientific and graceful art of throwing the artificial fly is a beautiful accomplishment but not so difficult as is generally imagined. In the months of May and June, the raft and lumberman from the Delaware and rivers of Pennsylvania are seen in the fishing tackle stores of New York, selecting with the eye of professors and connoisseurs the red, black and grey hackle flies, which they use with astonishing dexterity on the wooded streams in their mountain homes. Those therefore who have never tried this method of fishing, with such untutored examples before them, should make a little effort towards the successful practice of this branch of the art.[70]

Brown also advised his readers to "fish the Beaver Kill, the Mongaup, the Willewemack, and other kindred streams."[71] By 1848 the Erie Railroad skirted the western Catskills and followed the upper Delaware River through the borders of Sullivan and Delaware Counties. The railroad not only provided swifter transportation to and from New York but made the Beaverkill accessible to those outlying areas, now with rail connections to the city. The number of trout fishermen increased, and inn ledgers began recording guests from as far away as Kentucky, Maryland, and Pennsylvania.

Most Erie travelers, however, disembarked at Callicoon, along the Delaware River, where they were met by the buckboards of Murdock's, Flint's, Tripp's, or one of the newer Beaverkill boardinghouses, as more farmers were opening their doors to the additional fishing tourists. The road from Callicoon was long and rough, and travel was uncomfortable and tiring; once they reached their destination, anxious fishing parties often stayed for days or weeks before returning.

One who fished the Beaverkill often during these early years was Thaddeus Norris (1811–1877). Though he lived in Philadelphia, Norris spent many days in the 1850s fishing the waters of the Willowemoc and Beaverkill, experimenting with flies and fly-fishing techniques in the area of Westfield Flats (Roscoe). He usually stayed at the Boscobel, which was the name Chester Darbee called the resort previously owned by his mother, and which earlier fishermen had referred to as Mrs. Darbee's.

Norris was an expert fly fisherman, rod maker, fish culturist, and author. In 1864 his *The American Angler's Book* was published; the work was extremely popular and contained information on fish, tackle, trout and salmon fishing, as well as fly- and rod-making. The book greatly contributed to his being known, in his day, as the "dean of

Thaddeus Norris, author of *The American Angler's Book*, an important work during the early years of sport fishing in the United States. *Cyclopedia of American Literature*, 1881

American anglers," and it told of Norris's personal angling experiences on the Beaverkill, of his friendship with Chester Darbee, and of a number of noted artists and sculptors who together formed a small group of fly fishers that met at the Boscobel (Darbee House.)

In *The American Angler's Book*, Norris writes that he and "a few brethren of the rod" met for the first time fishing the Beaverkill in 1852 and became "drawn towards each other by a love of the gentle art." The men decided to form themselves into an association with the "unassuming name of the 'Houseless Anglers.'" The name was taken in "contradistinction of the old Fish-House clubs," associations known for their dinners and social gatherings rather than for their love of angling.

The Houseless Anglers were all fly fishermen who took their trout fishing seriously, and they met each season at Chester Darbee's. One of their goals was to not be boastful about their fishing and to follow the teachings of Izaak Walton—"that fishing, like virtue 'is its own reward.'" They adopted a policy of limiting their catch and not filling their creels, and they attempted to introduce this philosophy to other anglers and repress any rivalry or competition on the stream.

The group never exceeded ten members; "They were of various pursuits: amongst them were a few artists, professionally so, and two more who were merely amateurs."[72] Norris dedicated *The American Angler's Book* to "The Little Club of Houseless Anglers," and he wrote fondly of his experiences along the Beaverkill and the joy of a tradition he called the "Noonday Roast."

While they limited their catch, the fly fishers took great pleasure in meeting along the stream at a designated time and dining on trout. The proper necessities for a roast included bread, butter, salt, pepper, matches, and a bottle of claret or ale. Norris and his friends cooked over a wood fire along the stream bank. Once the fire was going, they collected flat stones for plates and placed them near the fire "to warm properly." For the roast they chose the smallest trout:

> [T]hose under nine inches are best; scour them well with sand, wash them clean, and open them, but allow no water to touch inside, as the blood and natural juices of the fish should be retained as far as possible; cut off the heads, score them (not too deeply), and pepper and salt them well inside and out.[73]

A couple of branches of "sweet birch" were cut, with as many twigs on them for the number of trout to be roasted. A fish was placed on each twig, running the twig along the upper side of the backbone, and then held to the fire. When the trout were done, they were placed on the hot stone and buttered while warm. The day's fishing was discussed, and stories were told of past and present trouting experiences. The camaraderie and the roast were memorable: "[I]f there *is* an objection to it, it is that one is never satisfied afterwards with the taste of trout cooked indoors."[74] The Noonday Roast was an important tradition to Norris, who described this break in fishing activity by stating "many pleasant hours have been passed under the dark sugar-maple or birch cooking, eating, smoking, chatting, sleeping, many a long story has been told, and perhaps occasionally a *long bow* drawn."[75]

Included among the group of Houseless Anglers were Chester Darbee and Peter Stewart, a well-known local hunter, angler, and woodsman; and William Morris Davis,

Thad Norris at his fly-tying bench. Considered the "dean of American anglers," Norris was knowledgeable about fishing, rod making, and fish culture. *The American Angler*, November 1917

who like Norris was from Philadelphia. Davis was the group's president; he was an abolitionist, author, and U. S. congressman from Pennsylvania. Artist members included Henry Kirke Brown and John Quincy Adams Ward, two of America's most noted sculptors; and other calculated members included the famous Hudson River School of landscape painters Sanford R. Gifford and Thomas Doughty, who were also friends of Brown. Doughty, like Norris and Davis, hailed from Philadelphia, and was known to be painting and fishing in Sullivan County in the 1850s.

• • •

Henry Kirke Brown (1814–1886) was an artist who had a passion for fly fishing and was among our earliest fly fishermen. Brown was born in Leyden, Massachusetts, and at the age of eighteen he apprenticed under a portrait painter in Boston named Chester Harding. While he started his artistic career as a painter, Brown soon discovered he had a talent for sculpture.

In 1842 he traveled to Italy to study, remaining there until 1846; upon his return he opened a studio in New York City and a few years later cast the first bronze statue in America, the figure of De Witt Clinton, for Greenwood Cemetery.

A lover of horses, Brown owned some of the finest purebreds, which he used as models. He possessed great knowledge of a horse's anatomy and "was the first American to disclose the possibilities of dignity and power in the monumental bronze equestrian statue."[76] Henry Kirke Brown became famous for producing equestrian statues, and his greatest work is said to be of George Washington, which was erected in Union Square and unveiled on July 4, 1856. (A replica of the Washington statue was erected at West Point in 1916.) This was the first important equestrian statue erected in America, and it was paid for by wealthy and patriotic citizens of New York. It is currently the oldest sculpture in the New York City Parks' collection.

Exactly when he began fly fishing or learned fly tying is not known, but most likely in the mid-1840s; he was an advanced fly maker and practiced the art of directly imitating natural flies at a time when it was rarely, if ever, practiced in America. As a fly tier he was well ahead of his time; he was innovative when most Americans were still dependent on English trout flies that were imitations of the natural insects found along English streams.

During the 1850s Brown fished the Beaverkill annually, and he did so often in the company of William Morris Davis and Thad Norris. The trio corresponded with one another regularly throughout the year and met each summer, usually in May or June, at the Boscobel near the junction of the Beaverkill and Willowemoc.

In 1861 Brown and his wife moved to Newburgh, where he lived and worked for the next twenty-five years. The move

Henry Kirke Brown, c. 1851. In addition to being one of this country's first sculptors of equestrian statues, Henry Kirke Brown was an avid fly fisherman and advanced fly maker. *Sartain's Union Magazine of Literature and Art,* February 1851

brought him closer to the Catskills, and undoubtedly fishing excursions became more frequent. In addition to trout fishing he was an accomplished salmon fisherman, and fished annually in Canada, with his usual companions being Sanford Gifford and John Quincy Adams Ward, whom he always referred to as "Quincy" Ward. Henry Kirke Brown was an excellent fly fisherman who knew and loved the sport; and while he was known to pursue trout on the waters of Long Island and the Adirondacks, his favorite trout streams were in the Catskills.

• • •

John Quincy Adams Ward (1830–1910) was born on the family farm in Urbana, Ohio. As a youngster he enjoyed fishing and hunting, and creating clay models of men on horseback and of farm animals. As a teenager he visited a sister who lived in Brooklyn, New York, and it was there that he began his life's work; at the age of nineteen he became an apprentice of the eminent sculptor and fly fisherman Henry Kirke Brown.

Ward was an excellent student and assistant, and he and Brown quickly became close friends. He assisted Brown with his equestrian statue of George Washington, perhaps his finest work, and Brown showed his admiration for Ward by demanding that Ward's name be added to the base of the statue. Ward worked for Brown for seven years and eventually opened his own studio in New York in 1861. During his years with Brown, Ward undoubtedly learned about fly fishing from him, as the two men often fished together, in the Adirondacks as well as the trout streams of Sullivan County.

After opening his studio, Ward became one of this country's greatest sculptors and a leader in his field; for half a century he was known as the "dean of American sculptors." Naturalism was the dominant feature of Ward's work, and two of his earliest and best-known sculptures are titled *The*

John Quincy Adams Ward, c. 1854. A one-time apprentice of Henry Kirke Brown, Quincy Ward became a famous sculptor with statues erected in New York City's Central Park. He and Brown made regular trips to the Beaverkill during the 1850s. Library of Congress, drawing by Henry Kirke Brown, 1854

Freedman (1865) and *Indian Hunter* (1868). The latter work marked the turning point in Ward's career.

The Freedman is a bronze statue of a slave, seated, looking at the shackles from which he has been freed. *The Indian Hunter*, conceived in 1857, was the first work by an American to be placed in New York's Central Park; the sculpture depicts an Indian with a bow holding back a dog. He also made a bronze figure of Shakespeare (1872) for Central Park, as well as one of a Civil War soldier for the 7th Regiment Memorial, and a statue titled *The Pilgrim*. His work is evident all over New York City; there is a statue of William E. Dodge in Bryant Park; and in Washington Square Park, the Alexander Lyman Halley Monument. Ward also crafted the sculptural decoration for the pediment of the New York Stock Exchange.

Ward's work included portrait busts, in bronze and marble, of many prominent individuals, and equestrian statues of famous American generals; he knew and loved horses, and his equestrian statues were considered his best work. In the world of art, "Quincy" Ward was a prominent figure, and was one of the founders of the Metropolitan Museum of Art, where he served on the board of directors from 1870 until 1901.

Thomas Doughty (1793–1856) was one of the first artists to specialize in landscapes in the United States. He began exhibiting landscapes as early as 1816 at the Pennsylvania Academy of the Fine Arts, and he became a full-time professional painter in the city of Philadelphia in 1820. Though he was born in Philadelphia, and his career began in that city, Doughty also took up residence in New York City and Newburgh. He made frequent trips to the Catskills, and was among the earliest to sketch Kaaterskill Falls.

Doughty was a fisherman, and his love for angling is often reflected in his paintings; many include fishing in their titles, or feature fishermen along a streamside landscape. Some of his works include: *Fishing in the River* (1828); *The Fishing Party* (1829); *The Anglers* (1834); *Fishing*; *The Trout Brook*; *The Trout Pool*; *Trout Fisherman*; *The Fishing Pool* (1850); and *The Fisherman*.

Doughty worked and fished in the Catskills during the 1820s and '30s, and while he sketched in the famous Kaaterskill Clove, he was also familiar with the wild regions of the upper branches of the Delaware River in Sullivan and Delaware counties, including the Beaverkill. Little is known of his trout-fishing experiences; however, he was quite familiar with the woods and waters of Sullivan County, where he

Thomas Doughty was an early American landscape painter and member of the Hudson River School of landscape painters. Many of his paintings contained fishing scenes, most likely because Doughty was himself a trout fisherman. *Graham's Magazine*, June 1854

painted some of his finest landscapes. His well-known painting *The Anglers* (1834) is said to be a scene along a stream in the western Catskills, most likely Sullivan County, where he was a pioneer trout fisherman and sketched and painted until the 1850s. The painting *Fishing Party* inspired his friend, noted author and poet Nathaniel P. Willis, to write:

> Come to the lake the shower is past
> And the bright sun is put at last,
> Come! Take your baskets and away,
> We'll to the rock for trout today.
> Our hooks are good; our flies are new,
> Our flexile lines are strong and true.[77]

● ● ●

Sanford Robinson Gifford (1823–1880) was born in Saratoga County, New York, and when he was about a year old his family moved to Hudson, within sight of the Catskill Mountains. In 1845, at the age of twenty-two, he moved to New York City to study art. At first Gifford painted portraits, but as with many artists, he soon realized he would rather paint landscapes.

Gifford was one of the first of the "second generation" of the Hudson River School to visit the western Catskills, and it was most likely that trout fishing lured him to the Delaware watershed. His sketchbooks reveal that he worked along the trout streams of Sullivan and Delaware counties, including the headwaters of the East Branch. He also did many sketches along the main Delaware River, one of which was of the famous confluence of the East and West branches at Hancock on September 3, 1849. The sketch appears to include a few anglers; and today's trout fishers, familiar with the pool, would recognize the location, even though the work was done more than 150 years ago.

In the fall of 1851 Gifford traveled to Sullivan County and explored streams and mountain views; he sketched along the Little Beaverkill and the Mongaup and Callicoon Creeks, and in early October sketched the "Forks of the Beaver Kill and Willaweemock." That Gifford found his way to the "Forks" is not surprising; even at this early date it was already a famous rendezvous for trout fishermen. Known today as Junction Pool, it is one of the most famous pools in angling literature, and was the subject of Inman's noted landscape, *Trout Fishing in Sullivan County, New York.*

Gifford liked to carry a small pencil sketchbook that he could produce at a moment's notice, even while traveling, to capture "the fleeting effects of nature." Fellow artist Worthington Whittredge once stated that Gifford was "always suspicious that if he stopped too long to look in one direction the most beautiful thing of all might pass him by at his back; the eternal truth Gifford sought was rare beauty . . ."[78]

In his *History of American Painting*, Samuel Isham states that Sanford Gifford turned "the usual painter's hobby of

Sanford Robinson Gifford, c. 1868. Gifford was a member of the Hudson River School of landscape painters, and it was said that he turned the usual painter's hobby of fishing into a passion.
Metropolitan Museum of Art, David Hunter McAlpin Fund, 1852

fishing into a passion." He went trouting in the spring, salmon fishing in the summer, and fishing for striped bass in the autumn.

● ● ●

Because of its inaccessibility, the Beaverkill for nearly half a century furnished twenty-five to thirty miles of as fine fishing as any trout stream in the state. With the coming of the railroad and an increase in fishing tourists, a greater burden was placed on its trout resources. New roads were built, and though they remained crude and primitive, they often paralleled the stream, allowing further exploitation by anglers who visited the fishing grounds by wagon and camped at streamside.

"Wagon fishermen" carried their comforts and luxuries with them, bringing bedding, a good supply of food, a stove, and lanterns. They found a comfortable place for their horses and made themselves at home. These men were not bound to any one place and lived right on the stream at all the best fishing spots. When one area was fished out, they moved to another and worked the stream relentlessly. During the 1850s reports circulated that the Beaverkill was being "fished to death," and its speckled beauties were decreasing in size, as well as in number. Veteran anglers saw wagon fishermen as an unethical lot who exploited the trout population of the Beaverkill.

Local newspapers seem to bear this out, as reports of incredible catches surfaced: "A party of gentlemen returned to

Camping along the stream. As new roads were constructed, they tended to follow streams, and this developed into a new type of fisherman known as "wagon fishermen." They brought many of the comforts of home and camped at one area until the stream was devoid of trout, then moved on to a new location and followed the same routine. *The American Angler*, December 1917

Easily accessible to wagon fishermen was Sherwood Flats, a lengthy, deep pool on the Willowemoc Creek. Lee Van Put

this village last week from a fishing excursion to our mountain streams, having caught about 1,400 trout during their absence."[79] And two weeks later: "A party of four gentlemen, from Kingston, returned last week, having caught between 1,700 and 1,800 brook trout."[80] Reports such as these were becoming all too common, as fishermen seemed "intent upon exterminating as many trout as possible."

Writing in *Harper's New Monthly Magazine* in the summer of 1859, author T. B. Thorpe claimed that in the past few years the best trout streams in New York State were being ruined. He believed that the ease of travel was affecting trout populations, and while he stated there were many reasons for this "great misfortune," his primary blame centered on saw mills and tanneries for their ruining the water quality and destroying spawning habitat.

Thorpe declared that during the 1830s the Beaverkill and Willowemoc were famous for their brook trout and they

were, at one time, favorites of the "lovers of piscatorial sports," but times were changing. Disturbingly, he wrote:

These haunts, where genius once found leisure from the toils of city life, with thousands of others which a few years ago abounded in game, are now deserted, and fret their way on to the ocean, stained by tan and thickened by the refuse wood that tumbles from the teeth of the grating saw. It has been very plausibly suggested that the constant clearing of the land precipitates the heavy rains so rapidly into the streams that they wash away and shift the game, destroy the spawn, and also the eggs of aquatic insects upon which the fish feed, lessening at the time the production of the fish and their food. The facilities of traveling have also had their effect in distributing anglers more plentifully over the country. Few streams or lakes can escape a thorough examination. The day is, therefore, rapidly passing away when tyros will be successful.[81]

Tanneries

It was not angling alone that began taking a toll on the trout populations of the region. The pristine waters of the Beaverkill and Willowemoc would soon also be choked with the odorous, noxious substances of the tanning industry. During the 1850s an increasing number of tanneries began to appear, up and down the watershed. Wastes discharged from this stream-related industry caused fish kills and loss of trout habitat, not only on the Beaverkill but all over the Catskills, and wherever hemlock trees grew in abundance. Commenting on the problem in his *American Angler's Book*, Thad Norris wrote:

> The tannery, with its leached bark, and the discharge of lime mixed with impure animal matter extracted from the hides, flowing in and poisoning the trout, have done more to depopulate our waters in a few years, than whole generations of anglers.

In the Catskills, the process of making leather with tannin, extracted from the bark of the hemlock, started as early as 1817. The first tannery appeared in Greene County, and the industry developed so rapidly that by 1825 tanneries in that region were producing more leather than in the rest of New York State combined. Tanners depended on hemlock, which flourished in the Catskills, especially on the northern and eastern slopes, where dense groves grew in moist, sheltered ravines and lower valleys. Hemlock was a limited resource, and when the trees were exhausted in Greene County, the competition for the bark forced the tanneries to move south, following the supply of mature trees into the heart of the Catskill range and into Sullivan and Ulster counties. Catskill hemlocks were said to be the richest in tanin; pioneer tanner Zadock Pratt once avowed that "the farther you go from the Catskill mountains, the less tannin you find in the hemlock."[82]

Another thing a tanner needed was a good supply of water. Streams provided inexpensive waterpower, as well as large amounts of fresh water necessary to the various stages of the tanning process. As was often the case, they were also considered convenient for ridding the tannery of its unwanted wastes, which were simply discharged into the nearby waterway.

Early on, it was deemed more practical to construct tanneries in the forest, and cart the hides in and out of the mountains, than to haul the bulky bark out. Hides were brought up the Hudson River by sloop, and then overland by oxen and horses to the tanneries. Many of the hides that were sent to the Beaverkill region originated from places as far away as Odessa, Russia, and Rio de Janeiro, Brazil. Some arrived by railroad at Callicoon and then were brought by wagon, over roads so rough that only two trips per week could be made; the wagons forded the Willowemoc at the present site of the Hazel bridge.

The hides were first limed or sweated. After the hair and excess flesh were scraped off, they were placed in a series of curing vats containing "ooze" made from the ground hemlock bark and water. As the hides progressed through the vats, they were subjected to solutions of increasing strength. Since large quantities of clean water were needed to control the tannic acid, the vats were sunk in the ground near the stream. Eventually, the hides were removed and dried, then treated with fish oil, then dried again and treated with tanner's oil. To tan a hide by the hemlock method took from six to eight months; the leather produced was mainly used for shoe soles, and it had a distinctive red-brown color.

During the peeling season, an army of men stayed in the forest, near the hemlocks, living in temporary log houses and crude shanties. One, who became a bark peeler at the age of thirteen, described his first experience in such a shelter:

One of them, about 16 by 20 feet, I was in. There were two beds, a fireplace, a small stove, some benches and a table in the one room downstairs. Above there was a loft where the men slept on the floor. There was a ladder alongside the chimney leading up stairs, and right under the ladder there was a big black bear chained. I tell you, my eyes stuck right out when I seen that bear, for I had come down from Prattsville, where there was a village. There was an old woman cooking and smoking a pipe over the kettles. In that house lived the owner and his wife, six children, four workmen, the bear and a couple of dogs.[83]

There were loggers, who felled the trees; bark peelers, who stripped off the bark; and teamsters, who hauled the bark back to the tannery. The work was difficult and dangerous; the men were not paid well, and the hours were long and tiring. Accidents were frequent, and when bark peelers were trapped and crushed under the heavy weight of a giant falling hemlock, they paid with their lives.

Life as a bark peeler, working for the tanners and living in the forest, was difficult and trying:

We had pretty hard sort of grub in them times and durned few of the barkpeelers saw fresh meat mor'n once or twice a year, less of a Sunday or a holiday some of the men dug out a woodchuck or caught a coon. There was plenty of deer around sure enough, but firearms wuz scarce, and cost a heap, so thet most of the time we ate salt pork and trout.[84]

The flow of sap in the spring made it easier to remove the bark, so it was peeled in late April, May, and June and hauled to the tannery in winter, on sleds and drays. The bark peelers referred to the sap as "slime" because of its stickiness; their predicament in dealing with this problem is best described by H. A. Haring, author of *Our Catskill Mountains*:

With the "slime" came much personal inconvenience. For, in their task of peeling the bark, the men would inevitably lean against the sticky sap. They would get stuck

Fleshing the hides. Hides were limed or sweated and the excess flesh scraped off.
One Hundred Years' Progress of the United States, 1870

against the tree, against the fresh bark, against the leaves of underbrush, even against each other! Then again, the sap dried on their clothes, which—it has been said—were never taken off during the two or three months of the peeling season.

It was commonly said in the Catskills, at the time, that "you could smell a barkpeeler coming—even before he left the woods." The tanneries, too, were a smelly business. The sap or slime on the bark would ferment and sour; and fish oil, animal hair, and the decaying flesh taken from the hides fouled the air. Curing vats, with their concoctions of tanbark and lime, were emptied into the waterways, killing fish and polluting the waters downstream.

In 1832 the first of the tanneries had appeared in the Beaverkill Valley when Linus Babcock constructed a dam across the river and built a tannery at the hamlet of Beaverkill. By the 1860s the demand for leather had increased to such an extent that there were eight tanneries operating in the area. One was located on the Little Beaverkill at Morrston; four were on the Beaverkill at Shin Creek, Beaverkill, Westfield Flats (Roscoe), and Butternut Grove; and three were along the Willowemoc, at Willowemoc, DeBruce, and Westfield Flats. The tannery at DeBruce was constructed in 1856, just downstream of Mongaup Creek, and was the largest, employing about one hundred men.

Competition for the hemlocks was great, as each tannery depended on the bark for survival; trees were cut down wherever they could be reached. Those found along stream banks were felled across the water, peeled, and left, bank to bank, obstructing the stream. While many of the hemlocks along the Beaverkill and Willowemoc were hauled to the river and rafted to market, it is estimated that 95 percent of the trees were left where they fell. Many deplored this wasteful practice of cutting down hemlocks, taking the bark, and leaving the greater part of the tree to rot. Trout fishermen were united in their dislike of the tanners and complained bitterly about how they despoiled the countryside and polluted the streams.

It did not take the tanners long to devastate the hemlocks in the Beaverkill and Willowemoc watershed. The industry peaked about twenty years after it had begun and then slowly declined, closing shortly after 1885. The tanners were so complete in their destruction of the hemlocks that many believed the giant evergreens would never return. Today, a little more than a hundred years after the industry left and moved

Unhairing the hide. As hides progressed through the tanning process, they were subjected to solutions of increasing strength, and hair was removed.
One Hundred Years' Progress of the United States, 1870

The tan yard. Large quantities of clean water were used to control the tannic acid, and vats were sunk into the ground in the tan yard near streams.
One Hundred Years' Progress of the United States, 1870

west into Pennsylvania, hemlock groves of mature trees are again found in abundance.

Because of the extensive abuses and wasteful practices of the tanning industry, there has been a common misconception that prior to this period the Catskills were dominated by hemlocks. The Catskill forest before the ravages of the tanners was similar to the forest that is present today, as depicted by surveyors' maps and field notes collected prior to 1812, before there was any considerable human disturbance or forest exploitation.

Records of early surveys are a useful means of determining what the forest was like; trees marked as witness or bearing trees and recorded on maps were an unbiased sample. Robert P. McIntosh, who studied surveyors' field records, found, "In 21 of 22 surveys of the Catskill forest, beech was the most common tree; and in most of these, hemlock was the second most common tree. Beech comprised 50% of the total density, hemlock 20%, sugar maple 13%, and birch 7%."[85]

One of the earliest survey records of the Beaverkill Valley, on file in the Ulster County Clerk's Office in Kingston, is a map by Jacob Trumpbour, dated 1809. The survey covers an area of 8,250 acres of the upper Beaverkill, in the present-day area of Turnwood, Alder Lake, and Shin Creek. As with the findings of McIntosh, this map depicts 56.4 percent beech, as the most common trees used as survey markers, followed by 17.6 percent maple, 10.3 percent birch, and 5.1 percent hemlock.

Pigeon Fever

Because of its abundance of beech trees and vast forest wilderness, the Beaverkill region was also famous as a gathering place for the phenomenon known as the wild pigeon. To the early settlers, they were a wonder of nature, coming north each March, filling the sky with numbers impossible to comprehend or describe.

The story of the wild pigeon, or passenger pigeon as it is now called, is one of greed, wastefulness, and senseless slaughter. To exploit a species so abundant and reduce it to extinction is unconscionable. The passenger pigeon was a beautiful, slender bird, fifteen to seventeen inches in length, with delicately pinkish-tinted gray feathers and a long tail of eight to nine inches. Passenger pigeons had a wingspan of twenty-three to twenty-five inches and resembled mourning doves, though much larger.

A bird of the wilderness, the pigeon chose to nest in the forests north of central Ohio, from the Mississippi River to New Hampshire. Sullivan County was well known for its vast nestings, as were the mountainous sections bordering Sullivan, Ulster, and Delaware counties. A favorite nesting area was the headwaters of the Beaverkill, Willowemoc, Neversink, and Esopus, stretching from Turnwood to DeBruce and Willowemoc, all the way over to Frost Valley and Denning. Passenger pigeons nested in immense numbers, covering thousands of acres; they chose areas of dense forest, with plenty of water and mast. While they ate a wide variety of seeds and berries, they preferred mast crops, especially the nutritious beechnut.

Their incredible flights were a wonderment to all, and attempts to adequately describe their numbers taxed the powers of even experienced writers. One of the earliest to try was John J. Audubon, who encountered passenger pigeons along the Ohio River in 1813 and gave this account:

The air literally filled with pigeons; the light of noon day became dim, as during an eclipse; the pigeons' dung fell in spots not unlike melting flakes of snow; and the continued buzz of their wings over me had a tendency to incline my sense of repose.[86]

Bringing darkness to daylight did indeed cause anxiety and apprehensiveness among those who witnessed these great flights of pigeons. Some early colonists of New England looked upon them with reverent wonder; they saw the flights as "ominous presages of approaching disasters"[87] and believed that pigeons were always more numerous in the springs of sickly years. Pigeons flying through the sky, wave after wave, in countless numbers, presented an image of "fearful power" and frightened beast as well as man: "Our horse, Missouri, at such times has been so cowed by them that he would stand still and tremble in his harness, whilst we ourselves were glad when their flight was directed from us."[88]

When pigeons arrived at the nesting grounds, they selected mates, and for the next two days went about the business of constructing a nest, entirely from sticks and twigs. They then took turns tending the nest, which usually contained but one or, at most, two eggs. Early in the day the males would leave to drink and feed, returning about midmorning; then the hens would leave, staying away until three o'clock in the afternoon. This pattern occurred daily, rain or shine, for twenty-eight days. After fourteen days the egg hatched, and the young, known as squabs, were cared for by both parents. For the next two weeks, squabs were fed a substance known as pigeon milk, which the parent birds produced in their crop, or throat lining.

Trees were filled with nests, often fifty or more in a single treetop. The nests were nearly flat, flimsy, and not very secure; any disturbance to the nesting bird usually resulted in the egg or squab being tossed to the ground. So many pigeons would collect in the trees that their accumulated weight would break the branches, leaving a nesting site desolate, as if a great hurricane or tornado had swept through the forest.

Noise and chaos were companions of a nesting ground, and the screaming and squealing pigeons made when roosting could be heard for miles: "From an hour before sunset until nine or ten o'clock at night there is one continued roar, resembling that of a distant waterfall."[89] Even when feeding on the forest floor, pigeons were a sight long remembered. They were so numerous and close to one another that the ground could scarcely be seen, and those who witnessed these events marveled at how they left not a leaf unturned in their search for beechnuts.

While pigeons were hunted and killed by hawks, owls, and every other predatory form of wildlife, their greatest enemy was man. When a nesting site was discovered, the news spread over the countryside, and all of the male inhabitants became afflicted with "pigeon fever." "Farmers, mill men, bark peelers, raftsmen, and tavern loafers"[90] would leave their customary occupations, intent on sport or plunder, to slay without limit. Shortly, they would be joined by professionals, netters and gunners, who descended on the roost with every variety of weapon and method known, to destroy or capture passenger pigeons while they tried to nest. The birds were shot, netted, poked out of nests with long poles, clubbed, and choked by men using pots of sulphur, "making the birds drop in showers."[91]

When they were in season, nothing was talked of, or eaten, but passenger pigeon. To those settlers trying to survive the rugged existence of Catskill mountain life, they were a welcome source of food. There was pigeon stew, broiled pigeon, pigeon potpie, and pigeon served in every style imaginable. They were salted down in barrels for winter use and shared with less fortunate neighbors whose food supply was not as plentiful.

While some were killed for home use, the greatest number found their way to markets in major cities. Commercially minded men were attracted to this great natural resource and killed or captured pigeons primarily for sale to restaurants and hotels. Before the advent of clay pigeons, gun clubs also purchased many of the birds for use as live targets.

Once a roost was located, rough roads were cut into the mountainsides to enable wagons to haul pigeons to market. Buyers would erect coops or cages for holding live birds and haul in barrels and ice for shipping dead birds. Day after day, two-horse wagons loaded with pigeons wound their way out of the forest, passing over the Newburgh and Cochecton Turnpike to the Hudson, to be taken by sloop or steamboat to New York. If a rafting freshet coincided with nesting pigeons, almost every raft leaving the upper Delaware carried a load of the birds, which were sold all along the river to Philadelphia.

The carnage that occurred when men invaded a nesting area is difficult for those living today to imagine. A mountain resident writes of a trip to a nesting at the headwaters of the Beaverkill and Neversink:

The flock is said to be spread over a space of ground some ten miles long and two miles wide. The trees there are filled with nests in every direction, and the ground is almost covered with eggs and dead pigeons. The hunters shoot into crowds, and when the birds do not fall within a few steps, they make no effort to find them, but try again. There was an immense number of hunters on the ground

Male and female passenger pigeon. Because of its abundance of beech trees and forest wilderness, the Beaverkill region was famous as a gathering place for wild pigeons. Louis Agassiz Fuertes, *The Passenger Pigeon*, 1907

and when the party from this place came out, they met some 150 or 200 persons armed and equipped—for the work of slaughter—who were just "going in."[92]

As long as passenger pigeons existed in great numbers, they were easy quarry for hunters. They were not shy or wary as most game, and they allowed men with firearms to approach them at astonishingly close quarters. This resulted in a most destructive fire, and the slaughter of pigeons was assured: "Many a time I have fired until the old gun became so hot I could scarce bear my hand on the barrels and was forced to cease for awhile to allow them to cool before I dared reload again. The flocks were so dense I literally made it rain pigeons."[93]

While some professional pigeon men resorted to the use of firearms, many more who made their living exploiting the birds used nets. One man who pursued pigeons for many years among the beechwood forests of the headwaters describes the method in graphic detail. After constructing a "bough house," a bed was made by leveling the ground nearby:

> Upon this we sprinkled wheat with anise seed to tempt the pigeons. A net was placed on one side of the bed fastened with saplings which sprung back so that when a rope was pulled at the bough house the net would be thrown over the bed. We had flyers and stool pigeons. Their eyes were sewed shut so they could not see; a flyer had a string attached to its legs. When thrown in the air it would fly up a short distance and drop down in a natural way as though it had found an inviting spot. This would attract the attention of pigeons which might be flying in the vicinity, sometimes drawing them from a considerable distance. Then the stool pigeon tied at the end of a lever that could be worked up and down with a string, would be made to fly. By and by down would come the flock of pigeons with a roar to the bed. While eating the grain the net would be sprung. Then a rush for the bed to hold down the net and kill the pigeons by biting them in the neck. The dead birds would be thrown in a basket, the feathers carefully picked off the bed, the net again set, when everything would be in readiness for the next flock.
>
> It's down right mean to kill them, but its business—business, not sentiment. I remember the first time I bit a pigeon and killed it. Ugh! I thought I tasted it for a week. Die easy? O, yes, just a little bite on the back of the neck, and the pigeon is dead before you can wink.
>
> It was always the rule to let one or two escape so as to bring back another flock to the same feeding ground. How many did we usually catch? Why, at one haul we could cover 150 perhaps, but the usual number was from 75 to 100. I knew a man near Kingston who netted 3,000 pigeons in half a day. It was an ordinary thing to catch 1,000 in a day. Those were great days my boy.[94]

While all must share responsibility for the extinction of the passenger pigeon, it was many people's conclusion that the netting of birds for market deserved most of the blame. The number of birds sold commercially was incalculable, and could only be reckoned in the billions. When railroads penetrated all parts of the country, they brought the prey closer to markets. In addition, the telegraph was used to apprise the netters as to the whereabouts of the pigeons. Express companies were anxious for the netters to know where the pigeons were, since they charged between six and twelve dollars per barrel and anywhere from four thousand to five thousand barrels were generally shipped from each nesting.

By the 1890s one hundred to two hundred men were engaged in netting pigeons all the time. With increased communications, netters, gunners, and buyers seemed to arrive at a roost at the same time as the pigeons, and they were joined by a multitude of hunters, amateurs and greenhorns, who surrounded and destroyed nesting grounds.

Reports by sportsmen repeatedly indicated that the passenger pigeon was in trouble. The size of the flocks kept diminishing, while the destructive forces exploiting them multiplied. The cry for their protection was a long time coming, and once the birds began their downward spiral, it was too late. An article calling for a closed season appeared in *Forest and Stream* as early as the fall of 1876, when there were still abundant numbers:

> If we wish much longer to hear over our heads on bright March mornings the rush of his breezy wings speeding in swift flight above the waking woods, battalion after battalion sweeping on from horizon to horizon almost in a breadth; if we wish our October lunch of his broiled tender flesh, or care for "squabs on toast"; even if we wish to pack them in a box, and liberate him only to cut short his sudden joy with our shot "at 21 yards rise," the pigeon, which is not only useful and beautiful, but a delight, must soon be protected by law from wanton capture in what should be for him as well as other birds, a "close season."[95]

By 1890 pigeons were scarce everywhere in the East. Traditional nesting grounds were now being abandoned, and the birds were being driven westward into the forests of Michigan, Wisconsin, and Canada. Even though everyone was aware of the wholesale slaughter of pigeons for commercial purposes, there were those who refused to believe the birds were in danger of becoming extinct. They believed that, owing to the birds' persecution, the pigeons simply disappeared to a distant and unexplored part of the country and hid themselves.

The last large flocks nested along the upper Beaverkill in 1877. In the final days, reports of passenger pigeon sightings grew scarce. The few that reached the public came out of the Catskills and, not surprisingly, from their old nesting grounds in the vast hardwood forest of the Beaverkill. When the birds were seen, the numbers were a pittance compared to their former abundance; but because of their scarcity, a flock of any size caused a sensation.

A few years after their disappearance, naturalist John Burroughs caused a stir when he gave accounts of passenger pigeon sightings to the readers of *Forest and Stream*. Pigeons were spotted at DeBruce in the fall of 1904 and, two years later, at Willowemoc. In 1907 Burroughs made a trip to Sullivan County to verify a report of about a thousand pigeons seen in May: "The locality was a few miles north of Livingston Manor, near the Beaverkill. I am fully convinced that the pigeons were seen,"[96] wrote Burroughs. Quite possibly, the last sightings were of a small flock preparing to nest along the Beaverkill in 1909, and a flight of about three hundred, seen over Willowemoc in 1910.

In 1914 the Cincinnati Zoological Gardens announced that its lone female, the last remaining passenger pigeon, had died in her twenty-ninth year. In 1878 the zoo had received eight passenger pigeons, and while a number of birds were hatched, all had died except Martha. Desperate to find a mate for the bird, the zoo had made an offer of one thousand dollars, but no one came forward to claim the reward.

The prevailing view of the people toward the extinction of a species so beautiful and so numerous was one of profound regret. Not everyone, however, took a sentimental view of their passing. Some found "its manner of life and vast numbers incompatible with agriculture interests." They determined that "when the wilderness ceased to exist, the earth had no place for the wild pigeon."[97]

11

"The Trout
Are Playing Out"

During the 1860s the Beaverkill's trout population received a small reprieve when the Civil War (1861–65) consumed men's passions. Those anglers who traveled to the stream during these years again found brook trout in abundance. Two men who journeyed over from Delhi and stayed at Murdock's wrote of their experiences to the editor of the *Bloomville Mirror* in June 1864: "We kept a record of each day's work, and the number caught by each, which gives the following result. . . a grand total for the three and a half days, 776 trout."[98]

Another interesting report of this period was found by Kenneth Sprague of Roscoe, while he was glancing through a diary his grandfather kept for many years. The entry was dated April 14, 1865: "Went fishing at Baxter's with Harry Mott; not much luck. Went to Buck Eddy [Willowemoc Creek, just upstream of Roscoe] and caught 109 trout. This night President Lincoln was assassinated."[99]

Several significant events were pivotal in the history of the Beaverkill; the first occurred when railroads penetrated the remote areas of the Catskills. Following the Civil War, an epidemic known as "railroad fever" spread across America. Visions of great commercial activity and national expansion were on the minds of everyone; bankers, manufacturers, farmers, and resort owners dreamed of prosperity and profits. Railroad construction became widespread, and new lines found their way from population centers even into the tiny, secluded hamlets bordering trout streams.

Construction started on the Rondout & Oswego Railroad in 1869. This line began in Kingston and wound its way up the Esopus valley, over Pine Hill, and into Arkville. A mere fifteen miles from Arkville, the upper Beaverkill was now accessible to anglers, who traveled up the Dry Brook valley,

over a wagon road, and around Balsam Lake Mountain to the headwaters. Even before it was completed, fishermen began using the line; and additional exploitation of the mountain streams was not only swift but dramatic. The *Kingston Journal* reported on the first trout shipped via the new railway, in the summer of 1870:

> Several thousand speckled trout from the brooks of Shandaken, Olive and other sections of Ulster, have been brought to town of late. The Rondout & Oswego railroad cars transverse the trout districts of the county, and not only afford cheap travel for those who indulge in piscatorial sports, but also bring fish to market in so short a space of time after being caught, that they are nearly as hard and fresh as when first taken from the water.[100]

A second railroad, and one that had an even greater impact on the Beaverkill and Willowemoc, began laying its tracks in 1868. The New York & Oswego Midland Railroad ran from New York to the very doorstep of the Beaverkill. The line traveled through Sullivan County to Morrston (Livingston Manor), along the banks of the lower Willowemoc Creek to Westfield Flats (Roscoe), and then followed the Beaverkill downstream, all the way to East Branch and on to Lake Ontario. At this time, Westfield Flats contained "3 hotels, 4 stores, 3 blacksmith shops, 2 wagon shops, 1 cabinet shop, 1 harness shop, 2 shoe shops, 5 saw mills, and 2 tanneries."[101] Known simply as the Midland, the railroad officially opened July 9, 1873. The last spike was driven on the banks of the Beaverkill at Whirling Eddy, a pool the raftsman called Hell Hole.

With the coming of the railroad, the Beaverkill was easy to reach. In fact, the Midland opened the door to a flood of anglers who could now get to the stream in a matter of hours and could commute regularly on weekends. Coincidently, trout fishing in the 1870s became increasingly popular, being fueled by the publication in New York of *Forest and Stream*, a weekly journal devoted to fishing, hunting, and outdoor life in general.

Forest and Stream made its debut on August 14, 1873, and in a short time began informing its readers on the pleasures of trout fishing and how to use the new railroad to reach the Beaverkill:

> One of the best trout regions within striking distance of New York lies on the borders of Sullivan and Ulster counties, and includes the famous Beaverkill and Willowemoc rivers. By taking the 6 o'clock morning train of the Oswego Midland Railroad the angler can reach Morrston at noon, distance one hundred and seventeen miles, enjoy the afternoon fishing, and fish all the next day until 3½ o'clock, when the train will bear him back to this city and land him at Cortland or Desbrosses street at 10½ o' clock, with his fish fresh and ready for the morning breakfast.[102]

Railroads brought the beautiful mountainous scenery of the Catskills, with its fresh air and pure waters, to the threshold of the metropolis. With low travel rates, good railway accommodations, and inexpensive board, it was not long before the entire region became one vast summer resort. Now city dwellers could escape the heat and toil of their fast-paced lives and spend time in the country, vacationing, much to the satisfaction of hillside farmers, boardinghouse owners, and hotel keepers.

Recognizing that trout fishing held a strong attraction for summer visitors, railroad officials began promoting the Beaverkill through advertisements in sporting magazines and journals. For many years the Ontario & Western, which replaced the Midland, ran "hunters' and fishers' specials," with Pullman drawing-room cars that carried the names of the famous streams, such as the Neversink, Willowemoc, and Beaverkill.

On the heels of the railroad came more hotels and boardinghouses, which catered to the new fishing tourists. In 1878 the Midland published the first of many annual guides to "healthful summer resorts among the mountains." This first edition informs anglers who arrive at Morrston:

The "Mountain Express." As new railroad lines found their way from population centers into secluded hamlets along trout streams, city anglers began to commute regularly to the Beaverkill Valley.

Fishing the Willowemoc Creek. A guest at the Hearthstone Inn, wearing a shirt and tie, tries his luck at the veneer mill bridge at DeBruce.
Jean Boyd

Here Emmet Sturdevant will meet you and take you to his house, or to Cooper's or Matt Decker's on the Willowe-moc, or good old Murdock or Jones Brothers will seat you in a springy buckboard for the Beaverkill. Who has not heard of "Murdock's on the Beaverkill"? Many a clergy-man and lawyer and business man has eaten motherly Mrs. Murdock's cakes and maple syrup during the last twenty-five years, and has gathered new strength and health from absorbing the perfect air as he struggled along the stream, and then came home, with a full basket, wet and hungry, to absorb his own trout as they came crisp and hot from her skillful hand.[103]

The enthusiasm for trout fishing continued to grow, and it received an added boost from the publication of a number of books on angling, most notably *I Go A-Fishing*, by W. C. Prime (1873); *The Fishing Tourist*, by Charles Hallock (1873); *Pleasures of Angling*, by George Dawson (1876); and another by Hallock, titled *The Sportsman's Gazetteer* (1877), which included a directory to fishing resorts in the United States.

This growing popularity was illustrated locally in an article that appeared in the *Ellenville Journal*:

The number of both City and Country who affect to be "trout fishers" is largely increased. It is said to be a rule in New York business circles that all applicants for positions of any kind, from that of bar-tender up through all grades of clerkships to a silent partnership, must be provided with a trout-pole, fly book and fishing basket. No man or boy can "come the gorilla" in the stock exchange who doesn't own or can't borrow a German silver mounted fly pole. No law student can be admitted to the bar until he knows the difference between a "Limerick" and an "Aberdeen," and owns a pair of hob-nailed "stogas." And the last time I was on the Beaverkill I encountered, rod in hand and creel on his back, a tailor's apprentice, fresh from Gotham, in a brand new suit of silver-grey corduroys! And in the country, the highway from boyhood to manliness leads through a trout-stream as certainly as through a cigar box. Hence the poor trout have next to no chance at all.[104]

The multitude of new anglers placed greater stress on the dwindling trout supply. Many believed that the railroads would be the end of trout fishing and that the streams would never recover from this new onslaught of fishermen, who fished so persistently. At this time, the trout population of the Beaverkill was still dependent upon the natural reproduction in the stream. No stocking or planting of domestic trout had occurred, and the native brook trout were still of the original strain.

With more and more fishermen vying for fewer trout, competition developed the practice known as "fishing for count." Eager to best one another, anglers no longer kept only the larger "saving" trout but began keeping every fish, right down to the smallest fingerlings, and then boasted of the numbers they had taken. Year by year, overfishing reduced the average size of the trout.

Because of their relatively small size, trout were hauled from the stream by a "jerk of the wrist," which served to make quick work of the fish while at the same time it did not disturb the water. Without laws to regulate anglers' success, the number of trout one angler could remove in a single day was extraordinary: "A party of five brought home 800 trout"[105]; "a party of twenty captured 1,500 in a single day"[106]; "There have been by actual count over 2,000 fish in the cellar [at Murdock's] at one time."[107]

The trout were disappearing, and it was a matter of time until the free fishing enjoyed by everyone was doomed. Until then, the public roamed the countryside, camping and fishing freely wherever they chose. Most farmers whose lands adjoined the Beaverkill took in fishermen and, like the inns and boardinghouses, allowed their guests to fish over their neighbors' water. But now the demand was greater than the stream could produce, and hordes of new anglers were tramping the stream, anxious to fill their baskets.

George W. Sears, the popular outdoor writer who used the pseudonym Nessmuk, bluntly told his readers:

> Salmo Fontinalis is becoming small by degrees, and deplorably scarce. . . It is the constant, indefatigable working of the streams by skilled anglers, who turn out in brigades, supplemented by the granger, who takes his boys along in a lumber wagon, camps on the stream until he has "salted down" several butter tubs full of trout, and saves everything large enough to bite. . . Anglers increase as trout diminish; and such streams are infested by anglers from April to August, to an almost incredible extent, nearly all of whom basket anything more than four inches long. . . The trout are playing out.[108]

12

Unlimited Trout

The idea of replenishing streams or ponds by stocking developed early in the history of sport fishing in America. Locally, stocking began long before there were fish hatcheries, before Americans even knew how to artificially propagate trout. The first reported Beaverkill watershed stocking occurred as early as 1833, when Benjamin and Jacob Misener transported brook trout they had captured from Pease Brook, Hankins Creek, and other nearby streams, and placed them in Long Pond (Tennanah Lake).[109] Afterward, and for many years, Long Pond was known for its large brook trout. During the 1860s and 1880s it was still furnishing anglers with an occasional brook trout that exceeded four pounds!

The first attempt at managing New York State's fisheries resources began with the formation of the Board of Commissioners of Fisheries in 1868. There was a Fish Commission even before there was a Forest or Game Commission; "Chapter 285 of the Laws of 1868 authorized commissioners of fisheries for the State of New York."[110] Its first members were former governor Horatio Seymour, Robert Barnwell Roosevelt, and Seth Green. Roosevelt was a sportsman/conservationist who served on the commission without a salary; Seymour was a former governor of New York who ran for president of the United States in 1868 and lost to Ulysses S. Grant; and Seth Green was a sportsman and fish culturist.

As a pioneer fish culturist Seth Green became known, not only in this country but throughout the world, as "The Father of Fish Culture in America." His career began in 1864 when he purchased a portion of Caledonia Creek and began artificially propagating fish; his experiments with brook trout led to the "dry method" of the impregnating spawn. This method of propagating fish created the means by which fish raised

for food could be supplied in seemingly unlimited numbers, and also pioneered the way to replenish depleted streams with trout.

When Seth Green began hatching, feeding, and raising thousands of trout in ponds, the word spread quickly across the country that there was no limit to the number of trout he could supply. At the time, there were few who believed the stories of what he was accomplishing at Caledonia; that is, until newspapers began publishing articles about Green's success. He had inaugurated American fish culture, becoming the first to prove that the hatching of trout on a large scale could be practical and profitable.

While Dr. Theodatus Garlick of Cleveland, Ohio, had fertilized the eggs of trout and hatched them successfully as early as 1854, it was Green who introduced to America the idea that trout could be artificially propagated and supplied in numbers never seen before.

Seth Green did not have the advantages of a higher education; his knowledge was self-taught, learned through personal experiences, and even though he was basically operating in a scientific field with no guidance, he was successful and achieved worldwide fame. At this time few men or women, even those of science or associated with universities, possessed knowledge of fish culture. The ease with which trout eggs could be taken and fertilized, producing thousands of fry from a single pair of fish, was seen as an extremely exhilarating idea.

With the help of A. S. Collins, Green, in 1870, published a book on hatching and raising trout, titled *Trout Culture*. In his book, Green encouraged others to take up the business of fish culture; especially farmers, who usually had a running stream, spring, or pond on their property. He encouraged farmers to take up raising trout: ". . . turn this water into profit, not only by raising food supply for themselves, but a supply for the city and village market . . ."[111]

It was also in the summer of 1870, two years after it was formed, that the New York State Fish Commission constructed a hatching establishment on Caledonia Creek on lands leased from A. S. Collins, who then owned the stream and ponds formerly owned by Seth Green. Green at this time resigned his position as a commissioner and was named the superintendent of fisheries. The Caledonia facility was in an excellent location for the distribution of hatchery fish; it was not far from Rochester, and railroad lines that ran within a mile of the hatchery connected with others that traveled to all sections of the state.

From the onset the fish commissioners focused their efforts and finances on fish propagation; they recognized that throughout New York State there were large bodies of water belonging to the "people generally," in which the public had the right to take fish, such as the Saint Lawrence River, the Hudson, Lake Ontario, and other large rivers and lakes.

The commissioners believed that if the fish populations were to be increased, it should be done by the state for "the good of all." And it was stated in their first annual report to the legislature that while many species of fish produce thousands of eggs, those eggs deposited in the wild had a low rate

Seth Green, c. 1870. Seth Green became known throughout the world as the "Father of Fish Culture in America." He introduced rainbow trout into New York State waters as early as 1875. *Trout Culture*, 1870

Securing trout spawn. Eggs are stripped from mature female trout and fertilized by an adult male. *Scientific American*, July 1, 1868

of survival, due to their being eaten by other fish, washed away by erosion, and smothered when covered by silt. It was claimed that the artificial method of hatching eggs from adult fish was superior and had a survival rate of more than 90 percent.

More favorable conditions could be created by placing eggs in trays or troughs with a steady flow of carefully filtered water with proper temperatures; if this was extensively carried out, hatchery fish could offset the problem of overfishing. It was written at the time that "the purpose of the pisciculturist is to imitate and assist nature."[112] And, to put it simply:

> The fish-farmer simply secures the eggs; sees that they are impregnated; watches their hatching; protects the young fish from their natural enemies and unnatural fathers; feeds them, and brings them to maturity. This is all; there is nothing elaborate or intricate in the operation.[113]

At first the commission agreed to focus its efforts on the hatching of food fish. This included increasing the number of shad in the Hudson River, and artificially hatching whitefish and salmon trout (lake trout), both popular food fish found in Lake Ontario and favorite fishes of commercial fishermen. Notices were published in newspapers advising the public to send for as many eggs or fry as they needed for stocking public waters; and for the next couple of years, whitefish and lake trout eggs and fry were supplied throughout the state. A few years later the commission began receiving criticism that it was focusing on stocking the larger rivers and lakes and was not replenishing the many trout streams found in New York State.

In 1875, five years after constructing their first hatching establishment, the Fish Commission enlarged its operations by purchasing the leased site of the state hatching house, as well as the hatchery Seth Green had started years before. The

The state hatching house was constructed in 1870 along Caledonia Creek on lands previously leased by the New York Fish Commission.
New York State Fisheries Commission, annual report, 1874

commission now had a larger, more complete facility and was now in the position to raise large numbers of brook trout and replenish the trout streams of New York. The annual report to the legislature stated:

> . . . there are thousands of small brooks and ponds crossing the farms of our people, or running by their doors, and in some cases within the jurisdiction of a single ownership. The larger varieties of fish do not inhabit these waters, and they are too valuable for fish of a coarser class. They are in fact natural trout streams, but have become exhausted by over-fishing or neglect. Formerly, perhaps, they yielded a bountiful supply of valuable and delicious food; now they are entirely worthless. Their restoration should be no longer neglected, for the benefit which would result from the restocking of these waters would accrue to the people at large.[114]

Prior to this date brook trout had not been raised at public expense, and in their report to the legislature, the commissioners announced that they planned to restock, within a few years, all the waters of New York State. The Caledonia hatchery expected to produce one million brook trout, for distribution to all persons desiring them, and to stock public streams and ponds. The fry would be sent to any address to those willing to pay the traveling expenses of a messenger to accompany the trout. The commissioners were now in a position to give as many young fish to applicants as they wanted, for streams that had been neglected and "barren."

It was believed that trout streams in New York State were being ruined by overfishing, pollution, and streamside industries that constructed dams that prohibited trout from reaching important spawning grounds. Sawmills and tanneries also polluted streams with their discharges of sawdust, tannic acid, and animal wastes, and some streams were becoming warmer from deforestation; in many cases they were no longer inhabited by brook trout.

In the fall of 1875 the Caledonia hatchery took eggs from brook trout, hatched them, and in the winter and spring of 1876 delivered more than one million brook trout fry to destinations throughout the state. One of the first stockings of brook trout was sent to the Beaverkill; on February 10, 1876, Charles Mead, a founding member of the Beaverkill Association, received twenty thousand brook trout fry. These trout were placed in the waters of the association (now Beaverkill Trout Club) and were one of the first shipments of brook trout ever made from the state hatchery.

It became the Fish Commission's policy to issue an annual news release advising the public that trout or other fish could be had for free, by ordering them directly from Seth Green, Rochester, New York. Every winter, newspapers throughout New York informed the public when it was time to order trout fry. All that was required was that the recipient give a general description of the waters to be stocked, how many fish were desired, and an affidavit that the fish were placed in public waters. Unless picked up at Caledonia, the fry were shipped in tins delivered by a messenger. In such cases, the person ordering the fish was to include directions specifying which rail route to come by and whom to call for settlement, since it was expected that the messenger's expenses would be paid.

Railroads became eager participants in the Fish Commission's plan to restore the state's trout streams. They ordered their baggagemen to carry cans of young fish and crates of fish eggs, and to assist anyone loading or unloading the same. "Conductors have also instructions to stop express trains at any streams, to leave fish, providing they can do so without missing connections."[115]

In addition to carrying cans free of charge, the Ontario & Western began stocking trout along its line. Trout fishing was an important asset to the railroad's passenger service, and officials determined early that stocking was necessary to ensure satisfied travelers. Their records show that in 1878 only twenty thousand trout were acquired. In just a few years the number of fish put into streams by the O. & W. grew dramatically: In 1884 they placed 310,000 fish; in 1885, 460,000; and in 1886, 900,000![116]

Stocking was deemed so vital to the railroad that in 1890 the O. & W. constructed a special car, designed strictly for transporting and distributing trout and other fish along the many miles of streams and lakes bordering their rail line.

• • •

Perhaps because he was an avid trout fisherman and fish culturist, Seth Green knew that there were also hundreds of miles of streams and rivers in the state that never did contain viable native brook trout populations. Some contained brook trout only at the headwaters, or in tributaries, because the lower portions of the streams or rivers had water temperatures slightly higher than those preferred by brook trout. He was well aware that there were many waters that brook trout would not live in, and he posed the question: "Shall we let them lie barren or shall we stock them with some fish that will live and thrive in them!"[117]

Green also knew that there were other species of trout that could inhabit these types of waters, and as soon as the commissioners had decided to stock trout in all of the waters of the state, he began the task of acquiring a species of trout that could survive in those streams not suited—or no longer suited—for brook trout. He had knowledge of the brown trout of Europe, and he had experience fishing for rainbow trout in California. While readying the hatchery in the spring of 1875 to produce a million brook trout, Green also imported brown trout eggs from Germany. In April he received at the Caledonia hatchery 2,500 "Bachforelle" eggs from the famous fish hatchery at Huningen. Unfortunately, when the shipping package was opened, the eggs were "in a horrible state of putrefaction."[118]

The German hatchery was located on the Rhine River and received its water supply from the Rhine and from springs located on the premises. Constructed by the French government in 1852, the facility was near Basle and the borders of France, Germany, and Switzerland. The celebrated hatchery became the property of Germany after the Franco-Prussian War in 1871, and was named the Deutscher Fischerei Verein.

Seth Green firmly believed that rainbow trout could inhabit most of the streams that brook trout would not, and that they were the most suitable fish for rivers such as the Upper Hudson, Genesee, Mohawk, and many other rivers and streams that were too warm for brook trout.

Green was more successful in his attempt to acquire rainbow trout from California and had actually received rainbow trout eggs before the brown trout eggs were received from Huningen. He became familiar with rainbows when, at the request of the California Fish Commission, he took live shad fry from the Hudson River across the country to California in 1871 and placed them in the Sacramento River. While on the West Coast he observed and fished for rainbow trout in their native habitat and, because of his angling experiences on California streams, he determined that rainbows could withstand higher water temperatures than brook trout.

Seth Green also visited California the following spring and, not surprisingly, found time to do some trout fishing; an item in the *Pacific Rural Press* of San Francisco dated April 13, 1872, reported that: ". . . Seth Green, who is considered good authority, after a day's sport in Marin County, said he had never seen more game fish or better eating fry than our California mountain trout."[119]

Under the comments on "California trout" in an annual report of the Fish Commission, it was stated: "We have reason to believe from the character of the streams in which they are found, and which are for part of the year roaring torrents, and part of the time a succession of half dried up pools, that they [rainbows] will endure a much higher temperature than our trout."[120] Because of such extremes, Green was also convinced that rainbows could withstand greater hardships than native brook trout.

California Mountain Trout

It is important to again note that once the New York Fish Commission decided to replenish the state's trout waters, Seth Green's plans to do so included rainbow trout from the West Coast. He believed that rainbow trout were a much hardier fish, withstood higher water temperatures, and that they would live in the many miles of streams that were not inhabited by native brook trout.

The first shipment of rainbow trout eggs that arrived at the Caledonia hatchery from California received notice on the pages of *Forest and Stream* on April 8, 1875. In an item authorized by Seth Green, titled "California Brook Trout," it was stated that "Ten boxes of California brook trout have been received at the New York State hatching house, the gift of the Acclimatation [*sic*] Society of the Golden State . . . We believe this to be the first arrival of the kind in this part of the United States."[121]

In referencing the shipment of California brook trout in the year-ending annual report of the Fish Commission, it was stated:

On March 31, 1875, 1,800 of the eggs of this fish were received. Of these, we regret to say, a number had been spoilt during transportation, occasioned, no doubt, by exposure to too high a temperature. Of the number that arrived safely, however, a fair percentage was hatched, and on January 7, 1876, there were 260 of them alive, looking fine and healthy, and about three inches long.[122]

The 1,800 rainbow trout eggs were sent by Dr. William A. Newell, president of The Acclimatizing Society of California, an organization involved in constructing ponds and propagating fish, birds, and game, and distributing them throughout California. The Society was founded in 1870 in San Francisco with the goal of introducing game, birds, and fish from Eastern states and Europe to California. The Society communicated with individuals about acquiring or trading various fish and wildlife that would transport easily. One of the first persons contacted by the Society was Seth Green, who sent Dr. Newell Eastern brook trout eggs from the Caledonia hatchery.

In the winter of 1871 Dr. Newell had been elected president of the Acclimatizing Society, and a trout hatching establishment was constructed at the corner of Fulton and Gough Streets, in the Hayes Valley section of San Francisco. The plan was to hatch the eggs sent by Seth Green and distribute Eastern brook trout throughout the state of California.

The Society also procured trout eggs from Lake Tahoe, as well as eggs of native rainbow trout from nearby San Pedro Creek, and hatched these eggs at the Hayes Valley facility. By the end of May abundant numbers of Eastern brook trout, Lake Tahoe trout, and native rainbow trout fry were moved about fifteen miles from the city to a site where the Society had constructed ponds, dams, spawning beds, and a hatching house along San Pedro Creek on sixty acres it acquired at Point San Pedro, in San Mateo County. In January of 1872 the Acclimatizing Society was hatching trout eggs in troughs at the hatching house at Point San Pedro.

By 1873 the Society was taking eggs from its own stock of Eastern brook trout from the ponds at Point San Pedro, as well as Lake Tahoe trout and native rainbow trout from San Pedro Brook,[123] and was hatching them at the site, as well as hatching trout eggs on the grounds of the University of California at Berkeley. The Berkeley hatchery was the first owned by the state of California, and the Society was paid by the California Fish Commission to hatch trout at the facility

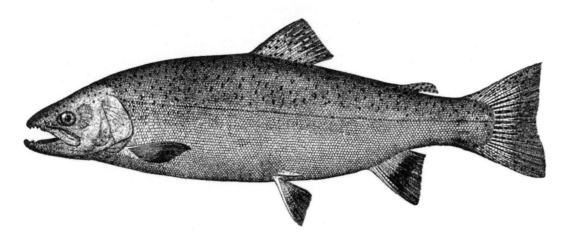

Steelhead trout. The trout eggs sent to Seth Green at the Caledonia hatchery in 1875 by Dr. Newell were from a stream containing both resident and migrant rainbow trout. *The American Angler,* Dec.–Jan. 1895–96

through 1873, after which the hatchery was operated by the state until it closed in 1877.

Strong evidence suggests that the rainbow trout that were sent by Dr. Newell to Seth Green at Caledonia were from San Pedro Creek where the Acclimatizing Society maintained their ponds and hatching house. San Pedro Creek is a small spring-fed stream that contained resident steelhead/rainbow trout and flowed directly into the Pacific Ocean. However, the Society at times also used other coastal steelhead/rainbow trout populations for propagation in the San Francisco Bay area. In either instance the eggs sent to Green were from streams that contained resident and migrant rainbow trout.

As stated previously, of the 1,800 eggs the Caledonia hatchery received in the spring of 1875 from Dr. Newell, only about 500 were in good condition; and of these Green was able to hatch 260.

• • •

The rainbow trout fry Seth Green received from the California Acclimatizing Society were carefully cared for in a pond separating them from all other trout. When they matured, at three years of age, they commenced spawning on March 19, 1878, and at this time, Green began referring to them as "California mountain trout." Those trout that spawned produced 64,000 eggs, and the fry were distributed throughout New York State, with the exception of 17,000 fry that were retained at Caledonia for breeders.

Stocking records reveal that only one stocking was made in the Catskills: On August 29, A. S. Hopkins of Catskill, New York, received 1,006 "California mountain trout" and placed them in the waters of Greene County.[124] Some of these rainbows, the first to be stocked in the Catskills, were placed in Kaaterskill Creek above and below the beautiful falls known as Fawn's Leap.

Three years after receiving the first shipment of rainbows from the Acclimatizing Society of California, a second shipment of rainbow trout arrived at Caledonia. For the first time ever, live rainbow trout fry, instead of eggs, were shipped from California to New York; on May 4, 1878, C. K. Green and J. Mason of the New York Fish Commission left the California State Hatchery at San Leandro with 150 "McCloud River" trout fry. The trout were donated by J. G. Woodbury, superintendent of the newly constructed San Leandro hatchery. When the men arrived at the Caledonia hatchery twelve days later, on the 16th of May, they had 113 live trout. This event was hailed as special; before this date only eggs, not live fry, had been shipped from coast to coast, and it was also believed to be the first time McCloud River rainbows were ever brought "to the Eastern States."[125]

Seth Green saw little difference between the two shipments of rainbows he received from California; he claimed the difference was primarily in their external appearances, probably because they came from different localities. He wrote that the McCloud River trout was the "true rainbow," and that it had a bright red band along the lateral line, whereas the mountain trout had the same markings, but with a fainter tint that in some was hardly visible. He believed the mountain trout had the "finest game qualities," and the McCloud River trout grew to a larger size. The McCloud River rainbows were kept separately, in different ponds from the original shipment of rainbows sent by Dr. Newell. The California mountain trout again produced 94,000 to 97,000 fry in 1879 and 68,800 fry in 1880,[126] and while 34,000 were kept at Caledonia, the rest were stocked throughout the state, but none were planted in the Catskills.

However, on April 23, 1880, forty thousand California mountain trout eggs were sent to John Goodwin of the Greene County Hatchery, Palenville, New York, and those fry were distributed in the streams of Greene County. In addition, fifteen thousand California mountain trout eggs were also sent on May 3, 1880, to Col. E. Z. C. Judson (Ned Buntline), Stamford, New York, for stocking in the West Branch Delaware River; these were the first rainbows placed in the Delaware River watershed.

It was not until 1881 that many of the well-known Catskill rivers of the Delaware watershed were stocked with California mountain trout, and these were descendents of the shipment Seth Green received from Dr. Newell (1875). The Caledonia hatchery produced more California mountain trout than brook trout in 1881 and planted more than a million fry throughout the state. On the 24th of June, twenty-five thousand rainbows were sent to E. D. Mayhew of Walton, New York, to be stocked in the East Branch of the Delaware River, and a few days later a shipment of fifteen thousand fry were sent to W. C. McNally, editor and publisher of the *Hancock Herald*, who placed them in a spring creek near the East Branch at Hancock.

The Beaverkill was stocked at Lew Beach on June 30, 1881, by Ed Sprague, who received fifteen thousand rainbow fry, placing part of them in Shin Creek; and on the lower Beaverkill, M. R. Dodge of Westfield Flats (Roscoe) stocked fifteen thousand rainbows on the 4th of July. All of the first rainbow trout stocked in the Delaware River watershed in New York State were California mountain trout, not McCloud River trout. At the hatchery at the time were thirty-five artificial holding ponds for fish, sixteen of which held California mountain trout, and only two contained McCloud River trout, none of which had been stocked.

That winter (1881), *The American Angler* published a column by George W. Sears, a popular outdoor writer and early conservationist, who wrote under the name of "Nessmuk." Titled "The Exodus Of The Trout," Sears detailed the demise of brook trout populations, and he asked, "What are we going to do about it?" He claimed that stocking had only moderate success, and it was useless to believe it would save the depleted streams. He blamed overfishing and those who kept everything that was "large enough to bite," even fingerlings; he stated, "anglers increase as trout diminish." In addition he pointed out the destruction of brook trout habitat by land clearing, log drives, and sawmills; and also asked, "Does anybody know a practicable way of preserving the brook trout in free waters?" Sears summed up his article by writing: "If the trout is to follow the elk, the Indian and the deer, it is well to look for a substitute; and the only hope in this direction seems to be the small mouthed bass."[127]

A few weeks later Seth Green, writing in the same outdoor journal, wrote a reply to the article by "Nessmuk": "I quite agree with the writer that the brook trout are bound to be exterminated before many years shall have elapsed."[128] And like Sears, he cited the loss of brook trout habitat through the destruction caused by sawmills, tanneries, paper mills, and the discharges of deleterious substances into streams and rivers; and overfishing by greedy, selfish fingerling fishermen. Green did not agree with Nessmuk's view that restocking streams was useless, and he added that he did not agree with his idea of stocking small-mouthed bass in trout streams, and wrote:

> In my opinion we have found a substitute in the California mountain trout, which New York State was the first to introduce in the East. They will thrive in the same waters with brook trout and will stand much higher temperature and endure greater hardships. Besides being hardy they are as gamy as the angler could desire. They are a fine table fish and grow to weigh from two to four pounds. We distributed last season, in New York State, over one million two hundred thousand young fry, and this coming season the supply will be much larger.[129]

For the next couple of years, millions of rainbow trout were stocked in the waters of New York State, and these continued to be the "California mountain trout" first received by Seth Green, not the McCloud River variety also kept at the Caledonia hatchery. Other major streams in the Delaware watershed receiving California mountain trout were Willowemoc tributaries on June 26, 1882; the Neversink River on July 7, 1882; and Callicoon Creek on May 12, 1885.

Shortly after stocking rainbow trout in streams, there was a general complaint that they disappeared from the waters where they were placed, and that they were rarely caught in the numbers that were expected. Rainbow trout began to develop the reputation that they did not stay in the streams in which they were planted. However, it was not too long before rainbows began to be caught in the large pools, eddies, and riffles of the Delaware River.

On May 3, 1883, *Forest and Stream* reported: "Two or three years ago some of the streams emptying into the upper Delaware were stocked with California mountain trout, and protection has been given them. A few days since an urchin of Hancock took a fine specimen of this fish, which shows they have thrived." And the following spring the *Walton Chronicle* of April 3, 1884, claimed:

> A boy was fishing in Big Eddy, in the Delaware River, at Narrowsburg, on Friday, and captured a California mountain trout that weighed over two pounds. Some fry of these fish were turned into the headwaters of the river, two years ago. Many fine specimens have been taken in the upper water since then but this is the first appearance of the trout as far down the river as this point.[130]

Confirming the fact that rainbows of large size now inhabited the Delaware River was a portion of a letter that appeared in *The American Angler* on July 4, 1885. Under the title of "California trout" it was stated: "I am told that there was a batch put into the Beaverkill, one of the branches of the Delaware River and that there have never been any caught near the locality where they were put in,

An early May afternoon along the lower Beaverkill. Lee Van Put

but about seventy-five or eighty miles below, where they found very deep water and large eddies, that they were quite plentiful."[131]

• • •

One year after Seth Green received the very small number of McCloud River rainbow trout fry from the San Leandro Hatchery, he received a shipment of eggs directly from the McCloud River. On March 26, 1879, J. B. Campbell of the U.S. Fish Commission shipped 7,200 eggs from the Baird Hatchery, located on the McCloud River, to Caledonia. Another shipment from Campbell of 6,078 eggs arrived at the state hatchery at Caledonia in April of 1880. It was not until 1883 that any McCloud River rainbow trout were stocked in any stream or waters of New York State; the first stocking of McCloud rainbows occurred on May 23, 1883, when twenty thousand McCloud River trout fry were stocked in the Mad River in Oneida County by H. W. Leonard, Camden, New York. Over time both the California mountain trout and the McCloud River trout were incorporated into the same ponds and generally referred to as rainbow trout.

13

Beecher, Burroughs, and Buntline

Three of the most notable and colorful anglers to fish the Beaverkill in the 1870s were James Beecher, John Burroughs, and Ned Buntline. Each, in his own way, enriched the lore of the Beaverkill. The Reverend James C. Beecher (1828–1886) was the brother of Henry Ward Beecher and Harriet Beecher Stowe. His sister, an ardent abolitionist, wrote *Uncle Tom's Cabin*, which became a sensation, ". . . the first powerful blow dealt to American slavery."[132] The book evolved into one of the most popular plays produced on the American stage. Henry Ward Beecher, too, was an antislavery leader, as well as a clergyman, and was one of the most conspicuous figures in the public life of his time. James, like his sister and brother, "ardently condemned slavery."

During the war over slavery, James Beecher fought in the Civil War, leading an all-black regiment: the 35th United States Colored Troops. Two years after the start of the war, President Lincoln authorized the recruitment of black soldiers to serve in the Union army. The governor of Massachusetts, John A. Andrews, formed the first black regiments, the 54th and 55th Massachusetts, and chose Brigadier General Edward A. Wild to lead the black soldiers and form a brigade. The governor believed that volunteer regiments of former slaves could be raised in Union-occupied eastern North Carolina to fill the brigade.

General Wild carefully selected officers who he believed were capable of meeting the demands of leading black troops and were "ardently committed to both abolition and temperance." As the commander for the first regiment he selected Colonel James C. Beecher of Hartford, Connecticut; having a Beecher at the head of a black regiment "was a powerful symbol."

Beecher had previous military experience serving as a lieutenant colonel in the 141st New York Infantry. He came from an abolitionist background, and his family worked against slavery prior to the Civil War; his father, Lyman, and famous brother, Henry Ward Beecher, were staunch abolitionists.

General Wild and Colonel Beecher established a camp at New Bern, North Carolina, and recruited men to join the 1st North Carolina Colored Volunteers; most of Colonel Beecher's soldiers came from eastern North Carolina and were slaves before they enlisted.

The regiment's battle flag was the gift of the black women of New Bern and Harriet Beecher Stowe. The banner portrayed "a rising sun with the word LIBERTY above it in crimson and black letters, and below it the inscription 'The Lord Is Our Sun and Shield.'" James carried the flag into battle at Charleston.[133] Shortly after the brigade was formed, the *Wilmington Journal* reported that the Confederate Congress passed a law dealing with black soldiers and their white officers: "All commissioned officers who shall be captured in command of negroes, shall suffer the penalty of death."[134]

The 1st North Carolina Colored Volunteers fought side by side with the 54th Massachusetts, the first black regiment formed by the governor of Massachusetts and made famous by the award-winning film *Glory* (1989). The units shared major battle experiences, both participating in the battle of Olustee, one of the bloodiest and the largest Civil War battle fought in Florida. The 1st North Carolina Colored Volunteers were later designated the 35th United States Colored Troops. Another engagement of the 35th Regiment occurred at the battle of Honey Hill, South Carolina, and once again Beecher and his men fought alongside the 54th Massachusetts Regiment.

Colonel Beecher was ordered to take the 35th forward, and during the attack he was severely wounded "but kept the field" and led his men in five separate charges against the rebel forces. After a bullet entered his thigh, he stood at the head of his troops until night, and then an officer of the 54th Massachusetts ordered two soldiers to escort him to the rear. During the battle Colonel Beecher was wounded three times, and his favorite horse was shot from under him.

After the war Colonel Beecher met a colonel from the Confederate army who was a part of the opposing forces at the battle of Honey Hill; the officer informed him it was no coincidence that Beecher and his great gray horse were hit so many times, as the word was passed among the Confederate soldiers to aim for the officer on the light gray horse. Beecher proudly served in the Union army throughout the Civil War and rose to the rank of Brevet Brigadier General.

Before the Civil War James Beecher had graduated Dartmouth and then went to sea, visiting China and for several years serving as a ship's officer in the East India trade. He then decided to be a minister like his father and brothers; he attended Andover Theological Seminary and served as a missionary in China.

Following the Civil War he became pastor at his brother Thomas Beecher's congregational church in Oswego, New York, and then moved to Poughkeepsie and became the pastor of the Poughkeepsie Congregational church, where he was well liked and received more than an adequate salary.

During the trouting season of 1874, the Willewemoc Club invited the Reverend Beecher, then pastor of the Poughkeepsie Congregational Church, to spend his vacation at their lodge at Sand Pond. The reverend loved nature and the outdoors; he usually spent his vacations fishing and camping in the most secluded parts of the country. On his visit to Sand Pond, he decided to explore the surrounding wilds of that primitive region and took off from the lodge with only his knapsack. After a lengthy journey through the forest, he discovered a lovely lake, encircled by high mountains with densely wooded peaks.

He was so delighted with the natural beauty of the place and its pristine surroundings that he camped along the lake's shore for six weeks, subsisting by hunting and fishing. Being a skillful angler, he did not have to venture far, since the lake had an abundance of brook trout. Believing he was the first person to discover the lake, he decided he had the right to name it Beecher Lake. This is somewhat understandable; maps of the region were rare. Even the most popular at the time, J. H. French's survey map, printed in 1858, failed to show any lake where Beecher found his, between Balsam Lake and Alder Lake.

The lake, its serenity, and the beautiful valley of the Beaverkill affected the forty-two-year-old preacher so deeply that he decided to abandon the comforts of city life. At the end of his vacation he resigned from his flourishing pastorate, giving up the lucrative salary of three thousand dollars, to live in the peacefulness of his newly found wilderness retreat.

Unbeknownst to Beecher, the lake that he found was called Thomas Lake and was owned by James Spencer Van Cleef. Van Cleef was willing to part with the lake, but with certain conditions. In September 1874 he sold it to Beecher, along with one hundred fifty acres, reserving the right to fish the lake for himself and members of the Willewemoc Club.

After purchasing the property, James Beecher decided to spend the first winter at the lake. He braved the punishing wind, cold, and deep snows alone, living in a tent. His only companions were "winter storms and the night cries of the mountain wild beasts."[135] There were no nearby neighbors, and the nearest road of any kind was seven miles away; yet he found the experience, with its solitude and peacefulness, uplifting:

> A sailor by nature and a minister by grace, I love to sit here by the hour and look out upon these surroundings. They are a source of never-ending enjoyment. During the winter months I am still more fond of this retreat, for as the beautiful snow lies so still and quietly all about us, there is nothing to disturb or discolor it. Here is true repose and communion with nature.[136]

All that winter, he walked through the woods and deep snow; it was nine miles to the nearest post office, where the

Colonel James C. Beecher was selected to command the 1st North Carolina Colored Volunteers, a regiment formed by men who had been former slaves in eastern North Carolina. Library of Congress

mail arrived once a week. James Beecher was a skilled and able carpenter, blacksmith, and glazier. He cleared land along the lake and cut a trail several miles through the forest so lumber could be hauled in for a permanent dwelling.

Along the lake, he constructed, with his own hands, a beautiful one-and-a-half-story house. After he and his family moved into the home, he avowed he would never go back to village life, even though he received many offers to return to the pulpit. "I can obtain more real enjoyment and comfort here with $300 a year, than with $3,000 in New York," he stated.

The Beechers were kind and caring people; Mrs. Beecher began teaching school and introduced books, for the first time, to the families of the backwoodsmen. They provided clothing to needy children who wore simple homespun. Their many acts of charity and good work endeared them to their neighbors; it was said that they gave to the poor of the valley so generously that they, too, were often "poor in purse."

Almost immediately, James Beecher began preaching locally at the two regional schoolhouses, and though he had to travel a great distance on horseback, he never missed a Sunday service. The scattered settlers journeyed by horse and wagon over the roughest of roads to Shin Creek (Lew Beach) to hear this Beecher, who had chosen to live among them.

Years later Frances Beecher, James's wife, wrote a lengthy article about the happiness and adventures she and her husband and three adopted children found in the wilderness of the Beaverkill. She wrote of the joy she found raising their children to appreciate the simpler things in life and learning about nature and the natural foods that could be found within the forest, especially the trout supplied by the lake:

> But the veriest gourmand could have asked no better breakfast than was furnished by those delicate trout, only half an hour from the pure water of the lake, half a pound in weight and dotted with the most brilliant colors, which neither oven nor frying pan could change. These trout, baked in cream and served with the best corn muffins and coffee, and discussed in the open air with one of Nature's loveliest pictures in full view, might well elevate the prosaic business into a fine art.[137]

Frances Beecher was also skilled with a fly rod and reminisced about catching the native brook trout in Beecher Lake: "A pretty sight it was when the first cool autumn sunsets came, and the shining trout were leaping up out of the water in every direction, as much as to say, 'Catch me if you can.'"[138] At those times she was proud of the fact that she could be the provider of her family's favorite breakfast. Taking her fly rod, and a companion to steady the boat, "she secured in twenty minutes"[139] enough trout to make everyone happy.

The house at Beecher Lake was a one-and-a-half-story building constructed by James Beecher shortly after he purchased the lake in 1874.
New England Magazine, July 1900

The Reverend James Beecher began preaching in the Beaverkill Valley at the two regional schoolhouses, and though he traveled on horseback, he never missed a Sunday service. *American Agriculturist,* September 1881

Those living along the Beaverkill came to love the "hermit" preacher, and they joined together and constructed a wagon road for him, from the post office to his home at Beecher Lake. To repay this kindness, he used his carpentry skills to place doors and windows in their crude log cabins or make other repairs and improvements. After the road was finished, he purchased a horse and wagon for Mrs. Beecher, but he continued to make his own journeys by saddle horse.

During the years he lived in the valley, James Beecher was at times visited by his famous sister and brother. Henry Ward Beecher, too, was a "lover of the trout-rod" and undoubtedly fished the Beaverkill when he came to Beecher Lake; he and his sister were known to pitch tents near Quaker Clearing along the Beaverkill. On occasion, he even served as guest preacher and delivered Sunday services. He was a preacher of national fame, known for his originality of thought and his highly emotional and florid sermons. For nearly half a century he was pastor of Plymouth Church, where he "fearlessly preached freedom for the slave, and [his] words have electrified a continent and sent a thrill to the heart of the whole English speaking race."[140] When President Lincoln visited New York and was asked what he would like to see, he chose Plymouth Church in Brooklyn, where Henry Ward Beecher delivered his antislavery sermons.

Henry Ward Beecher was an extremely popular figure. Though he had a great many admirers and was known across the land as a fiery orator, in the backwoods of the Beaverkill even someone of his stature and reputation could go unnoticed. One legend that has been preserved in the valley tells about the time when he was delivering a sermon and in the audience was an equally famous man by the name of Joe Jefferson. Jefferson was a veteran fisherman who had visited the stream for many years, frequently staying at Murdock's. He relaxed by sketching the natural beauty of the Beaverkill, but it was the stream's trout that he was after; and while he was a great success as an angler, Joe Jefferson was best known as an actor. He was a star of the stage, especially his role in *Rip Van Winkle.* From 1866 on, he played annual tours, and children across the country were taken to see "Rip." Jefferson became one of the best-known and best-loved figures in America, and his performance was recognized as "one of those rare and precious things which come only in a generation."[141]

On this particular Sunday, the service was held at the little one-room schoolhouse above Shin Creek;[142] since it was a warm summer day, the sermon was given from the doorway. During the service Henry Ward Beecher saw and recognized Joe Jefferson, who, he noticed, was not paying close attention. "They would not know me, but maybe my dog Schneider would," he said, louder than necessary. "Jefferson looked up (for that was Rip's dog's name) and said, 'who am I listening to?' and they told him it was Henry Ward Beecher."[143]

James Beecher died in August 1886. Upon his death, the Poughkeepsie *Evening Enterprise* commented on the "hermit" preacher's life among the settlers of the Beaverkill:

He had endeared himself to the dwellers of that mountainous region by his simple mode of life and his continuous acts of kindness and benevolence. During his entire residence among them he was always ready to help the poor and suffering with hands and money; foremost in every good work, and with all his eccentricity, he was looked upon by those people as a good man, worthy of their highest respect.[144]

● ● ●

Another who enriched the lore of the Beaverkill through his writings was John Burroughs. Famous throughout America as a naturalist, poet, philosopher, and writer, this Catskill native was an early saunterer and trout fisherman of the Beaverkill. Born in Roxbury, Delaware County, in 1837, Burroughs had fished mountain streams since boyhood, acquiring his love for the sport from his grandfather Edmund Kelly.

John Burroughs, like many who grew up on farms in Delaware County, learned to fish the small brook trout streams that seemingly flow through every farmer's field. Even today, these little streams are important to country

John Burroughs. Known throughout America as a naturalist, poet, philosopher, and writer, Burroughs was also an early saunterer and trout fisherman of the Beaverkill. *Scribner's Magazine,* January 1877

youngsters, who find in them not only the delightfully pretty "native" trout but also small adventures. They provide a challenge; a boy or girl can bring home a treat for the table, gaining praise and respect as an angler, or fail to deliver, and experience humility. Such trout streams build character.

In July 1860, when he was a grown man of twenty-three, Burroughs set out with a friend to find the source of the Beaverkill and to fish in famous Balsam Lake. Off in the wilderness, far from settlements, they camped and lived on the fish and game they captured. Perhaps they heard the howl of wolves, or the screech of a bobcat or panther; whatever the cause, their first night in the wilds of the Beaverkill was a memorable one. They took turns keeping up the fire; Burroughs had the first watch and "fired shots in several directions lest the creatures which seemed to be lurking out there in the darkness should close in on them."[145]

They survived the night, and the following day camped on the shores of Balsam Lake, where they tried to fish for trout; but they couldn't manage the flies until some men came along and showed them how. In the years that followed, Burroughs made other trips to the area, to the Willowemoc and Mongaup as well as the Beaverkill.

In 1868 he and some friends set out to fish Thomas Lake (Beecher Lake), the small trout pond hidden in the forest between Alder Lake and Balsam Lake. They hiked in from Mill Brook valley, and while the distance was not great, the terrain was steep, and the going was rough and difficult. The

men got lost and were about to give up and return home, but Burroughs convinced them to stay. He went ahead and eventually found the lake; then he returned and got everyone lost again:

> I would have sold my interest in Thomas's Lake at a very low figure. I heartily wished myself well out of the woods. Thomas might keep his lake, and the enchanters guard his possession! I doubted if he ever found it the second time, or if any one else ever had.[146]

At last they found the lake, and along its shore a crude raft, which they used to cast their flies for the trout they were assured were there. They did not catch very many during their stay and had to be satisfied with catching sunfish, which took the hook more readily. But it was Balsam Lake that really charmed him—which is not surprising, since it is beautiful and secluded, and its infinite population of trout was always eager to take the hook. In his ever-popular work *In the Catskills,* he described a trip made in 1869:

> Balsam Lake was oval-shaped, scarcely more than half a mile long and a quarter of a mile wide, but presented a charming picture, with a group of dark gray hemlocks filling the valley about its head, and the mountains rising above and beyond. We found a bough house in good repair, also a dug-out and paddle and several floats of logs. In the dug-out I was soon creeping the shady side of the lake, where the trout were incessantly jumping for a species of black fly that, sheltered from the slight breeze, were dancing in swarms just above the surface of the water. The gnats were there in swarms also, and did their best toward balancing the accounts of preying upon me, while I preyed upon the trout, which preyed upon the flies.[147]

Writing to a friend about this particular trip, Burroughs declared:

> I wish you could have had some of the trout we caught. At Balsam Lake, during a thunder shower that drenched Johns and me to the skin, I caught from a dug-out 75 as beautiful trout, in about two hours, as ever swam. It was such fun! Sometimes I would haul in two at a time, as I had two flies on my line.[148]

John Burroughs was a great observer, an angler who took the time to look closely at his catch and appreciate the great natural beauty of the native brook trout:

> It pleased my eye so, that I would fain linger over them, arranging them in rows and studying the various hues and tints. They were nearly uniform in size, rarely one over ten or under eight inches in length, and it seemed as if the hues of all the precious metals and stones were reflected from their sides.[149]

Burroughs was inspired by his beloved Catskills, their farmlands and mountain streams. He wrote with a unique style and shared with the world his observations of rural life and nature. Trout fishing often found its way into his writings. His trips to the Beaverkill Valley first appeared in *Wake-Robin* in 1871; in *Locusts and Wild Honey* (1879), he included the wonderful essay "Speckled Trout." Burroughs's writings endeared him to the American public, and by the turn of the century he was considered the foremost among American nature writers. He camped with Theodore Roosevelt and enjoyed the friendship of such noted men as Oliver Wendell Holmes, Ralph Waldo Emerson, Henry Ford, Thomas Edison, Walt Whitman, and John Muir.

John Burroughs loved fishing for the native brook trout of Catskill streams. He had the heart of a fisherman and possessed the special gift of being able to write with simplicity and beauty of his experiences:

> The fisherman has a harmless, preoccupied look; he is a vagrant, that nothing fears. He blends himself with the trees and the shadows. All his approaches are gentle and indirect. He times himself to the meandering soliloquizing stream; he addresses himself to it as a lover to his mistress; he wooes it and stays with it til he knows its hidden secrets. Where it deepens, his purpose deepens; where it is shallow he is in-different. He knows how to interpret its every glance and dimple; its beauty haunts him for days.[150]

● ● ●

No one who fished the Beaverkill was as widely known as Colonel Edward Zane Carroll Judson. Judson, who went by the pen name of Ned Buntline, was one of the most famous and colorful literary figures in America. He, too, was a native of the Catskills, born in Stamford, Delaware County, on March 20, 1823; and like John Burroughs, he developed a childhood love of trout fishing, the outdoors, and writing. However, that is where any similarity between the two men ends.

As a child, Ned Buntline learned to fish from his father, who made his own rods, tied his own flies, and was an expert on a trout stream. From him, Buntline developed a lifelong

John Burroughs fished all the major Catskill streams and many of their tributaries for a period that spanned seventy-five years. *Cold Brook Gazette*, May 1921

love of fishing, and when not off to a war or similar adventure, he could be found fishing in the Adirondacks, Catskills, and Poconos.

He had a burning desire to be an American hero, and he spent the greater part of his life trying to reach that goal. Ned became an adventurer at an early age, running off to sea as a cabin boy and serving as an apprentice in the navy. When he was but thirteen years old, he rescued the crew of a vessel that collided with a ferry boat and received from President Van Buren a commission as midshipman for his bravery.

Ned Buntline's wild and romantic life almost ended in 1846. In Tennessee he killed a man whose wife he was having an affair with. At the trial, the man's brother opened fire, and Ned escaped by leaping out a courthouse window. He was recaptured and hanged by a mob in the square; however, friends cut the rope and saved his life. Another version of the story is that the hangman's noose broke when the trapdoor was opened, and Ned, with his neck intact, was, by law, freed!

That year he began writing cheap, sensational fiction. He was the first of the dime novelists, and is credited with pioneering the technique. In time, Ned Buntline became known as the "King of the Dime Novels." This "fertile writer of fiction" wrote more than four hundred of the adventure books, and in many of his earliest stories he was his own hero; later he exploited "various more or less authentic Westerners."[151] His confrontations with the law continued, however, when a few years later he was convicted of leading the famous Astor Place Riot in New York and spent a year in prison. In 1852 he was indicted for causing an election riot in St. Louis, in which several persons were killed and houses and property destroyed.

Constantly seeking adventure and guided by intense patriotism, Ned took part in every war he could. He was a veteran of the Mexican War, the Seminole War, and the Civil War. When there were no wars, he found other ways to pursue danger and excitement. He was once a bounty hunter, and he roamed the Yellowstone region as a fur trader; he saw much of the old West when it truly was "wild."

After years of controversy, his public image soared shortly after he met William Frederick Cody at Fort McPherson, Nebraska, in 1869. At the time, Ned Buntline was reputed to be the best-paid writer in America, and Cody was the regimental butcher and buffalo scout. Ned conferred on him the name Buffalo Bill and proceeded to write a series of dime novels that featured Buffalo Bill as the hero. *Scouts of the Prairies*, a very successful play, followed; it starred Cody and introduced him to eastern audiences, who were eager to see the famous plainsman. Through his writings, Ned also immortalized the legends of Wild Bill Hickok and Texas Jack.

Always fond of firearms, Ned once had the Colt factory make him an order of guns. The Buntline Special was a unique .45-caliber six-shooter with a twelve-inch barrel and an overall length of eighteen inches. The weapon also had a

Ned Buntline was one of the most famous and colorful literary figures to ever fish the Beaverkill. Known as the "King of the Dime Novels," Buntline wrote more than four hundred novels and introduced to the American public such figures as Buffalo Bill, Wild Bill Hickok, and Texas Jack. *My Angling Friends*, 1901

detachable walnut stock, which allowed the owner to convert it into a small repeating rifle. Engraved on the walnut butt of each gun was the name NED. Buntline presented one of these guns to famed lawman Wyatt Earp, and it is reported that twenty years later the Dodge City marshall was still wearing his Buntline Special.

Age began to slow Ned down—age, and the many wounds he had received in campaigns and gun scrapes. His face and hands were scarred, and he had begun to feel the pain of a few unextracted bullets, which had made him somewhat lame. He was aging rapidly and looking older than his years. In 1871, at the age of forty-eight, a wealthy but weary Ned Buntline retired permanently to his Catskill roots at Stamford.

He was now content to challenge the trout and find excitement along the waters of the Beaverkill. And the stream must have filled his need for adventure, as he made numerous trips and annual pilgrimages from his elegant residence, called Eagle's Nest—so many, in fact, that he had a special wagon constructed to travel the rough and narrow roads leading in and out of the Beaverkill region. The wagon was extra long, with back-to-back seats, and was pulled by a pair of fancy bay horses.

Ned and his wife, Anna, spent a good part of each summer visiting Catskill trout streams. She, too, was an accomplished angler, and Ned, proud of her skill with a fly rod, let everyone know she had "deftly drawn her share of the speckled beauties from their native element to the shore."[152] Ned Buntline regularly opened the season along the banks of the Beaverkill, a tradition he looked forward to every year. He loved the Beaverkill, and in the last years of his life the stream gave him tremendous pleasure. In his special wagon, among the fishing gear, Ned packed a large American flag; whenever he stopped at an inn or boardinghouse in trout country, the flag was hoisted. On the Beaverkill he stayed at Tripp's Brookside Paradise, just upstream of the Turnwood covered bridge, and they always flew the Stars and Stripes in tribute to his intense patriotism. City sportsmen learned to look for this emblem as a sign that Ned Buntline was on the stream.

Even in the backcountry, Ned Buntline could draw a crowd. In the summer of 1871, while camping in the meadow near Beaverkill Falls, he described in his diary a talk he gave in Sunday school, where he found a large crowd "who had been informed that I would talk to them. Did so, with temperance for my theme, and the beauties of nature and the wilderness for my text."[153]

Ned Buntline also contributed to sporting literature, writing fishing articles for such publications as *The American Angler*, *The Rod and Gun and American Sportsman*, *Forest and Stream*, and *Turf, Field and Farm*. He wrote about the Beaverkill, and since his wife fished alongside him, he became enthusiastic about female anglers. In the fall of 1881 he wrote an article for *The American Angler*, recommending that more women enter the sport and write of their experiences. He ended the piece with an appeal: "What I want most to see now in *The American Angler*, is some live, spirited, true—sketches from some of our Female Anglers. There are plenty of them—so come on ladies and blest be he, who first cries—hold enough!"[154]

"Fishermen are born such—not made!" he wrote in an essay for Orvis and Cheney's *Fishing with the Fly*, published in 1883. And while he did not consider himself a great caster, or as skilled as some of his talented companions, he understood trout and possessed the practical experience and cleverness of one who had grown up along trout streams, and he believed the statement applied to him. And he was a good fisherman, holding his own with the best of them; he once took a beauty of a native brook trout out of Alder Creek, which flows into the Beaverkill at Turnwood. The trout weighed 2¼ pounds, and like many of the largest fish taken from the Beaverkill, it was captured in a large, deep pool created by a milldam.

Ned Buntline died in July 1886. His funeral was one of the largest ever held in the Catskills; special trains were run on the Ulster & Delaware Railroad to bring more than eight hundred people to Stamford. Mourners and citizens watched in admiration as two hundred veterans of the Grand Army of the Republic marched over to Eagle's Nest to accompany his remains to the cemetery. Throughout his life, Ned Buntline was a controversial figure. He was "both hymn writer and inveterate duelist, he could lecture on temperance while being accused of drunkenness."[155] Ned possessed a flamboyant and vain nature, which caused some people to despise him, others to admire him. He was a bona fide rabble-rouser and tremendously popular. The rugged old sportsman was friends with the best anglers of his day and fished with many of them, including the legendary Seth Green.

Fred Mather, a noted fish culturist and one of the earliest writers for *Forest and Stream*, wrote a series of articles titled "Men I Have Fished With," which evolved into a book with the same name, featuring many of America's best-known anglers. Writing about Ned Buntline, Mather states:

> When I fished with Ned in the Catskills, the drift of his talk would give an uninformed person the impression that his services to the country were equal to those of Grant, Sherman or Sheridan. His vanity was not balanced by modesty or humor, yet he was always clean of speech, as I knew him.
>
> Only last week, Col. Kerrigan wrote me: "When you write up Ned Buntline, don't put wings on him. He was a grand, good man all the same, and there is no use in trying to hide his faults, for he had plenty of them; other people have worked up Ned's faults, and you know that he was a man in whom the good predominated."[156]

Clubmen

During the 1870s overfishing had become a major problem; and one solution that was gaining in popularity among landowners and anglers was the establishment of private, or posted, water. In this era trout-fishing clubs were founded on the Beaverkill, and for the first time notices began to appear along the stream, advising anglers that they were no longer welcome.

Trout populations must have been in a deplorable state, as evidenced by the fact that legislation was introduced in Albany to halt trout fishing. This desperate attempt occurred in the spring of 1874, when "an Act for the preservation of fish, commonly called speckled trout" was introduced to the legislature. The bill prohibited anyone from catching or fishing for trout, in any stream, in Ulster and Delaware Counties, for a period of two years. While the bill passed in the assembly, it failed in the senate.[157]

Stream posting actually began in the Catskills on Willowemoc Creek in 1868, when the Willewemoc Club was established at Sand Pond. The club leased four miles of the Willowemoc upstream from the tannery at DeBruce. In a letter to *Forest and Stream*, dated March 19, 1874, Cornelius Van Brunt, club president, advised readers that he and several others had formed the Willewemoc Club, not only to have a pleasant place to fish but, more important, to put a halt to the destructive practice of keeping every fish, no matter how small. Immediately they met with opposition; however, attitudes changed as landowners witnessed an increase in the stream's trout population. The founders of the Willewemoc Club set in motion a policy of stream preservation through private ownership that exists on the Beaverkill and Willowemoc to this day.

In 1872, Junius Gridley, Edward B. Mead, Daniel B. Halstead of Brooklyn, and Robert Hunter of Englewood, New Jersey, spent the entire summer boarding on the upper Beaverkill. They slept in tents the first year and constructed a small clubhouse, approximately a mile and a half upstream of Beaverkill Falls, in 1873. These men were the parent group of the Salmo Fontinalis Club; whether they operated their club in the traditional manner or leased and posted the stream is not known.

Posting on the Beaverkill began in earnest downstream of Shin Creek, on the farm of Royal Voorhess. Like other farmers whose lands adjoined the stream, Voorhess received a substantial portion of his income from boarding fishermen. And like others, he was concerned, because his guests were bringing in fewer fish and were traveling farther upstream, where trout were more plentiful. Most farmers were reluctant to post their lands and prohibit fishing. They were afraid they might incur the wrath of anglers, who had always fished over their waters, and they held a "fear of some secret attempt at retaliation."[158] Something, however, had to be done, and Royal Voorhess believed he had found the answer.

On July 1, 1875, Voorhess obtained leases along the stream from several adjoining landowners for the "exclusive rights of fishing, and preserving of the trout and other fish." The leases included a ten-foot strip along either side of the stream and were for a period of five years, with an option for five more. After obtaining the leases, Voorhess and several of his regular boarders filed a certificate of association and founded a society known as the Beaverkill Association: "The business of said society shall be fishing and other lawful sporting purposes."[159]

The leases and the certificate of association were filed and recorded in the Sullivan County Clerk's Office on September 9, 1875. The original trustees of the organization were Royal

Voorhess, Whitman Phillips (Franklin, New Jersey), Edward A. Hastings (Brooklyn, New York), Henry Bacon, and Charles Mead (Goshen, New York). This filing was the first of its kind in either Sullivan or Ulster County, making the Beaverkill Association the first fishing club of record on the Beaverkill. In the years ahead, the Beaverkill Association would evolve into the Beaverkill Trout Club, which yet today maintains the Voorhess homestead as its clubhouse.

The practice of posting had begun, and soon others would follow. On July 5, 1877, the *Walton Weekly Chronicle* reported that the Mead brothers, from Brooklyn, would build a boardinghouse on the one thousand acres they owned at Quaker Clearing, and that no one would be allowed to fish on their property except their guests.

The Meads built their resort at the headwaters, far beyond where others had settled. The land had been partially cleared long before by a Quaker who had abandoned the idea of farming in such a rugged area. This was the most remote section of the Beaverkill and the last to be inhabited. Visiting anglers were surprised to find not only a homestead but notices prohibiting fishing as well. One angler who visited the Meads during their opening season felt a touch of pity for these city people who found themselves far off in the wilderness, and stated:

> It saddens one to see refinement buried alive in such a place. Over twenty miles to the nearest town, no church, no doctor, no neighbors, and no prospect for any advance in civilization for a lifetime. In the summer one vast forest, in the winter one expanse of snow, the only visitors are an occasional deer, or a starving bear; their lullaby, the screech of a wildcat, the howl of a hungry wolf, mingled with the roar of a biting wind which seeps through the valley with a restless fury.[160]

Those most concerned over the trout fishing in the Beaverkill were the veteran anglers who had fished the stream before its slide into mediocrity. One such angler was George W. Van Siclen, who fished its waters each season for many years. He, like Royal Voorhess, became convinced that measures had to be taken to halt the overfishing.

Van Siclen was a founding member of the Willewemoc Club; along with other club members, he would hike three miles through the forest from Sand Pond to fish the Beaverkill and Balsam Lake. Now, in 1878, after obtaining a lease and the cooperation of adjoining land owners, he and other club members formed a new fishing club known, appropriately, as the Beaverkill Club.

Van Siclen was an authority on angling and an expert caster; he helped organize some of the first casting tournaments in Central Park. He also contributed articles and letters to *The American Angler* and *Forest and Stream* on a variety of angling subjects. One letter that appeared in *Forest and Stream* must certainly have upset many who fished the Beaverkill:

NO MORE TROUT FISHING IN THE UPPER BEAVERKILL

No more trout fishing in the upper Beaverkill. Please give notice through your columns. Last summer, while I was at Weaver's there came down from "Quaker Clearing" three men on a buckboard, and they boasted "over four hundred trout"; I could not see nor imagine where they had so many stowed away, but after a while they opened a twelve-quart butter firkin and showed me the poor little things. They claimed four hundred, "and I guess they told the truth." I think that not one of the "fish" was six inches long. Now this sort of thing must be stopped, and I have made up my mind to stop it on that stream. How many of us have fished the Beaverkill! We used to put up at Murdock's or Flint's, or Walmsleys, or Leal's, or camp out, and catch our creels full; but now-a-days the smallest creel half full of seven inch trout is good luck.

After the sight of those poor little innocents my plans were soon laid. I obtained the next day, from Joseph Banks, a long lease of the stream across his two lots; I have since made an arrangement with Mead Brothers, at the old Quaker Clearing. Van Cleef and Van Brunt, the owners of Balsam Lake, have joined me, and so has Ransom Weaver. I have hired a patrol to guard that stream from Balsam Lake down to Weaver's west line, and have posted notices, and the fishing of the upper Beaverkill in Sullivan and Ulster counties, New York, is going to be preserved. All gentlemen sportsmen will keep away from there after this notice, unless they have my permission to fish, and all others will wish they had stayed away if they disregard it. It is unpleasant for me to write in this positive manner— it sounds boastful and ungenerous—but somebody had to take hold or the fishing would be gone from there in another two years; and, as I have fished there almost every season since 1856, it falls to my lot not unfairly. Since recording my lease, eight of my friends have agreed to share with me the expense of preserving and the pleasure of catching. We shall not increase our number above twelve or fifteen, and in two or three years we hope to have the lake and stream full of trout as they were less

George West Van Siclen. A founding member of the Willewemoc Club and the Beaverkill Club, he made the decision to post a large section of the Beaverkill in 1878 because of the dwindling supply of catchable native brook trout.
The Year Book of the Holland Society of New York, 1887–8

Beaverkill Trout Club, formerly the Royal Voorhess property and home of the Beaverkill Association which, in 1875, obtained leases along the Beaverkill on adjoining properties.

than twenty years ago. No tannery nor saw mill has ever polluted the waters of this part of the Beaverkill.

This notice will undoubtedly cause great disappointment to many, especially to sportsmen of Ulster, Delaware and Sullivan counties, New York, but I do hope that it will be regarded, because we have the legal right and title and the means to enforce it, and we shall certainly do so. It is but fair to add that anyone stopping at Weaver's or Mead's, will be allowed to fish over their respective pieces of stream, but not on Balsam Lake nor the "Bank's" lots. The increasing fondness for real sports sends more hunters and fishermen afield every year, and forests and streams near the great cities are almost stripped of fin and feather. Those who cannot take time to go far have but one resource—to preserve the game by restricting the privilege.

Yours Respectfully,
Geo. W. Van Siclen[161]

The stream section referred to was several miles in length and included practically all of the water upstream of Beaverkill Falls. To make sure that local anglers also were notified of the upper Beaverkill posting, Van Siclen followed up by writing to newspapers all over the Catskill region. He requested editors to give his letter space before the fishing season opened, since "this is a matter of such general interest" to the fishermen where their paper circulated.

Virtually every newspaper in the mountains published a letter similar to the one that appeared in *Forest and Stream*. Van Siclen again stated how he disliked the idea of preventing fishing that had been, for so long, free to all, and he emphasized that the fishing was gone, due to careless fishermen who killed every trout they caught.

The trout population must have indeed been low on the Beaverkill, and the public must have sensed the urgency or recognized the need of Van Siclen's action. There was no outcry, at least not in print, nor were there any angry follow-up letters on the stream closing. For that matter, the only editorial comments looked favorably on the idea. The *Hancock Herald* told its readers that the trout once so numerous were now scarce, and the cause was the careless and destructive fishing by the public. The paper urged landowners and lessees to protect their fishing interests and post their water.

More posting did follow, and on the Beaverkill there were few, if any, complaints by the angling public, which seemed to recognize the action as justified and necessary for the preservation of trout fishing. Another area newspaper, the *Ellenville Journal*, chose to speak out against the exploitation of Balsam Lake. Even though the lake was remote and travel difficult, men continually raided the lake's trout population, in winter as well as summer:

> Every winter barrels of trout are scooped out with nets through holes cut in the ice on Balsam Lake and whose business is it? Parties of ten or a dozen "campout" for a week at a time on the shores of these secluded ponds; each one fired with the ambition to beat his fellows in the numbers of trout taken. Hence it is fish, fish, from dawn to dusk, and everything that bites from two inches to twenty, must be kept and counted.[162]

This type of outcry was not lost on the owners of Balsam Lake. In 1878, Cornelius Van Brunt and James S. Van Cleef broke up the boats at the lake, posted it, and hired a watchman. In response, the *Kingston Freeman* reported that as Balsam Lake was now "guarded by a mountaineer with a big dog and a Springfield musket, it is not a popular place with the public generally."[163]

By this time, a rough road or trail ran over the mountains from Seager, in the Dry Brook valley. It traveled the west side of the foot of Graham Mountain to Samuel's Clearing on the Beaverkill. The road was steep, windy, unreliable, and fraught with hidden dangers. While it made the lake more accessible, it was a deplorable road, and was best described by Ned Buntline, who in 1881 was invited by the owners to fish Balsam Lake. Buntline made the trip with his special buckboard, which was followed by an ox sled loaded with two boats to fish from. They traveled "through swamps hub deep, over roots, fallen logs, rocks as large as a small house stuck up edgeways, lengthways, crossways and every other way, making turns so short that we had to lift the latter end of the wagon around to pass and even unhook traces to get between huge trees."[164] Buntline avowed that should he be elected to join the club, the only way he would ever visit Balsam Lake again would be as a passenger in a hot air balloon!

In 1884 a clubhouse was constructed on a hillside overlooking the lake, and the Balsam Lake Club, which had been founded the year before, began operations. The parent group of anglers forming the organization was the same as the group that had formed the Willewemoc Club in 1868 and the Beaverkill Club in 1878. Just as he had been the first president of the Willewemoc Club, Cornelius Van Brunt also became the president of the new organization.

In 1886 the Balsam Lake Club began leasing portions of the Beaverkill and acquiring others. By 1887 they owned four and a half miles, including waters previously leased by the Beaverkill Club. Through continuing land purchases, the club amassed more than three thousand acres, including six miles of the upper Beaverkill, by 1894.

From the time settlers began salting down barrels of its trout, Balsam Lake has maintained a seemingly inexhaustible population of brook trout. The main reason for this bountiful supply is the small stream entering the lake at its north end.

The stream has ideal spawning habitat, and each fall great numbers of trout enter its waters to reproduce. They do so very successfully, thereby replenishing the lake with an apparently infinite number of new trout.

The reputation of Balsam Lake was that its trout "always seem to be hungry and bite very freely."[165] Yet even during the year-round slaughter they remained abundant, and no matter how many were removed, the trout maintained a length generally between 6 and 8 inches.

One angler who fished the lake for almost forty years, beginning in 1845, remarked after his last visit that he "found to my surprise no appreciable diminution in number and size of the trout in it. They are uniform in size, from three to five ounces."[166]

Records of the Beaverkill Club in 1880 reveal that 1,364 brook trout were kept, with a total weight of 205¾ pounds.

Cornelius Van Brunt became the president of the Balsam Lake Club; the club erected a new clubhouse overlooking the lake in 1884. Bill Goetz

The average trout taken weighed .15 pound, which, according to conversion charts, would be a trout of approximately 7.5 to 7.9 inches. When the Balsam Lake Club took over the lake, it, too, enjoyed incredible catches of brook trout. Early records reveal the following:

1885	2,135
1886	3,521
1887	3,163
1888	1,879
1889	2,350
1890	2,030
Total	15,078

While the lake's trout were small, they were generally of the same size as those found in the club's headwater section of the Beaverkill. Club members were not concerned with the size of trout, though; they enjoyed the outdoors and the quality of the fishing experience. The same year the Balsam Lake Club was founded, Charles Orvis and A. Nelson Cheney published a collection of articles written by well-known anglers of the 1870s, titled *Fishing with the Fly*. One of the contributions was by club member George W. Van Siclen. It was a sentimental essay about a day on Balsam Lake titled "A Perfect Day."

Van Siclen was a lover of trout and nature, and he did an excellent job conveying to his readers the happiness he found in the tranquility and beauty of Balsam Lake. He thoroughly enjoyed his escape from business cares and the din of the city. On this day Van Siclen reflected on the pleasantness he found about him:

> Soon seated in my boat I paddle to the shade of a tall, dark hemlock and rest there, lulled by the intense quiet. Ever and anon as I dreamily cast my ethereal fly, a thrill of pleasure electrifies me, as it is seized by a vigorous trout.
>
> I have long classed trout with flowers and birds, and bright sunsets, and charming scenery, and beautiful women, as given for the rational enjoyment and delight of thoughtful men of aesthetic tastes.

15

No More Free Fishing

Fishing clubs were formed because of the scarcity of trout and a desire for social communion. They were important to the preservation of the trout resources of the Beaverkill. In the 1870s fishing clubs protected the remaining population of brook trout by immediately reducing fishing pressure. Before there were laws and officials to enforce them, clubmen initiated their own strict regulations on members by reducing daily creel limits and restricting angling to fly fishing only. In addition, by employing a watcher to patrol the stream on a regular basis, they further protected the trout from illegal fishing, such as netting, poisoning, and dynamiting.

"No More Free Fishing." Once posting began, other landowners quickly followed suit, and by 1895 most of the upper Beaverkill was posted.

Early on, posting was accepted by the public, at least on the Beaverkill. However, as it grew in popularity and spread to other streams, where more and more water was being leased and posted by newly formed clubs, it began to be resented. On Rondout Creek, most of the headwaters were acquired by the Peekamoose Fishing Club; on the Willowemoc, by the Willewemoc Club; and on the West Branch of the Neversink, by the newly formed Neversink Club. Through leases, clubmen were acquiring all of the best trout-fishing water in the Catskills. In the spring of 1885, a reporter for the *New York Times* wrote that the Beaverkill, Neversink, and Willowemoc were no longer open to public fishing; and that natives who had fished these waters all of their lives, as well as visiting anglers, would be considered poachers if they attempted to do so.

No stream posting angered the public as much as the closing of the West Branch of the Neversink. The stream had been very accessible to anglers, especially those from the Kingston area. When a Kingston newspaper carried the notice that the public could no longer fish in those waters, it triggered a war of words that raged for years.

The conflict began with letters and editorials in local newspapers, and then spread to sporting journals. One area newspaper decried the idea of leasing streams as "preposterous" and declared, "Why, there are men enough in New York City with money to control every trout stream in Ulster and Sullivan County."[167] An outdoor writer compared posting to monopolizing sunsets! He added, "And only those of sufficient wealth should see the recurring glories of the evening sky."[168]

One of the most persistent and outspoken critics of the clubmen was Robert E. Best, a Kingston fur dealer, who had fished the Neversink for many years and did not take kindly

Fishing a small stream. With the posting of so much water that had been previously open to public fishing, anglers turned their attention to smaller tributaries, at least to those that still held populations of trout. *Scribner's Magazine,* January 1915

to the idea of the posting of his favorite stream. In a series of blistering letters, he questioned not only the legality of leasing trout streams but the very character of the men doing such an "un-American" deed:

> These migrating vagabonds hailing from New York, forming themselves into clubs, and leasing fishing streams for their selfish purposes, have been on the increase for some years. As a rule they spend but little or no money in the county where their nests exist, and where they have their drunken orgies, and sing their obscene songs. A few barrels of rum brought with them from New York, and what chickens they can steal from hen roosts, and the trout they can catch from the stream that has been stocked from the State hatcheries and placed there with Ulster County people's money, form their stock of summer substance.
>
> It is but two years ago that an old and gray-haired man, born near the waters of the Beaverkill stream, wandered to its edge to catch a small mess of fish for a sick daughter.

He was ordered off by two members of a club, who had leased that portion of the stream, upon which they told him he was a trespasser, and because the old man in his infirmity could not move fast enough to suit them, they cruelly knocked him down, and kicked him when down in a most brutal manner. One of the assailants, a member of the New York City club, was the keeper of a house of prostitution, and the other, the keeper of a gambling den in New York City. Pretty specimens indeed of humanity to come to Ulster County to teach the natives to obey the laws of New York . . .

In this free country, thanks to God, the rich and the poor are equals. Let the man be a millionaire or a bark peeler, let his hands be soft and white, or horny and brown, give him free fishing and free fowling in free America. However humble may be the man's calling in his home the dainty and delicious trout is one of God's good gifts to earth to his children. He has vouchsafed it to all whether his smoke curls from a palace chimney or a bark peeler's shanty.[169]

Charles Hallock, past editor of *Forest and Stream*, laid much of the blame for stream posting on the Fish Commission, for allowing the streams to deteriorate. He took issue with the commission, which seemed to believe that stocking more fish was the solution to improving trout fishing. He pointed out that after years of stocking, the fishing was not any better and argued that the Fish Commission should abandon the idea that stocking alone was the solution to good fishing. Hallock stated that the commission followed a policy of spending the public's money on "making fish so abundant that they can be caught without restrictions and serve as cheap food for the people at large, rather than to expand a much larger sum in 'protecting' the fish, and in preventing the people from catching the few which still remain (or did remain) after a generation of improvidence."[170]

Forest and Stream also took issue with Best's assessment of the clubmen and came to their defense: "Knowing the high character of the gentlemen composing the Neversink Club, the Balsam Lake Club and the Willewemoc Club, most of whom are personal acquaintances, we regard the article written to the '*Freeman*' as a most vile slander."[171] Streams were being purchased and "preserved," and many felt that only men of wealth would be allowed to "enjoy a day's sport in fishing for trout."[172] Another noted angling authority who spoke out on the situation was William C. Harris, editor of *The American Angler*:

Men have felt galled to see legal notices prohibiting them from taking fish from streams where their fathers fished before them and where they had as freely angled away the Saturday afternoons of their boyhood.

This is a natural and by no means ignoble sentiment, but a little consideration will show any man that it is no more practically possible to leave all fishing waters free to all than it is to do away with farm fences and turn the crop fields of the country back into meadow-grazing lands free for all.

We have nothing whatever to say for or against this system. We only point out a known fact and draw the plain conclusion that every angler who cares to provide for his enjoyment in years to come had better lose no time in securing some good angling privilege somewhere.[173]

Fishermen were not the only ones upset over the leasing of trout streams; hotels, inns, and boardinghouse owners also became alarmed at the amount of stream mileage lost to posting. Such businesses had increased steadily ever since the railroad came through the region, and they viewed free fishing as vital to their success in attracting tourists. Boardinghouse and resort owners prepared petitions that they hoped would influence legislators into preparing a bill preventing the leasing of trout streams.

One club member responded to their concerns by stating:

If the fishing in these streams would always remain as good as it was when the hotels were built and railways

introduced into this section, their argument would be better, but unfortunately the reverse is the case. Four years ago I ceased fishing the Beaver Kill and adjacent waters, the river almost devoid of fish; that parties from a distance were in the habit of visiting the streams with the apparent view of carrying away as many fish as possible, regardless of size, hiring small boys to increase the catch, and making use of other unsportsmen like ways of depleting the streams. I have heard parties boast that they had carried away 1,100 fish (some of which were scarcely two inches long), the result of three days fishing, besides all they ate.[174]

The most persistent argument put forth by those opposed to the leasing of streams was that if the stream was stocked with trout by the Fish Commission, it should remain open to the public. Stocking, it was stated, brought the streams back to their original value as trout waters and was done at public expense. Therefore, it was reasoned, the trout in the streams were public property, and it should be illegal to post such waters.

Clubmen did not disagree that the state owned the fish, even in their wild state; but, they argued, they had the "right of property, and can exclude any person from trespassing upon their grounds for the purpose of fishing."[175] In effect, they granted that individuals had the legal right to catch state trout, as long as they did not trespass over private land to do so.

When streams first began to be stocked, they were, for the most part, free to everyone; and when trout were planted in those streams, the public benefited from the stocking. Although not public waters in the strictest sense (since they flowed over and through private lands), they were public waters for all intents and purposes, since the public had "unrestrained" access and use of them for fishing.

As the growth of angling increased, the fishing privileges grew in value, and these waters that had always been free were posted and became in fact what they had always been legally: private waters. All that the Fish Commission required of one ordering fish was an affidavit that the trout would be placed in public waters. Frequently, those ordering and stocking the fish were not stream owners, nor did they have permission of the owners. Yet "free" fishing advocates insisted on fishing the entire stream, on the grounds that the stream had been stocked at public expense.

One stream owner remarked:

The result has been that many of our finest streams have been practically destroyed by stocking through acts of trespass to which the State has really been a party, and it is a grave question whether a claim for these injuries to the rights of riparian owners could not be successfully made to the Court of Claims of this State.[176]

The argument over the public's right to fish in streams once stocked by the state continued for years and led to more frequent confrontations between fishermen and the stream watchers hired by the clubs. These disputes were, at times, taken before a judge; however, trespassers hauled into court were usually released, as it was almost impossible to procure a verdict against a man guilty of trespassing on private club water. Most often these arguments were settled with fists, stones, and even drawn revolvers! Some fishermen refused to recognize the rights of the clubs to prohibit fishing and when asked to leave hurled insults at the watchman. When this occurred, the watchman would fill his pockets with stones, follow the trespasser, and throw stones in the water ahead of him, spoiling his fishing. This occasionally escalated into a fistfight, where one side or the other was treated to uncomfortable bruises or a good ducking in the stream.

Not all watchmen were challenged in such a manner; one who was usually avoided was Sturgis Buckley, who patrolled the Beaverkill for the Balsam Lake Club. Buckley acquired a reputation as a determined, uncompromising stream watcher. It was said, rather sarcastically, that he wore a "winning smile," which "made would-be poachers fish or cut bait."[177] Those daring enough to fish "his" water did not do so openly; they would hide along the stream, wait for Buckley to pass by, follow him until it was time for his return trip, and then follow him again. When they became familiar with his pattern, they would fish the area that he had just left.

The idea of posting also began to catch on with farmers. While some refused all attempts to "fish over them" and would threaten to shoot, others gave permission to fish for a fee of twenty-five cents a head. Farmers did not have time to patrol their water, nor could they afford to pay someone else to do so. One way to keep an eye on the water was to pasture an angry bull next to the stream; another was the practice of having a large, aggressive, hungry-looking dog run freely. When someone was fishing, the dog let it be known,

and an uneasy angler was only too happy to toss a quarter to the farmer and be rid of the annoying beast.

After years of exploitation and overfishing, trout fishing on the Beaverkill seemed destined to improve. One *Forest and Stream* writer reported:

> We are glad to hear from some of the veterans who have for many years made it a point to fish these brooks, that last season's catch showed a very marked improvement over the previous years as that did over the one of 1888, both in size and number.
>
> This happy state of affairs has been partially brought about by the liberal stocking of these waters by the wise management of the Ontario & Western R. R., but there is another cause which has helped the brooks, and that is the headwaters of the two streams [Beaverkill and Neversink] are controlled by clubs and private parties who limit the fish caught both in size and numbers, and absolutely prohibit fishing in the little side streams where the fingerlings seek shelter from their larger brethren, thus assuring a constant source of supply. Reasonable people begin to see the advantages of having parts of streams controlled in this way, as it certainly improves the whole of the waters. They cannot lock up the fish, and they naturally will drop down stream, particularly as they grow large.[178]

Once posting began, it spread quickly. Undoubtedly it became a case of self-preservation; as water became posted it placed an even greater burden on that which remained open. Commenting on the increase in posting, the Livingston Manor correspondent to the *Walton Reporter* wrote:

> Fishing is very poor around here this season. The primary causes are undoubtedly excessive legislation and the profusion of notices posted on the banks of the stream in endless variety of form and nearly every language from Hebrew to Choctaw, which has so bewildered the trout that they know not what to do.[179]

16

"Who Would Not Be a Game Protector?"

Year after year, season after season, ever-increasing numbers of anglers were removing more and more trout from the Beaverkill and other area streams. They did so without restrictions, as there were virtually no laws. The only law was one of common decency, which was adhered to by those fishermen who considered themselves sportsmen: anglers who knew it was unwise to keep fingerlings and who killed only reasonable numbers of trout. Laws restricting the number of trout that could be taken or setting limits on the size of the fish did not appear until 1876, and many believed it was too little, too late.

In New York State, fish and game laws are based on the premise that ownership of all fish and wildlife is vested in the state. This principle has been handed down from the common law of England, and while a statewide law restricting the use of seines was adopted as early as 1813, most laws were enacted to meet the specific needs of a particular locality. These early fish and game laws were enacted by county government, through the Board of Supervisors. Enforcement was the duty of all sheriffs, constables, and other police officers.

One of the earliest laws pertaining to trout in the Beaverkill watershed was enacted by the Sullivan County Board of Supervisors on April 3, 1849, and was titled "An Act for the Preservation of Deer, Birds and Fish, and for the destruction of certain wild beasts."[180] Section No. 7 of the law prohibited the use of the berry *Coculus indicus* or any other poisonous substance for the purpose of fishing. Section No. 10 set a season for trout, protecting the fish during the spawning season between August 1 and November 1. And Section No. 11 allowed that:

All penalties imposed by this act may be sued for and recovered by any individual or by the overseers of the poor of the town where the offense is committed in a suit to be commenced in two months after the commission of the offense and when sued for by the overseers of the poor shall be for the use of the poor of such town.

The act also established bounties to be paid: for wolves, ten dollars; panthers, five dollars; wildcats or catamounts, two dollars; and foxes, fifty cents. In 1857 the state legislature passed a law prohibiting the taking of trout with anything other than a hook and line; they could not be taken by "net, seine, weir, basket, spear, grapple or trap." A feature of this law, and of fish and game law in general, was that all penalties imposed by the act could be sued for and recovered, with one-half going to the complainant. Known as the moiety system, it allowed any person to bring suit and recover one-half of the fine, with the other half going to the poor. Though the system continued for many years, it was generally disliked by law enforcement officials.

In 1871 changes by the legislature gave more power to the county Board of Supervisors. A law provided for the election of game constables, with powers similar to civil constables, to be nominated at town meetings. Laws continued to be made at both state and county levels of government; one law passed by the Ulster County Legislature in 1876, dubbed Murdock's Trout Bill,[181] was proposed by Hardenbergh supervisor and longtime resort owner James Murdock. Murdock had witnessed decades of Beaverkill trout exploitation, and he believed a size limit was necessary to halt the keeping of undersized trout, especially fingerlings.

Concerns about overfishing became obvious when, just a few years later, the Sullivan County Board of Supervisors provided the ultimate protection to a nearby stream. In 1882 the board created, in a sense, an early no-kill regulation by passing "an Act for the preservation and protection of Brook trout in the Middle Mongaup Stream and its tributaries in the Town of Liberty, Sullivan County."

Section No. 1 of the law stated: "No person shall kill, or attempt to kill or catch any brook trout in the water of the Middle Mongaup River."[182] The stream was protected for a period of three years, and a fine of twenty-five dollars was imposed for violating the law; one-half of the penalty went to the complainant, one-half to support the poor in the town of Liberty.

While increasing concern over diminishing trout populations brought about more restrictive laws pertaining to fishing, enforcement of these laws was, for the most part, nonexistent. Reports of trout being taken illegally with nets, spears, poisons, and dynamite were common and were the cause of public outrage. There were too few game constables appointed by the county to be effective. Sheriffs and other law enforcement officers were generally involved with what they considered more serious crime.

Finally, in 1880, the governor was authorized to appoint eight state game protectors, and while this was the beginning of fish and game protection, a more accountable and effective force was not established until 1888, when the Fish Commission appointed a chief protector and fifteen game and fish protectors. These men were empowered to begin suits in the name of the people; one-half of the penalties recovered in civil actions would go to the state, and the other half would go to the game protector or the individual bringing the suit.

These pioneer game protectors had a most difficult time carrying out their duties; they had to bring suit, and in return they could be sued personally if they made a mistake, with no assurance that the state would back them up with an attorney. Laws pertaining to fish and wildlife were not always respected or readily accepted. Many people still adhered to the belief that in America the woods and streams were free, and laws limiting this freedom were looked upon with contempt.

Sometimes, game protectors were ridiculed for not enforcing the law, and then mocked when they did—often on the front pages of area newspapers. Some of the same editors who lamented the deplorable conditions of trout streams took issue when the lawbreakers were brought to justice, siding with the violators and claiming they were poor victims, ignorant of the law. There was also great animosity shown toward game protectors over the fact that they received one-half the fine, even though the money could go to anyone making the complaint.

An example of how difficult the job of game protector was can be seen in the experiences of Seth Walley, who enforced the laws in Delaware County, which included the lower Beaverkill. In the summer of 1893 Game Protector Walley received a complaint from a citizen about three men spearing fish in the waters of Trout Creek. A Walton newspaper, with a touch of sarcasm, reported on the incident: "Here was an opportunity which [Walley] embraced at once of showing the people of Trout Creek that the suckers still had rights, and at the same time scooping in a nice little fee."[183]

Two of the men were immediately brought to justice and charged with illegally taking fish; the penalty of each offense was one hundred dollars, of which Walley received half. In an effort to extract some satisfaction by outwitting Walley, the third violator had his brother charge him with the crime before a justice in Walton. The defendant pleaded guilty and was fined one hundred dollars; but since the brother who brought the suit was entitled to one-half the fine, it was thus "kept in the family" and did not go to Game Protector Walley!

By doing his job and enforcing the law, Seth Walley became a very unpopular man, especially in the hamlet of Trout Creek. A year after the spearing incident, the *Hancock Herald* wrote openly of the desire to tar and feather Seth Walley: "But the self-constituted avengers were doomed to disappointment, for at sundown Mr. Game Protector quietly folded his tent and stole away. Whether he 'smelled a mice' or not, deponent sayeth not. Who would not be a game protector?"[184]

Two days later a Walton newspaper reported:

NOW THEY ARE AFTER SETH

Fish Protector Walley does not find his path strewn with roses in his pursuit of the infringers of the game laws. On the contrary the animosity of some has been aroused and their hands are "lifted up against" the officer of the law. Trout Creek has been a favorite field of operation for Mr. Walley and he has reaped a rich harvest from some of the farmer boys of that little hamlet and its environs. But this has been done at the cost of popularity, and 'tis whispered that before the dark shades of night surround that village Seth takes care that he is safe without its bounds. The lively young men of that vicinity have organized a "vengeance club" with the avowed purpose of "getting even" with Mr. Walley and are patiently biding their time when the unpopular official can be caught at some favorable opportunity, and then, woe be unto him.[185]

Such obviously biased reporting could only have made it harder for Seth Walley, or any game protector, to enforce the law. And it delayed the acceptance of laws restricting or regulating fishing, as well as their receiving respect and recognition as being in everyone's interest. By August of 1894 Seth C. Walley was removed from his position as a Special Game and Fish Protector. At a meeting of the Commissioners of Fisheries, Chief Game and Fish Protector J. Warren Pond recommended Seth Walley be removed, "such removal being for the good of the cause of game and fish protectors."[186] Chief Pond was directed to report, at the commission's next meeting, any other protectors whom complaints could be made against or who were lax in doing their duty.

Checking undersize trout. Size limits on trout appeared as early as 1876, and many believed it was "too little, too late." *The Country Gentleman,* May 1924

Laws continued to be made by the county Board of Supervisors until 1895, when they became the duty of the state legislature. In general, trout season in the Catskills opened on May 1 and closed August 31, to give the trout more protection throughout their spawning seasons, with no fishing allowed on Sunday. This short season—only 106 days—

continued for many years, from the early 1870s until the 1920s, and may have been responsible, as much as anything, for the fishing remaining as good as it did.

The Indian, too, had seen the importance of protecting trout during certain times of the year. This early wisdom is revealed in a tale by Dr. E. A. Bates, who supervised relations

In 1882 a law was passed prohibiting anglers from taking trout from Middle Mongaup Creek. It lasted three years. In 1969 a similar regulation began on 3½ miles of the Willowemoc Creek; it is still in effect today. Lee Van Put

between the Agricultural College at Cornell and Indian reservations, and persuaded many Native Americans to come to Cornell:

> In the olden moons, at such a time, the boys of the village cut a long pole of sinewy willow, and at the end of a tough line made of the inner bark of the elm, they tied the sharp pointed fish hook made of bone. With a juicy piece of bear fat, they fooled the trout.
>
> Then one trout-fishing moon came when few trout were caught. The next spring, this happened again. Finally, a wise old fisherman opened one of the trout with his sharp stone knife and found it was full of eggs. So the council drew from the wisdom of the old fishermen, and

a careful watch was made, and then it was found that the trout always swam over their spawning beds just before the wild apple bloomed.

> From that moon on, and even today, the redman stays far from the home of the trout until the apple trees are in full bloom, for he dreams of a trout-fishing moon for his grandchildren.[187]

Size limits may have helped also, as they both increased and spanned an even greater time period. In 1876, with the passage of Murdock's Trout Bill, the size limit was five inches; by 1885, it had been increased to six inches, and by the late 1930s, it climbed to seven inches.

17

Enter
Salmo fario

---

red Mather, like Seth Green, was an early fish culturist who was interested in fly fishing for trout and writing about angling. However, he disagreed with Green and the Fish Commission about the rainbow being the salvation of New York's trout waters. In a paper read before the American Fish Cultural Association in 1884, Fred Mather, then fishery editor of *Forest and Stream*, registered doubts as to their worth:

I have suspected the so-called rainbow trout to be identical with the steelhead salmon, *S. gairdneri*, which is a migratory fish.

We have been waiting and watching the habits of this alleged trout with great interest in order to learn if its habits might not show it to be, in some respect, different from the steelhead. The evidence of the Commission tends to show that it is a migratory fish and, if so, it may escape to the sea and be lost.

The promise of the rainbow trout was that in it we had a quick growing fish, which was not as sensitive to warm water as our own "fontinalis," a desideratum which now promises to be filled by the brook trout of Europe, *Salmo fario*.[188]

While fishing in Europe, Mather became familiar with brown trout, and he so admired the fish that he resolved he would introduce the species to America at the first opportunity. That occasion arose in 1883, when Mather took charge of a new hatchery located at Cold Spring Harbor on Long Island. The facility was a joint venture of the United States and New York Fish Commissions.

On December 28, 1882, he wrote to Professor Spencer F. Baird, of the U.S. Commission of Fish and Fisheries:

My Dear Professor,

We think it desirable to introduce both European brook trout (*Salmo fario*) and the grayling at the new hatchery at Cold Spring. Should you have any offer of any from your foreign correspondents we will be glad to receive and care for them.

Very Truly Yours,
F. Mather

The next day, the commissioner replied that he had been offered plenty of trout eggs but had always turned them down. He would, however, ask Herr Von Behr, president of the Deutschen Fischerei Verein.

Professor Baird wrote to Friedrich Von Behr, announcing he was sending a shipment of eggs of lake trout, whitefish, and brook trout, and concluded his letter: "Mr. Mather is about starting a new hatchery on Long Island, near New York, in which he will do a great deal of work for the United States. He thinks he would like to have some eggs of the European trout. Can you send him some?"[189]

Fred Mather began operations at the Cold Spring Harbor hatchery on January 1 and had barely had time to set up when he received, on the 28th of February, 80,000 brown trout eggs from Germany: 60,000 large eggs, and 20,000 from upper Rhine tributaries, which were smaller but were of the same species. Mather reported sending 10,000 large and 2,000 small brown trout eggs to the state hatchery at Caledonia, and 2,000 large and 3,000 small eggs to the U.S. Fish Commission hatchery at Northville, Michigan.[190]

In the above correspondence, it appears that the introduction of brown trout into America was due to the suggestion of Fred Mather but was accomplished by Professor Spencer

F. Baird.[191] Hardly had the brown trout arrived in this country when anglers with European fishing experience began describing their merits in the pages of sporting journals. Some were convinced the brown trout would be welcomed by all, since they grew larger and were warier, gamier, and, therefore, superior to native brook trout. They stated that brook trout were easier to catch, took the fly more readily, and did not require the delicate approach that was practiced in England. One angler noted, "On many English streams the fish can only be taken with a dry fly, a practice unknown, so far as I know, in America."[192]

These comparisons annoyed more than a few anglers who loved their native brook trout and in no way thought it inferior to any fish. When English authorities declared their trout was "only a charr," American anglers took offense. One writer asked indignantly, "In what respect is a trout superior to a charr? Certainly the American charr is handsomer than the brook trout of Europe."[193]

In time, the brook trout of Europe would be judged on more than looks alone, and while discussion varied on the values of the fish, almost everyone agreed that the new trout should be placed in American waters. Meanwhile, at Cold Spring Harbor, Fred Mather was having trouble hatching and raising the trout he received from Friedrich Von Behr. Those of the large type all died shortly after hatching. The smaller eggs taken from upper Rhine tributaries did better, with some 4,000 being placed in rearing ponds. These too, however, proved difficult for Mather and his staff:

> We were so proud of these fish that we often caught them to show them to visitors, and as often as we disturbed them we would find dead ones on the ground the next day.
>
> Those specimens jumped out of the wooden rearing ponds, and it was only when their numbers had been severely thinned by it that we learned that they seemed prompted to it every time they were disturbed either by putting a net to catch specimens to show to visitors or at night by some animal swimming in the pond. In November, 1884, when they were a year and a half old, we removed them to a large breeding pond, and the next morning the ground was covered with them, although this pond had banks a foot higher than those of the rearing ponds. At present not over fifty are left, and learning their habits has been expensive.[194]

Fortunately for Mather, Von Behr made another shipment of eggs, which was received on February 15, 1884, and on the 25th the hatchery received five thousand brown trout eggs from England. These were a gift of R. B. Marston of the London *Fishing Gazette* and were eggs taken from two of England's most famous trout streams: three thousand from the Itchen and two thousand from the Wey, a tributary of the Thames.[195]

Secure in the knowledge that he now had backup stocks of the European trout, in May 1884 Fred Mather began placing forty thousand brown trout fry directly into New York public waters in and around Long Island. The following spring, in 1885, the Cold Spring Harbor hatchery expanded its range when it distributed 28,900 brown trout into the waters of Queens, Suffolk, Westchester, and Rockland counties. In November of that year both Cold Spring Harbor and Caledonia reported taking eggs from brown trout hatched from the original shipment, received in 1883.[196] In the spring of 1886 the Caledonia hatchery stocked its first brown trout, sending one hundred sixteen thousand fry throughout the state, with one shipment reaching the Catskills. On March 20, four thousand brown trout were sent to E. D. Mayhew for placement into Spring Creek, near Walton. In December 1886 the New York Fish Commission announced that it would have a limited number of "German trout" available next season for stocking the public waters of the state.

It was in the spring of 1887 when Montgomery Dodge purchased a round-trip ticket and traveled to Caledonia to pick up the first brown trout to be placed in the Beaverkill. "Gum," as he was known, owned and operated a hotel located just

Fred Mather was an early fish culturist and is credited with receiving the first shipment of brown trout eggs from Germany in 1883 at the hatchery at Cold Spring Harbor, Long Island.

Modern Fish Culture, 1900

BROWN TROUT (*Salmo fario*).
151

Brown trout. The first brown trout eggs that arrived in New York came from lakes and tributaries of the Rhine River. *The Book of Fish and Fishing,* 1915

upstream of the Forks, on the Rockland flats. He was a genial host, well-known to fishermen and, for that matter, the traveling public. It was said that men would ride half the night just to spend the other half at his popular Excelsior Hotel.

The records show that Dodge received ten thousand "German trout" at the hatchery on the 25th of March.[197] The trout fry were so tiny that had he peered into the large tins that accompanied him on the train it is doubtful whether he could have distinguished them from the native trout he was so familiar with. He had ordered the fish from Seth Green during the winter and was no doubt encouraged by the reports on the European import. Perhaps on the return trip he pondered how this new trout would do in the lower Beaverkill. It was said that they did well in larger, warmer waters, and that they would not wander off, as did the rainbow. He may have even envisioned a trout season lasting through the summer and ultimately increasing his hotel business. It is unlikely he could have realized the tremendous impact the stocking of brown trout would have on the Beaverkill.

"Gum" Dodge did not make the trip to Caledonia alone. Jefferson Campbell of Roscoe also picked up an order of ten thousand German trout; these fish were for Warner Sprague, who placed them in the nearby Willowemoc.[198]

A little more than a week later, E. R. Sprague, who owned the Mountain View Villa at Lew Beach, picked up an order of fourteen thousand German trout and placed those fish into the waters of the upper Beaverkill and Shin Creek. On the 4th of April J. G. Stevens of Livingston Manor received seven thousand fry and stocked them in the upper Willowemoc and its tributaries. Now this trout of Europe, whose noble lineage descended from the Itchen, the Wey, and the Rhine, was well distributed throughout the Beaverkill and Willowemoc.

In the lower river, brown trout found an environment that was extremely beneficial to their growth and survival. It was

the most productive section of the Beaverkill, and the habitat was excellent: pools were large and deep, riffles rich in aquatic insects. Mayflies were abundant and, coupled with a large and varied minnow population, formed a wonderful food supply. Perhaps most important, the water was generally too warm to support brook trout and so was virtually free of competing game fish. These circumstances not only ensured their success but allowed brown trout to have a swift and dramatic impact on the fisheries of the Beaverkill.

Brown trout grew rapidly, and while some from the original stocking of 1887 may have been caught previously, the first reported catch did not appear in local newspapers until May of 1890. Irving W. Finch, a veteran Roscoe angler, came into town with a German trout that measured 15⅝ inches in length, and weighed 1 pound and 9 ounces.[199] This trout, a little over three years of age, was one of the fry that had traveled on the train with "Gum" Dodge on his trip from Caledonia. Later that summer an even larger trout was seen living in Palen's millpond, which was located on a split channel of the Beaverkill, along the flats upstream of the Forks. Every man in Rockland was said to be after the trout, but only "Gum" Dodge succeeded in hooking, and then losing, the big fish.

Over the next couple of years, reports of trout weighing two or three pounds became common. Before long, even larger fish were caught, as brown trout began to inhabit and dominate most of the best water on the Beaverkill, especially the large pools formed by milldams.

After the introduction, the U.S. Fish Commission attempted to have the new trout from Europe become known as the Von Behr trout. In 1889 Commissioner Marshall McDonald proposed "to give to this trout a name which is intended to perpetuate in America the memory of the man to whom we are much indebted for this valuable addition to our list of noble fishes."[200]

The "Big River"

The trout-fishing history of the lower Beaverkill coincides with the stocking of brown trout. Their introduction created many more miles of trout water, as browns began inhabiting the water previously avoided by native brook trout—virtually all of the lower river below Roscoe and the junction of the Willowemoc. While there may have been controversy in the stocking of these foreign trout, their introduction to the Beaverkill was one of the most significant events in the stream's storied past.

Previously, Morsston (Livingston Manor) was where anglers disembarked from the train. From there, they traveled the DeBruce road to the fishing grounds at Willowemoc and DeBruce or the Beaverkill road to Beaverkill, Lew Beach, and Turnwood. In 1886 Roscoe listed only one resort in the O. & W. Railroad's *Summer Homes* guide.

Now, with brown trout well established in the lower Beaverkill, anglers no longer concentrated their efforts upstream. More and more fishing tourists were making Roscoe their headquarters and plying their skills on the lower river. As its popularity grew, trout-fishing regulars, especially local anglers, referred to the water below Roscoe as the "Big Beaverkill" and, more often, the "Big River." An increased demand for accommodations saw major new hotel construction up and down the stream: Central House (1890), Beaverkill House (1893), Beaverkill Mountain House (1894), Bonnie View (1895), and Campbell Inn (1901).

During these years, additional rail travel spurred the O. & W. to construct a new railroad station at Roscoe in 1895. Upon its completion, Jeronimus S. Underhill, a wealthy Brooklyn sportsman, presented the railroad with a handsome weathervane topped by a stately trout. The trout was a fitting symbol for the village, as the stocking of brown trout brought new prosperity to the Beaverkill in the 1890s.

Jeronimus Underhill was a New York shipbuilder who fished the Beaverkill for more than fifty years, making his first trip to the stream in the 1840s. While he was known to be a skilled angler, he is best remembered for the wonderful gift he bestowed on the railroad station and the village of Roscoe.

In the years ahead, the trout weathervane greeted thousands of anglers who traveled the O. & W. seeking their favorite sport in the waters of the Beaverkill. Stepping off the train, passengers eagerly cast their eyes on the great copper trout to get the wind direction, which in some cases determined not only where to fish but whether to fish the dry fly upstream or the wet fly down.

The big trout remained on the Roscoe station for many years, serving as a landmark to several generations of Beaverkill anglers. It remained there until the 1950s, when a bankrupt railroad gave way to improved highways, increasing auto, truck, and bus travel. The railroad ceased operations in 1957; and shortly thereafter, before the old railroad station was razed, someone climbed onto the roof and removed the weathervane. Frank Trinkner, an outdoor columnist for the *Liberty Register*, wrote an interesting story on its demise:

> Back when Roscoe was the trout fishing capital of the country and anglers came from just about every state in the union to fish the far-famed waters of the Big Beaverkill, the Little Beaverkill, the Willowemoc and dozens of smaller streams in the area, one of the first sights that greeted their eyes as they disembarked from the old O. & W. R. R. was the weathervane on top of the depot, topped by a fine figure of a trout that seemed to represent the very essence and spirit of the village which

Beaverkill House, one of several fishing resorts constructed in Roscoe in the 1890s.

Village of Roscoe. A look down Stewart Avenue with the Roscoe House visible at the opposite end of the street.

Roscoe railroad station. Located in the center of town, the railroad was an important link for trout-fishing tourists.

J. S. Underhill's famous gift weathervane on top of the railroad station. Trout fishermen would often look at the weathervane to determine if they would fish upstream with a dry fly or downstream with a wet.

catered to fishermen from every walk of life. While many eyes [that] glanced upward to it at the beginning of a day's fishing to see if the wind was in the right quarter are now closed in a long sleep, there are still many anglers who will always remember Roscoe's trout weathervane as a golden symbol of the good times and good fishing of another age, for it maintained its proud position atop the station for 62 years.[213]

Trinkner notes that he telephoned the Roscoe state police and was told that no one had lodged an official complaint about the theft of the old landmark. He then contacted Doug Bury, the proprietor of the Antrim Lodge, who told him that he knew the "old trout" was missing and admitted cheerfully that he had his eye on it himself. One longtime customer of the Antrim had suggested that Doug steal it for him—and he was thinking of doing the deed when the weathervane disappeared "right from under his nose." Doug told Trinkner that he had a good idea where it went and that it was not very far away. "In fact, he thought that a fellow with a sharp eye might see the hot trout appear in the environs of Roscoe, after it had cooled off a bit." Trinkner concluded his column by stating that he hoped that Doug was right, since "we think that a lot of old time anglers would prefer to see their famous landmark stay in Roscoe, trout-famous for years."[214]

While the railroad station is long gone, the weathervane is not; today, a "fellow with a sharp eye" can still see the trout that was such a familiar sight to those anglers who traveled the rails to fish the "Big River" and meet the challenge of the brown trout.

If there ever was a golden era for trout fishing on the Beaverkill, it was, without a doubt, those introductory years, especially after brown trout began reproducing naturally in the stream. In the decade from 1894 until 1904, brown trout enjoyed a superiority in numbers and sizes that would never be equaled or surpassed. In August 1894 three of the largest trout ever to be taken from the Beaverkill were captured within days of one another. Jasper Barnhart caught a twenty-six-inch, six-pound trout at the covered bridge at the hamlet of Beaverkill, and Joseph Kelley took another six-pounder under Wagner's bridge (Craig-e-clare). The biggest, however, was not caught but found floating in the Beaverkill, severely wounded though not quite dead. The giant brown had been speared; it measured thirty-two inches and weighed 8¾ pounds.

Anglers were, in fact, unaccustomed to catching such big fish, and more often than not these huge browns smashed tackle and got away. The following year, in the summer of 1895, even more large trout found their way from the river into the spotlight of the local inns, taverns, and newspapers. Alex Voorhess of Lew Beach caught a five-pound, two-ounce German brown; Lee Davis caught another weighing five pounds. Joseph Kelley again caught a monster trout under the bridge at Wagner's, this one weighing six pounds and fifteen ounces. Upriver, under Charles Sliter's dam, John Tompkins captured two beauties weighing 3½ pounds and 4½ pounds; and one week later, also under Sliter's dam, Egbert Tripp of Turnwood caught a four-pound, five-ounce

trout and another monster German trout measuring thirty-one inches and weighing ten pounds—by far the largest ever caught in the Beaverkill!

One other brown trout would make headlines in 1895; that June, a huge fish was again seen in Palen's millpond, which was located just downstream of the new state hatchery in Rockland. The magnetism of the trout was apparent when more than two hundred people turned out to witness its capture. The millpond was drawn down, and personnel from the Beaverkill Hatchery placed a net across the outlet. Somehow, in the excitement, the big trout managed to jump the net and escape into the raceway. George Cochran, who had been watching from the bank, leaped into the millrace and succeeded in capturing the fish with his hands. It was immediately placed in a nail keg, transferred to a tank of water, and taken to the hatchery.

The giant trout, which measured thirty-one inches and weighed nine pounds, may have been from the original stocking of 1887. At the hatchery, it was placed in a display tank; in just a few days, several hundred visitors, from all over the state, came to view the huge fish. In time, the trout succumbed to injuries it had received when captured and died. It was such a grand specimen that the supervisor sent the trout away to Rochester to be mounted, and upon its return it was placed on exhibition at the Beaverkill Hatchery.[215]

Over the next several years, many more record-setting browns were taken from the waters of the Beaverkill. Each

Palen's millpond and raceway, home of the giant brown trout that was exhibited at the Beaverkill Hatchery in 1895. The trout measured 31 inches and weighed 9 pounds.

Roscoe House. A favorite gathering place of old-time Beaverkill anglers. Proprietor William Keener was known as one of the best trout fishermen in the valley.

four-pound smallmouth bass; the bass took the end fly, and the trout, the dropper.

He was fishing with Louis Rhead, who mentioned their longtime friendship and Keener's renown as a fly fisherman in his *American Trout Stream Insects* (1916). Rhead wrote of the piscatorial feat in *Fisherman's Lures and Game-Fish Food* (1920) and again in *Forest and Stream* in August 1923, where he devoted an entire article to describing Keener's unusual catch. Though the two fish often inhabit the same waters, hooking a trout and a smallmouth at the same time is a rare occurrence, even for those who regularly fish with two flies. In all probability, Keener's landing of those two large fish will never be equaled. William Keener was so well-known and respected by sportsmen everywhere that when he died in 1924 *Forest and Stream* printed his obituary on its editorial page, which was edged in black. Commenting on his character and contributions to trout fishing, it stated:

Considered an expert angler, William Keener was known for catching a number of large trout, often at Junction Pool. Fishermen came to the Roscoe House to learn from him what was hatching and what flies the fish were taking. Doug Bury

Trout and Bass drawing by Louis Rhead. The drawing depicts a catch made by William Keener of a 3-pound, 9-ounce brown trout and a 4-pound smallmouth bass. *Forest and Stream,* August 1923

By nature he was unusually mild and gentle-hearted, with a fund of native Irish wit and humor, well known to that race. It was as good as a play, to hear his quips and sallies on those boasters and braggarts one so often meets out fishing. His own nature was the very opposite, modest in the extreme, generous, charitable, and possessed of a very winning manner to his intimate friends, of whom he had many. The thousands of anglers whom now enjoy the fine fishing of the Beaverkill and Willowemoc are much indebted to Mr. Keener, who has for many years upheld the best traditions of the craft, and used uncommon sense in properly stocking the streams, by placing the young fish in situations where they had ample food and quick growth. No angler in the entire state of New York was better known, and none more esteemed.[222]

Appropriately, William Keener's final resting place is not much more than a long cast to the waters of the Beaverkill. This friend to so many anglers lies buried in a small hillside cemetery overlooking his beloved Junction Pool.

By far, the largest trout ever taken from the Beaverkill was a brown, first reported in the fall of 1903. On November 4, the *Walton Reporter* carried a story of a 38-inch "German" trout found dead near Cooks Falls. The enormous fish was taken to Leighton's store and tipped the scales at nearly 15 pounds! Other New York newspapers ran the article, and the story culminated in the pages of *Forest and Stream*, which published the following two letters on January 9, 1904:

A BIG BROWN TROUT OF THE BEAVERKILL

Middletown, N. Y.—Editor, Forest and Stream: About election time a squib went the rounds of the papers hereabouts that a large trout had been found dead in the Beaverkill at Cook's Falls, Sullivan County, which measured thirty-eight inches long and weighed fifteen pounds, and that it had died from fatty degeneration of the heart or starvation, or probably old age, nobody knew which. A

whopping lie I said to myself, and let it go at that. On the 16th of November the Daily Press of this city again published another big trout found dead at Rockland. That made two big 'uns, and I thought I would investigate; so I wrote to my friend "Bill" Keener, the genial proprietor of the Roscoe House at Rockland, and, as luck would have it, I struck the right man and the same fish, as you will see by the enclosed letter. Friend Keener is an all-round sportsman, and is an authority on fishing, particularly in the Beaverkill and Willowemoc country. I am glad this big fellow has gone to the happy hereafter, the place where all big ones ought to go.

John Wilkin

Mr. Keener wrote:

I can tell you about the big trout. I am the first one who saw it after the two small boys found it. On November 1, I was down the track about three miles below here and met the boys coming down with the trout strung on a cane, carrying it between them. I measured it, and it was plumb 3 feet 2 inches long. They took it down to Cook's Falls and it weighed 14¾ pounds. It was very poor; if it had been fat it would have weighed 20 pounds at least. This is no fish story. Lots of people saw it. It was a German brown trout. It was found down by the old stone mill between here and Cook's Falls. The time of the high water last month it ran up a little spring brook between the track and the river; when the water went down it could not get back, and I suppose starved to death. I don't think it was dead when the boys found it, but the boys were afraid of the law and said they found it dead. I had a hound dog with me and the trout's head was as large as the dog's. It does not appear possible that there could have been such a fish in the river, but it is true.

William Keener

The small spring brook next to the railroad bed where the largest brown trout ever to come out of the Beaverkill was captured. The giant fish measured 38 inches in length and weighed 15 pounds.

I was so intrigued by this story that shortly after reading it, I decided to find the stream where this incredible trout's life came to an end. The timing of the incident coincided with the spawning season for brown trout. What stream could entice such a grand trout? My interest increased when the topography map of the area did not show any streams in the vicinity described by William Keener: three miles below Roscoe, between the railroad and the Beaverkill.

On a summer day, I crossed the river opposite the Red Rose Motel and found the old railroad bed. Walking in the direction of Cooks Falls, I soon came upon the stream, which Keener described as a "little spring brook." Its source was a large spring, welling up in a partially hidden glen, less than a couple of hundred feet away. The little stream of springwater flowed to, and then alongside, the railroad for a short distance, then ran through a culvert to the opposite side. Here, between the railroad and the Beaverkill, there was a small plunge pool a foot or more deep and several feet wide, after which the stream flowed overland and shortly disappeared, hundreds of feet short of the river.

Only during floodwaters could any trout reach the spring run, and only during such high flows could they leave. Incredibly, this little stream, its total length only six to eight hundred feet, maintains an isolated population of brook trout.

On this particular day there were more than two dozen nice trout trapped in the pool; and my approach sent them scurrying wildly, to and fro, seeking to get under anything that would give them shelter. This was, without a doubt, where the boys found the great trout, in a weakened condition, with no place to go and no place to hide; the fish could not escape them.

No one knows which pool this noble trout called home, but my guess is that it moved up from nearby Mountain Pool. Large and deep, it has long been a favorite of Beaverkill fishermen; combined with the Lower Mountain Pool, it forms some of the best-looking water on the lower river.

● ● ●

Louis John Rhead (1857–1926) was an Englishman who came to the United States in 1883. By profession he was an artist, and a good one, painting in oil as well as watercolor, exhibiting in American and European galleries. At expositions, Rhead

Facing page: "Selection of the Best Trout Insects for the Month of August and Corresponding Artificial Flies Tied by the Author." A page from Louis Rhead's *American Trout-Stream Insects.*[223]

captured gold medals for his artistic posters, but he is perhaps best known as an illustrator of books and magazines. Many of the books he illustrated were juvenile classics such as *The Swiss Family Robinson*, *Gulliver's Travels*, *Robin Hood*, and *King Arthur and His Knights*. His work was so popular that it is still produced today by Children's Classics in New York. Rhead began fishing in 1888 or 1890 and became an enthusiastic angler. He wrote several fishing books and numerous fishing articles, many of which appeared in *Forest and Stream*, for which he also produced a number of magazine covers.

Local newspapers first reported on his visiting the Beaverkill in 1901. That summer he stayed at the Campbell

Louis Rhead fishing Junction Pool. Rhead spent three years studying and collecting aquatic insects of the Beaverkill for his book *American Trout-Stream Insects*. Charles Scribner's Sons

Inn, overlooking the Forks, and gathered material along area streams for a book he was editing and illustrating titled *The Speckled Brook Trout*. The book, which was well received, sported a unique cover design, with trout flies on imitation birch bark. It featured articles by such well-known angling writers as William C. Harris, the editor of *The American Angler*; Charles Hallock, the editor of *Forest and Stream*; and A. Nelson Cheney, New York State fish culturist. One article titled "An Angler's Notes on the Beaverkill," by Benjamin Kent, contained valuable information on fishing the Beaverkill at the turn of the century. *The Speckled Brook Trout* also featured excellent illustrations by Louis Rhead, depicting scenes on the Beaverkill, the Willowemoc, and Mongaup Creek.

Louis Rhead became a Beaverkill regular, spending more than twenty years fishing his favorite water, below the Forks on the lower Beaverkill. He frequently stayed at the Campbell Inn or the Roscoe House, where he enjoyed the friendship of William Keener. On occasion, he fished the Willowemoc and, like most anglers of his day, made his headquarters at DeBruce, at the Hearthstone Inn, hosted by Elizabeth Royce.

Rhead believed strongly in the theory of exact imitation; in 1914, he wrote a seven-part series for *Field & Stream* titled "The Entomology of American Trout Streams." While he would go on to write several books of his own, *American Trout-Stream Insects*, published in 1916, was his most noted work. Some have hailed the book as "the first American work on trout stream insects,"[224] and others as "America's first angling entomology."[225] In preparation for this ambitious undertaking, Rhead had spent three years studying and collecting the aquatic insects of the Beaverkill. Unfortunately, he lumped all aquatic insects together: mayflies, caddis, stoneflies, and so on were identified only by a monthly insect chart. While he included plates of naturals, they are not identified other than by names he devised, such as "Female Green-Eye," "Male Green-Eye," "Broadtail," "Greenback," or "Yellow Tip."

He may have started out to write an angling entomology, but his work was amateurish and fell well short of the goal. At the very beginning of the book, on page five, Rhead made the impetuous remark, ". . . I deem it wise to brush aside the science of entomology . . ." *American Trout-Stream Insects* is not an entomology and should not be considered one.

Louis Rhead went on to design almost one hundred different flies, but it is impossible to match these with the natural insects he set out to imitate. In fact, Rhead excluded the dressings of his "nature flies," as he called them, in an obvious attempt to control their manufacture and sales. He sold the flies from his home and through the New York firm of William Mills & Son, which had the ". . . exclusive rights to make and sell all my new patterns."[226] He often promoted these flies in fishing articles and advised his readers

Louis Rhead fished along the Beaverkill and Willowemoc and often collected aquatic insects for use in creating his "nature flies."
Lee Van Put

that they could be obtained by writing to his editor at *Forest and Stream*.

In Rhead's many articles on trout fishing, he was constantly discovering new flies that were more killing, and he had no qualms about making boastful claims about himself or the flies he invented. He created "nature flies," "metal bodied flies," "shining fly minnows," and so on; his flies, he told his readers, were better than all the rest.

American Trout-Stream Insects was not this country's first entomology; it was, however, the first book devoted to the theory of exact imitation. Louis Rhead believed strongly in directly imitating the more prolific aquatic insects trout feed upon, and he tied his flies as true copies of the naturals. He dubbed the standard flies of his day "fancy flies" and saw them as useless: "If an exact copy of the natural insect is offered to the fish, it is sure to entice and lure a trout more readily than a fancy fly." How ironic it is that not one

of the numerous flies he designed and promoted is known by the fly fisherman of today, while many of those he saw as useless are still favored, seventy-five years later, by trout fishers everywhere.

One who fished with Louis Rhead on the lower Beaverkill was William Schaldach. Like Rhead, he, too, was an artist and an angling writer; his career with brush and pen was just beginning:

Louis Rhead had a great devotion to the natural-imitation theory, and he tied lifelike replicas of crawfish, hellgrammites, nymphs and adult flies. He would fish these diligently, day after day, and the empty creel with which he often returned never dampened his spirits. Anglers called him a luckless fisherman and kidded him unmercifully; but usually, when things were at their worst, he would show up with a brownie or rainbow of prodigious size and silently slay his critics.[227]

Creating New Trout Waters

During the 1890s two new fishing clubs acquired more than seven miles of the Beaverkill and, in so doing, made virtually all of the water on the upper river private and posted. In 1895 a few avid fly fishermen from New York formed the Fly Fishers Club of Brooklyn and acquired a one-mile stretch of the Beaverkill that flowed through the farm of Ben Hardenbergh, at Craig-e-clare. The club bound itself to three rules: No trout under seven inches would be creeled; members could fish only with flies; and the stream would be stocked with adult or yearling trout, persistently and liberally.

A few years later, a small group of anglers from Binghamton began acquiring leases and strips of land bordering the stream, from Beaverkill Falls downstream to the Bonnie View resort. They made their purchases from farmers, sawmill operators, and boardinghouse owners, put together a holding of approximately six miles, and became known as the Beaverkill Fishermen's Association. In 1903 this group's holding was acquired by the Beaverkill Stream Club, which made its headquarters at the Bonnie View.

With more of the best stream water on the upper river becoming posted, serious attention was given to creating private trout preserves by constructing artificial lakes and ponds. During the 1890s, a number of these man-made impoundments made their appearance in the Beaverkill (and Willowemoc) watershed; private trout hatcheries were constructed on their premises to replenish the lakes on a regular basis. A few became well-known trout-fishing resorts, adding to the history of the Beaverkill. The first trout hatchery to appear in the Beaverkill region was established in 1890 at Alder Lake.

Alder Lake

Actually, Alder Lake was at one time a natural body of water. When the region was first surveyed in 1809, by Jacob Trumpbour, the lake was quite small. In his field notes, Trumpbour wrote that lots 190 and 191 contained "about 14 acres of Aulder Pond, and [are] watered by its outlet on which is a fall of about 10 feet, a good mill site."[228] As with most of the farm lots surveyed in the Beaverkill Valley, the land was "steep and stony" and "a poor lot." These surveyor descriptions readily explain, in a few words, why the land was not settled for nearly a half century after being subdivided.

It was not until 1856, when Asahel Bryant of Andes purchased "Aulder Pond" and lots 190 and 191, that the land became occupied. This pioneer settler constructed a log cabin and worked diligently to convert the wilderness into an "improved farm." Farming was never easy in the rugged, mountainous country; winters were long and sometimes punishing. During the first spring, Bryant lost fourteen of his thirty head of cattle due to a late snowstorm. A deep snow fell in April, catching him out of forage; far from any neighbors and surrounded by forest, it is a wonder he did not lose them all.

In 1861 Bryant's brother, William, took over the farm and continued making improvements. He constructed a sawmill at the falls and replaced the primitive log cabin with a more permanent dwelling. Learning, perhaps, from the hardships of his brother, he drained Aulder Pond and turned it into a rich meadow, which in turn provided his cattle with enough hay to last the long winters. The Bryants farmed the land successfully for many years before trading farms with Julius (June) Smith of Dunraven in 1889.

June Smith had a different vision for the farm carved out of the wilderness. He knew about trout, having been a guide in the area since 1866; but more importantly, he knew about trout propagation. Instead of a meadow, he saw a lake full of leaping trout. Many farmers on the nearby Beaverkill enhanced their incomes by boarding fishermen, and Smith decided to flood the farm, create a lake, and build a fishing resort, which would attract trout-fishing tourists.

He found the financial means to carry out his dream when he formed a partnership with Colonel Charles H. Odell. Odell was a wealthy Pittsburgh steel manufacturer with a Wall Street address. The two men were from vastly different backgrounds, and how their unusual alliance was formed is not known. Perhaps it was their Civil War experiences that brought the two together; June Smith had seen plenty of action as a member of the 3rd New York Cavalry. It was said that he was a veteran of more than sixty battles before he was discharged. The two men also shared another bond: a love for trout and a desire to improve trout fishing.

A large dam was constructed and a new, larger, deeper Alder Lake now covered fifty-five acres. The lake was stocked with native brook trout taken from the Beaverkill; and given added space, with cold, clean water and no competition, they grew large and plentiful. To enhance the fishery, June Smith constructed a hatchery below the dam, in a narrow ravine along the lake's outlet.

At the rear of the lake, where spring feeders flowed, shallow ponds were made by building small dams with fishways, which allowed spawning trout to enter. Once in the ponds, the trout were captured in nets and taken by buckboard to the hatchery, where ripe trout were stripped of their eggs, then returned to the lake. In time, when the fry were large enough, they, too, were placed in Alder Lake.

The partnership between Colonel Odell and June Smith dissolved in 1891, and a corporation was formed with the name of the Alder Lake Club. Membership was limited to forty, and most members resided in Kingston. Samuel D. Coykendall, a millionaire railroad and steamboat company owner, was its most prominent member. A large clubhouse was constructed, along with a barn and ice house.

While some members traveled from Kingston by wagon, and even on horseback, transportation to Alder Lake was generally provided by the Ulster & Delaware Railroad. The detraining point was Arkville; from there, members traveled the fourteen miles by carriage or buckboard. The lake quickly developed a reputation as a great trout preserve. Its members regularly returned to Kingston with catches of large brook trout, some in the 2-pound class; occasionally, they would

The Brooklyn Fly Fisher's Club was formed in 1895 and followed three rules—trout had to be 7 inches in length; fly fishing only; and the stream would be stocked "persistently and liberally." Jack Niflot

The old hatchery at Alder Lake. This hatchery was constructed by Julius Smith, who used the building to strip and fertilize brook trout from Alder Lake and hatch their fry for distribution.

even bring back a trout of 20 inches. On May 28, 1892, the *Kingston Weekly Leader* reported:

> The finest mess of trout ever seen in this city was brought in town on Thursday afternoon by Abraham Hasbrouck, President of the National Bank of Rondout. He captured them in Alder Lake which is the property of a fishing club [of] which he is a member. The catch weighed 15 pounds, and none of them weighed less than a pound and the largest weighed two pounds.

"Any luck?" is a question fishermen hear all the time. Most experienced anglers, however, will tell you that luck has little to do with catching fish. It is skill, or knowledge, or maybe even perseverance, they will say, that makes for successful fishing. An incident, though, that clearly demonstrates how luck—both good and bad—can be involved occurred on a day in June 1895.

Jansen Hasbrouck, an Alder Lake Club member, was fishing with two hooks on his line and caught what fly fishermen call a "double": two trout at once. Unfortunately, the pair of speckled beauties became snagged on the bottom and broke

Hasbrouck's leader—an apparent case of bad luck. Later in the day he hooked another trout, which fought furiously, swimming to and fro with seemingly increasing strength. When Hasbrouck finally was able to bring the fish to the net, he saw that the trout had become entangled with his lost double, and he landed all three—an obvious example of good luck!

When the trout season opened in the spring of 1899, Samuel Coykendall was the new owner of Alder Lake. He purchased the shares of the other club members and planned to create a stylish estate and fishing preserve. On a knoll overlooking the lake, Coykendall constructed a stately mansion of grand proportions. More than a hundred men were employed during its construction; all materials were hauled from Livingston Manor, sixteen miles distant.

By June 1900 the magnificent three-story building was completed. In addition, Coykendall added hundreds of acres of forest lands to his lake holdings and constructed a new road, mostly at his own expense, over Cross Mountain from Arena. While the road may have made the trip a little shorter and more pleasant, it also made it easier for poachers to find Alder Lake. Once word had gotten out about how good the trout fishing was, poaching became a problem. There was always a resident caretaker; at times, the club employed as many as seven men to patrol the lake's shore. Confrontations were common and especially troublesome at night, when patrolmen were occasionally assaulted by determined poachers. But poachers, too, paid indirectly for their indiscretions. Old-timers tell of hasty escapes and injuries sustained while fleeing in the dark, tripping over rocks and logs.

The late Catskill fly tier Harry Darbee told the story of three poachers who were caught at Alder Lake with more than one hundred trout over the legal limit. The state police were summoned; the trespassers and their catch, which was in a burlap bag, were placed in the rear of the troop car for a trip to the judge in Livingston Manor.

All the way down the road leading out of the Beaverkill Valley, on the way to the Manor, the men quietly and efficiently tossed their illegal catch out of the car's rear windows. Upon arriving at the town justice, a red-faced trooper discovered that he had no evidence! I can still see the glint in Harry's eye and hear his laughter as he finished telling the story with a slap on his knee. While he frowned on their greedy deed, Harry admired the poachers' ingenuity and their ability to outwit the law.

Samuel Coykendall owned Alder Lake for many years, enlarging his estate to more than sixteen hundred acres, which also included Beecher Lake. To reach Beecher from Alder, he improved a rough wagon road, which had been an ancient Indian trail, running between the two lakes. The stewardship of Alder Lake by the Coykendall family ended in 1945, when the estate once again became a trout-fishing club. A new Alder Lake Club emerged, only this time, its membership came from Liberty, in Sullivan County. This club maintained the lake for fifteen years before conveying the holdings to the Nassau County Council of Boy Scouts.

For the next twenty years, the lake and its woodlands were used as a summer retreat by the scouts from Long Island. In 1980, Alder Lake and the sixteen hundred acres surrounding it changed hands for the last time. The lands were acquired by New York State and added to the forever-wild Catskill Forest Preserve.

Orchard Lake

During the 1890s June Smith went on to construct other private trout hatcheries in Sullivan County. He became a well-known expert in trout propagation, pioneering, at least locally,

Alder Lake is presently owned by New York State and maintains a population of native brook trout.

Orchard Lake Hatchery was also constructed by Julius Smith in the 1890s. *Forest and Stream,* May 3, 1913

an industry whose time, it seemed, had come. In 1894 Smith established the Orchard Lake Hatchery at the headwaters of Sprague Brook, a Willowemoc tributary. This facility was owned by Stoddard Hammond, a tanner and acid manufacturer, who constructed a dam, creating a forty-acre lake he named Orchard Lake Trout Preserve.

In 1911, the Hammond family sold the lake to a group of New York City sportsmen, who became known as the Orchard Lake Club. With a hatchery located on the premises to ensure a constant supply of trout, it was not long before Orchard Lake developed a reputation as a fine producer, especially of large brook trout. In 1915, one club member even captured the *Forest and Stream* contest prize for catching the largest trout on a fly.

Membership was about fifty, and while the lake's excellent fishing was the main attraction, another important activity was the club's clay pigeon shooting. In time Orchard Lake Club amassed two thousand acres and changed its name to the Trout and Skeet Club of New York. In 1955, after a span covering more than forty years, ownership of Orchard Lake, too, passed on to the Nassau County Council of Boy Scouts.

Waneta Lake

Another trout hatchery that began operations during this period was constructed immediately below Lew Beach, on a spring tributary of the Beaverkill. It was built by Bruce Davidson in 1895, the same year he created a trout preserve farther down the Beaverkill road. A year earlier he had purchased an "alder swamp" and employed a large force of men to cut trees and burn brush, clearing more than thirty acres. He then built a stone dam across the small stream flowing through the wetlands and created Waneta Lake. Davidson

stocked the waters with trout, constructed a fine boardinghouse, and, for many years, provided his paying guests with excellent trout fishing.

Forest Lake

Another trout preserve that made its appearance about this time was Forest Lake, located opposite the Salmo Fontinalis Club water. In 1894, William Bidwell built a small trout pond where a series of springs flowed over his property.

Searching for a place to enjoy trout fishing, Frank and Charles Andrus of Roxbury, Delaware County, purchased the Bidwell property, constructed a new dam, and enlarged the pond to twelve acres. After a few years, the Andrus brothers sold their lake to a small group of anglers, mostly from Roxbury, who became incorporated under the name of Forest Lake Club. For many years, club members enjoyed trout fishing in their spring-fed waters with individual catches of brook trout at times numbering in the hundreds.

Hodge Pond

One of the most bizarre attempts at creating a trout fishery occurred in 1899, when a Brooklyn contractor named Patrick H. Flynn attempted to "blow up" a lake in order to rid it of undesirable fish and then restock its waters with trout. Flynn purchased more than two thousand acres surrounding a beautiful, mountaintop twenty-acre lake named Hodge Pond. The land was heavily forested; the lake, deep and cold, straddled the divide between the Beaverkill and the Willowemoc.

Flynn's goal was to have a game and trout preserve in the wilderness, and he began by importing deer from New Jersey and Wichita, Kansas, and turning them loose on his property. He built a road into Hodge Pond and constructed a large summer residence high on a hillside overlooking the lake. For transportation to and from his preserve deep in the forest, Flynn brought to Livingston Manor the first automobile ever seen there. A local newspaper reported, "It is a curiosity to the people living along the route, and is inspected most thoroughly by horses that chance to meet it."[229]

Hodge Pond had all of the physical requirements necessary to be an excellent trout pond, but it was populated by pickerel, perch, bullheads, and sunfish. Flynn was determined to wipe out the existing fish population by the novel use of explosives. In preparation, he hired a dynamiter and acquired between twelve hundred and twenty-five hundred pounds of explosives.

In the early spring of 1899, a crew of men worked for a week, drawing off water to lower the lake by three feet. As it was still covered by more than thirty inches of ice, they drilled two hundred holes, fifty feet apart. Each hole was wired with dynamite, which was lowered to within four feet of the lake bottom. From five to thirty-five sticks were placed in each hole and connected to three circuits, which were timed to explode seconds apart.

On the day of the big event, a crowd of nearby residents gathered at the lake to witness the unusual occurrence. They made their way by horse and carriage or buckboard; and, as they gathered along the lake's shore, speculation among the multitude was varied. Some believed Hodge Pond would "go heavenward," others "didn't think it would budge an inch," and a few were "absolutely sure it would blow the whole bottom out."[230]

At the sound of a pistol shot, the electric spark was sent, discharging the explosives. The earth shook, and the detonation was accompanied by a roar similar to "a hundred claps of thunder":

> With the first plunge of the batteries fifty-four holes were exploded, and a sight as grand and awe inspiring as one could wish to see met the eager eyes of all. There is nothing with which to compare it, and description will not avail. From fifty-four holes as many columns of ice and water ascended simultaneously to a height of one hundred, to one hundred fifty feet, each column being ten to fifteen feet in diameter.[231]

Within a second of the first explosion, there was another, and then a third equally as large. The result was "one of the grandest spectacles ever witnessed." Several days later, when an assessment of the experiment could be carried out, it was discovered that though the lake bottom was covered with dead fish, many remained alive: "While the experiment was an underwater pyrotechnical success from a spectator point of view, so far as exterminating the finny tribe is concerned it was a gigantic failure."[232]

Punch Bowl Pond

One other noted trout preserve was developed during the 1890s; it was constructed by Jeronimus S. Underhill, the Brooklyn sportsman who had gifted the Roscoe railroad station with the famous trout weathervane. In 1892 he built a dam across Meadow Swamp Brook, a spring tributary of Abe Wood Brook, which flows into the Willowemoc just upstream of Junction Pool. The pond he created was small, a little over six acres; unfortunately, shortly after it was constructed, the dam sprang a leak and drained. After reconstruction, continuing leakage problems caused the oval-shaped pond to maintain a half-full appearance, similar to a punch bowl, and it thus became known as the Punch Bowl, or Punch Bowl Pond.

Underhill also built a large, rustic, three-story clubhouse overlooking the valley and the village of Roscoe, providing a "bird's-eye view for miles around."[233] Alongside the building, high in a hemlock, flew an enormous American flag. It measured thirty feet by eighteen feet and was suspended from a huge tree more than one hundred feet high that had been trimmed for the purpose. The glorious flag could be seen for miles, capturing the attention of fishermen and travelers. Atop the mountainside, it could be spotted from the veranda of the Beaverkill House, opposite the railroad station, where curious travelers marveled over who lived in such a wonderful location.

Punch Bowl Pond. A small pond constructed by J. S. Underhill, a Brooklyn sportsman. The pond was about six acres in size but had a continuous leakage problem, which maintained a half-full appearance, and thus it became known as the Punch Bowl.

stream in falling upon the rocks, is converted into a white foam, producing a noise that is almost deafening, and throws off a watery mist handsomely illustrating in miniature, the great Niagara.

The rain had now ceased, and I was soon lost in contemplating the grandeur of the scene around me. Wild flowers bloom upon either bank in rich profusion, imparting their fragrance to every breeze that sweeps through the valley. Ever and anon, the joyous song of some feathered warbler near me, would mingle with the war of the waters, as he fritted from bough to bough among the giant hemlocks that skirt the banks of the stream, while a glance over the dark blue waters of the basin beneath the fall, discovered to the eye, numerous trout leaping from their watery element after flies that were skimming over its surface. Stopping short in my musings, I commenced fishing. As in imitation of the real, I drew my artificial fly lightly over the water. It was eagerly seized, and one fine trout after another, came floundering upon the bank near me.[236]

Historically, the fishing experience described above is important, since this Delaware County angler was certainly not fishing wet flies in the traditional style. His description borders on dry-fly fishing at a time when the method was not known or practiced in this country. He appears to be fishing one fly on top of the water. While he does not mention it, he most assuredly had to false cast or dry the fly in order to have it at or near the surface, especially after catching a trout.

In the years that followed, the Falls Lot, like other portions of the Beaverkill, was despoiled, its appearance debased by a sawmill and forest exploitation. In 1874, John and Robert Jones constructed the mill, dammed the water above the falls, and began manufacturing lumber, shingles, and wooden trays. While the mill destroyed the scenic aspects of the falls and affected its trout resources, anglers still flocked to its waters. One of Beaverkill Falls' most dedicated users was the famous Ned Buntline.

Whenever his large American flag was flying at Tripp's, Ned was sure to be found fishing at the falls pool. It was his favorite, and he was a familiar figure there, standing midstream with his cherished Orvis rod, casting a pair of wet flies straight upstream into the foamy water at the base of the falls. He liked to use a Coachman, Black Gnat, General Hooker, or Seth Green. However, if flies were not working, Ned would not be opposed to using worms and split shot to reach the large trout that lived in the depths of the "grand pool at the foot of the Big falls."[237]

The Jones brothers halted their mill operations in 1891, when they sold the Falls Lot and all of their stream holdings to Colonel Charles H. Odell. Odell intended to make a trout preserve, and he began by constructing a summer residence he called Troutholme. The first trout fisherman to own the falls, Colonel Odell was determined to restore the fisheries. Under his stewardship, the Falls Lot began to recover from the effects of the mill and nearby forest degradation.

In 1892 he improved the fishery by stocking brown trout above the impassable waterfall and initiating a program of stream habitat improvement. Colonel Odell employed Robert Jones, who had operated the sawmill for many years, to supervise the construction of in-stream structures of logs and stones. Jones knew the power of the Beaverkill; he had seen the damage its high flows were capable of. The stream work, done with oxen, proved to have created the most durable and effective improvement structures placed in the Beaverkill. They were sensible, stable, long lasting, and not only pleasing to the eye but appealing to the trout as well. With only minor repairs, these structures have withstood countless floods and ice-outs, and they have lasted for more than 125 years—a remarkable achievement!

The structures were built using hemlock logs and large flat rocks; they raised the level of a pool one to two feet upstream of the structure and created a plunge pool, three to five feet deep, on the downstream side. Aesthetically they are pleasing to the eye and have a general appearance, unlike many of the structures created from logs and planks by the New York State Conservation Department from the 1950s through the '70s, which looked artificial and needed constant repairs.

When I began working for the Conservation Department in 1969 in the Bureau of Fisheries, Burt Lindsley, a state conservation officer with the department, made a special point to show me the in-stream structures on the upper Beaverkill above the falls constructed by Colonel Odell back in the 1890s. Burt knew of my interest in trout fishing and also that I would be involved at some point with trout habitat improvement with the state and wanted me to see what, in his opinion, was the best stream work found in the section of the Catskills he patrolled, enforcing fish and game laws.

The stream section was impressive and while there may have been a couple more structures than were necessary, the structures blended with the stream environment, so much so that for a moment one might believe they were a part of the natural landscape. The overall appearance of the stretch above the falls was that it was a special fishery. My thought was that the landowner held trout fishing in high regard and desired to make the stream a better place for the trout that inhabited his waters and yet keep as natural an appearance as possible.

Perhaps one of the best descriptions I ever read about this stretch of the Beaverkill was written by Dana Lamb back in the 1960s. In an article titled "After All These Years," in which he reminisces about fishing the Beaverkill, Dana, a veteran Beaverkill fly fisher and excellent writer, describes the stream from its confluence with the East Branch all the way up to the private water of the Falls Lot:

Five miles above, nature with its waterfall and early owners with their great stone dams, have compounded the river's innate beauty and here indeed even today the privileged angler reaches Nirvana. Here, or on the Fontinalis water just above, I seldom stop or linger long lest envy, which should have no place within the angler's makeup, begin to enter mine, but turn where the road permits, drive back down from this deer-haunted fairyland toward the present day realities of open water in a land where heavily traveled roads run everywhere and the majority seek fish rather than fishing.[238]

The next owners of record were the Snedecors: Jordan L., Abraham, and Eliphadeth. They were a family of fly fishermen, very much involved with every aspect of the sport, and were known socially by most of New York's large fly-fishing community. During the years the Snedecors owned the falls, one of their guests was the legendary Theodore Gordon. At the time, Gordon was using the dry fly but had not yet perfected his famous Quill Gordon. One thing is for certain, though—he made an impression on his hosts:

J. L. Snedecor and his two sons owned for a number of years the famous high falls stretch of the Beaverkill (now the Jenny Henderson water) above Turnwood, and I remember Abram Snedecor telling me of Gordon stalking and catching a very large trout with one fly tied on the end of his leader and cocking it beautifully.[239]

In 1912 the Falls Lot changed hands, as the Snedecors sold their interests to Gifford A. Cochran, a famous yachtsman and wealthy Yonkers carpet manufacturer. Two years after acquiring the property, Cochran conveyed the falls to the Beaverkill Stream Club, which owned the adjoining downstream water.

Later that same year the Beaverkill Stream Club sold the falls back to Cochran, and in an obvious attempt to preserve Beaverkill Falls, placed a series of unique restrictions in the deed. In addition to barring every known form of manufacturing or establishment, the list protected the falls from "any place for public amusement, circus, theatre, menagerie, or other store of any description, or any trade business or calling whatever." The deed restrictions further safeguarded the falls by not allowing the owner to "throw or allow to run into any waters in the premises herein conveyed and above described any dyestuffs, coal tar, refuse from a gas house, sawdust, shavings, tanbark, lime or other deleterious or poisonous substance whatever injurious to fish life."[240]

In 1921 Gifford Cochran relinquished title to the falls to Malcolm D. Whitman of Manhattan. During Whitman's tenure, the Falls Lot was leased, in 1954, to a small group of

One of Colonel Odell's habitat improvement structures constructed more than one hundred years ago. The improvements still function as intended and are not only pleasing to the eye but provide habitat for trout.

Beaverkill Falls in an early summer flow. Judy Van Put

A stream permit for Theodore Gordon. Theodore Gordon is remembered fishing at Beaverkill Falls, stalking a large trout and catching it on a dry fly.

fly fishers who mostly came from Connecticut. Inspired by the finding of a framed card giving guest privileges to Theodore Gordon, the men decided to call themselves the Quill Gordon Associates. The card was dated May 17, 1902, and had been used by Gordon while the Snedecors owned the falls.[241] The Quill Gordon Associates' lease of the water ended in 1984, when the Whitman family sold the Falls Lot and its adjoining lands to Larry Rockefeller. The noted environmentalist added the property to his Beaverkill Valley holdings. From 1749 to the present, a period of nearly two hundred fifty years, ownership of Beaverkill Falls has been limited to just seven families. It is comforting to know that the falls will be preserved, in their present state, for years to come.

23

"Dancing Feather Creek"

Mongaup Creek may be the most beautiful and best-known tributary flowing into the Willowemoc Creek. The stream flows out of Mongaup Pond and travels four miles through forest lands, entering the Willowemoc at DeBruce. Along the way, many large springs add their icy-cold waters, creating excellent habitat for native brook trout. The stream begins at an elevation of 2,139 feet; at first, its gradient is rather moderate, but after a short distance the Mongaup descends rapidly, plummeting more than three hundred feet in the next two miles. Its swift current carries the stream through a series of cascades over solid bedrock, falling wildly, swirling and churning, agitating the water into a foaming, hissing body that culminates in beautiful waterfalls encircled by emerald ferns, hemlocks, and moss-covered ledges. After the falls, the stream settles down and continues on its way at a more gentle, less hurried pace.

The Mongaup is an excellent trout stream, with good habitat and cold, clean, well-oxygenated water; its riffles and pools are capable of holding the largest trout. The stream's reputation as a fishing ground was founded during the earliest days of Catskill trout fishing, and its abundance of native brook trout caused anglers to stray from the Willowemoc and work their way up the Mongaup, assured that in doing so they would return with a heavy basket. The naturalist John Burroughs fished its waters, and while he was enamored with the name of the Willowemoc, he found the Mongaup more productive: "When fishing in the Willowemoc, the beauty of that lovely stream's lovely name enhanced for him its charm: 'Thy name casts a spell upon me, Willowemoc, Willowemoc!— but we take more trout from the Mongaup!'"[242]

The stream's beauty and the abundance of trout attracted many fishermen and other pleasure seekers—too many, it seems, as early on local anglers fabricated a story to frighten away visitors. A tale was told of a huge panther, or mountain lion, that frequented the Mongaup in search of tourists; one story even went so far as to state that the monster panther was seen in the act of eating a fisherman!

At the beginning of the trouting season of 1882, the *Hancock Herald* reported:

> It is about time to hear something about that DeBruce panther. The animal generally puts in an appearance in April or May, just about the time the trout up the Mongaup are aching to be caught. The last time seen by a reliable correspondent up that way the animal had a pair of fishermen's boots dangling out of his mouth.[243]

In time, angling was restricted along the Mongaup, as its waters became private and individuals acquired large portions of the stream, turning them into fishing preserves. The first to establish private water was O. M. Cleveland of Newburgh, who purchased a couple of miles in 1895.

In 1922 Robertson Ward constructed a rustic fishing lodge and trout hatchery along its banks. Guests attracted to Ward's preserve included celebrities of the day, such as the famous world heavyweight champion Gene Tunney and Irvin S. Cobb, a noted American humorist, novelist, and short story writer. Both men enjoyed fishing and found the trout and pleasant scenery of the Mongaup much to their liking.

One other large landowner of note was John Karst, who moved to the Mongaup in 1907. Karst was a premier wood engraver of school texts in the country, and he enjoyed a nationwide reputation as an artist who raised the standard of textbook illustrations. Considered a man of culture, he collected rare prints, old books, antiques, weapons, paintings, clocks, and historical furniture. His home was described as a museum, crammed full of priceless relics, including a number of books from the library of Henry Ward Beecher.

John Karst (1836–1922) was born in Nauheim, Germany, and came to this country when he was two years old; his family first settled at West Point, New York, and then in New York City. As a young man he trained as an apprentice to a wood engraver and after two years he became skilled enough to work on his own. He was an extremely talented engraver whose skills could make crude drawings into "spirited" pictures. Perhaps he is best known for his illustrations for the McGuffey Readers; the books were graded primers and widely used as textbooks in American schools. It is estimated that at least 120 million copies of the books were sold between 1836 and 1960, with sales ranking alongside the Bible and Webster's Dictionary. Even today McGuffey Readers are still in use in some private schools and by parents for homeschooling purposes; they continue to sell at an estimated rate of thirty thousand copies a year. Karst prepared all the illustrations for the six McGuffey

Dancing Feather Creek is the Indian name for the Mongaup Creek that flows into the Willowemoc Creek at DeBruce. The name is quite appropriate, as the stream plummets more than three hundred feet in two miles.

Readers, choosing the subjects that were used and supervising the work.

At the outbreak of the Civil War he went to work for Frank Leslie, who published a popular weekly journal titled *Frank Leslie's Illustrated Newspaper*. Karst was the superintendent of the engraving department and after the Civil War he became an independent engraver with a shop on Canal Street in lower Manhattan. He made many engravings for *Harper's*, *Scribner's*, and other periodicals and for artists such as Edwin Austin Abbey, Thomas Moran, Frederick Church, and Winslow Homer. He is also known for producing illustrations for the Beadle & Adams Dime Novel series, publications that were said to help develop the reading habits of Americans.

When the art of wood engraving gave way to photoengraving and improved photographic techniques, John Karst retired to an "ancient house" on eleven hundred acres in what was known as "Whipple Hollow" near Mongaup Mountain and DeBruce. It was here that he enjoyed his love of fishing, hunting, reading, and grafting apple trees. The house, constructed in 1804, had great ceiling beams and huge fireplaces, one almost covering an entire wall—in bygone days strings of fish had hung from the rafters to dry. The house was built in the time of tenant farms, when a feudal system reigned over the Catskills, and it had been a meeting place for farmers who were "anti-renters," who during the 1840s revolted against an unjust system of land tenure.

John Karst lived in retirement with his daughter, Esther, and when he died in 1922, she inherited his estate and made the home a museum, exhibiting many of her father's treasured belongings and "fine examples" of his art. The 1804 house became known as the John Karst Historical Home Museum and was maintained as an historic site in New York State.

It was during the early 1930s that Esther Karst became embroiled in a controversy that caused a barrage of letters to appear in area newspapers. At issue was her desire to change the name of Mongaup Creek, an idea that incited not only local residents, summer residents, and former residents, but even nonresidents.

Esther wrote to the *Livingston Manor Times*, suggesting the stream be renamed because it was confused with the Mongaup River, which had branches that began in the nearby town of Liberty. She invited readers to think of a new name. A month later, the newspaper reported that the state historian recognized that "some change seems advisable" and suggested that interested readers who desired to submit new names should address the editor.

Esther Karst began to circulate a petition for the renaming and again urged readers to send in their suggestions. One of the first to write and object was Ada Cooper. Her grandfather had been a pioneer settler of the area, and for many years she had owned and operated the Homestead, a popular fishing resort at DeBruce:

John Karst. A premier wood engraver of school textbooks, one of his best-known works were his illustrations for McGuffey Readers, which are still in use by homeschoolers. House of Beadle & Adams

From the earliest days of De Bruce and vicinity, it has been known to sportsmen as Mongaup Creek.

As long ago as when fishermen came from Ellenville with three-seated-buckboard wagons, before the O. & W. RR was built, it was known all over the country by sportsmen as Mongaup Creek, the outlet of Mongaup Pond.

It grieves me, to think anyone would want to change the old Indian names which have come down from the history of the early days of this part of the country.

Mongaup means "Dancing Feather." What better name could be selected.[244]

Another letter, signed "A Lover of the Forests and Streams," favored a name change and even suggested Esther Creek, in honor of Miss Karst. This letter was followed by many others opposing a name change. A writer from New York City stated:

To change the name now to a surname or nondescript female name would be most confusing; would lose this stream its identity among trout fishermen as a picturesque trout stream and would not be in keeping with the other Indian and historic names of the neighborhood.[245]

Esther Falls on Mongaup Creek, named after Esther Karst, whose family owned much of the surrounding lands.

Esther retaliated with another letter in defense of her petition. She suggested calling the stream "Hunter Creek" or "Mountain Creek" and proposed that "as wild orchids have been found near it, the name 'Wild Orchid Creek' would be appropriate."[246] Another writer with an opposing view replied:

> It is difficult to understand how anyone can conceive of changing the name of one of the beautiful trout streams flowing through that valley.
>
> It is not difficult to imagine the soft shod Indian wandering through our woods and coming upon the babbling Mongaup and calling it by a name that its ripples suggest, despite the fact that another river many miles away is called by the same name. Certainly this is no argument to deprive that river of its beautiful name and us trout fishermen of something very near and dear to our hearts. We don't call it the Mongaup River nor the Mongaup Creek, but just plain "Mongaup."[247]

Esther Karst lost out on her bid to alter history and change the name of the Mongaup; and while she stirred up the ire of many, there was never any lasting ill will directed toward her. Indeed, in a circuitous way, her name is honored; she is remembered, perhaps immortalized, by the beautiful waterfalls of the Mongaup, which are still known today as Esther Falls.

24

Acid Factories

Beaverkill anglers of the 1890s had a couple of reasons to celebrate. The stream and its tributaries were finally beginning to recover from the abuses of the fading tanning industry, and the introduction of brown trout was proving extremely successful. But any celebration was to be short-lived: Just as the tanneries were closing down, a new, larger, and even more destructive industry developed in the watershed. Like the tanneries, it too exploited the forest, fouled the air, polluted the water, and destroyed trout fisheries. This new industry was the manufacturing of chemicals from wood by hardwood-distillation plants, known locally as "acid factories." These forerunners of today's chemical industry were well suited to the Catskills. They required an abundance of hardwood, large quantities of water to cool their distillation machinery, and unskilled labor to harvest the forest and work in the plant.

There were many more acid factories than tanneries, and while the tanner laid waste to the hemlock, the acid men were not as selective and cut down whatever was standing. Thousands of acres of beech, birch, maple, oak, and chestnut were felled, cut, and split into four-foot lengths. Mountainsides were devastated by clear-cutting; a single plant consumed up to thirty cords of wood in a single day, and between five thousand and ten thousand cords per year. (One cord is a stack four by four by eight feet.)

Cordwood was placed in retorts, or ovens, and subjected to heat by a coal fire. Approximately 60 percent of the wood was converted into a liquid, called pyroligneous acid, from which wood alcohol, acetate of lime, and wood tars were obtained. Wood alcohol (methanol) was used as an antifreeze and solvent. The rest of the wood was reduced to charcoal, which was removed and sold.

The first plant appeared along a Trout Brook tributary, at Acidalia, in 1878. In time, as the industry grew, there were sixteen wood chemical plants operating in the Beaverkill watershed, with many being constructed during the 1890s. Along the Willowemoc, there were acid factories on Sprague Brook, at Willowemoc, Livingston Manor, and Hazel, a tiny hamlet located between Roscoe and Livingston Manor. On the Beaverkill, factories were located at Cooks Falls, Horton, Elk Brook, and Peakville and along Spring Brook, Horton Brook, Russell Brook, and Trout Brook.

From the beginning, the wood chemical industry proved it was not compatible with trout streams. Reports of fish kills followed the construction of plants, and many people believed they caused more injury to trout fishing than the tanneries and sawmills ever did. Fish kills became a regular occurrence downstream of virtually all acid factories. They generally occurred when streamside tar pits, or cesspools, which were filled with residue wastes such as insoluble wood tar, known as "oil of smoke," overflowed or leached into nearby waters. They were also caused by carelessness and incompetent laborers; valves were left open, and vats of acid overflowed into the stream. Some plants constantly discharged their lethal poisons directly into the stream and did not kill trout or other fish, simply because there were no trout or other fish life located below them; their wastes kept the stream permanently depleted of all aquatic life.

Streams below acid factories were smelly from their putrid discharges, and samples taken near them often recorded that the water contained "zero" oxygen. The bed of the stream generally contained a "vigorous growth of gray, slimy organic matter."[248] One angler who spent a week fishing the Beaverkill, in the area of Cooks Falls and its acid factories,

Acid factory in Livingston Manor along Cattail Brook. In May of 1930 thousands of fish, mostly trout, were killed in Cattail Brook and the Willowemoc Creek when acid overflowed into the stream. *The Wood Chemical Industry in the Delaware Valley, 1986*

complained bitterly in the pages of *Forest and Stream* of his lack of success:

> I caught a few California trout in the Russell Brook about two miles above the Beaverkill River and ruined a pair of boots from the refuse of a wood alcohol factory that empties its chemical filth into, what otherwise has the natural condition for a good trout stream. The Beaverkill is a great stream for chubs, bass, wood alcohol and lemons.[249]

Prior to 1890 laws pertaining to pollution were relatively weak and rarely enforced. In 1892, however, a new law prohibiting pollution was passed:

> No dye-stuff, coal tar, refuse from gas houses, saw dust, shavings, tanbark, lime or other deleterious or poisonous substance shall be thrown or allowed to run into any of the waters of this State, either private or public, in quantities destructive to the life of, or disturbing the habits of fish inhabiting the stream.[250]

All mills and factories were given notice of the new law and time to correct any discharge problems. But the new law did little to halt pollution. Most of those discharging into streams continued to do so, as game protectors found it

difficult to enforce laws of this nature. Fish kills were the most obvious evidence that deleterious or poisonous substances were dumped into the stream, but often by the time a game protector was notified and drove the many miles by horse or wagon to the site, the fish kill would be over and the discharge long gone.

Those who did undertake to sue acid factory owners met with stiff resistance. Factory owners were generally influential men who might ask, "Would you have us throw all these men out of work because we kill a few fish that some rich fisherman might otherwise catch?"[251] Cases against them sometimes took years, as they would repeatedly be knocked off court calendars. When they were tried, the fines were so small that owners continued doing business as usual, as it was cheaper to run wastes into the streams—and kill fish—than to remove the cause of the pollution.

Letters deploring stream conditions in the vicinity of wood chemical plants appeared in local weekly newspapers and in sporting journals. A. Nelson Cheney, a state fish culturist, was appalled at conditions he found when he visited the Beaverkill, especially in the area of Spring Brook. Only a few years earlier a tank at the Spring Brook factory had burst, dumping acid into the Beaverkill, killing "a ton" of trout—by estimate, more than four thousand trout, of between 2 and 18 inches in length. In an article titled "Trout and Acids," Cheney let it be known that the state would discontinue stocking trout in any stream receiving acid factory wastes, and he reported:

On a recent visit to the region of which I am writing, I found it infested with acid factories that were running their refuse into the streams and thus killing the fish.

One of the factories was on Spring Brook, one mile from the point where it empties into the Beaverkill, and the brook is two miles above the State hatchery. I sent a man to procure some of the water and put a trout of known size into it and note the result. He reported that a 6 inch trout placed in the bucket of water lived four minutes, and when I saw the sample of water, I was surprised that the fish lived as long as it did.[252]

The problems associated with the Spring Brook acid factory continued, and it was but a few years later that a veteran Beaverkill angler wrote to a local newspaper:

I saw and smelt something that made me feel very sad, namely, the condition of Spring Brook . . . It was covered with some stuff from the acid factory, making it full of soapy bubbles, and on getting out the smell was very perceptible all along the main stream. Is there no way to stop it? There are few enough fish in the river now, and if this continues there will be less.[253]

It continued, and six months later there were less—many less—fish in the Beaverkill. In the middle of the spawning run, when adult trout moved up into Spring Brook, a chemical spill caused the stream to be strewn with dead fish. One man alone picked up twenty trout that weighed twenty pounds total; every trout below the factory perished.

Writing in *Field & Stream*, the noted fly fisherman George M. L. La Branche deplored the stream-discharging practices:

There is another condition over which no control is exercised, but which might and should be brought under strict regulation: I refer to the pollution of these waters. Chemical companies, or "acid factories," as they are called, pour their refuse into the stream in direct defiance or contempt of the law which is supposed to prohibit it. These men tell you, if remonstrated with, that running water purifies itself every hundred feet or so, which may be true, but not when sludge is incorporated with it—and trout are actually prevented from negotiating many stretches from this cause, which bars them from reaching the spawning beds in the fall. Some day some courageous man will be placed at the head of the Forest, Fish and Game Commission, and these offences against public health and privilege will cease.[254]

But it was not just trout and streams that were the victims of the wood chemical industry. Thousands of acres of forest lands were sacrificed as woodchoppers marched through, cutting virtually every tree greater than three inches in diameter. What they left behind looked like a wasteland, and the devastation caused by clear-cutting did not go unnoticed.

Regarding one of the most remote and heavily forested areas of the watershed, the Willowemoc correspondent to the Livingston Manor *Ensign* asked:

What will this country look like in ten years from now if the axe and saw, six steam mills and an acid factory continue on in their destruction of our beautiful forests? To see the hillsides denuded and laid bare by the woodsmens axe spoiling the watersheds and drying up the streams and the damage done by freshets in time of heavy rains is a sad thing to many of us.[255]

And downriver, the editor of the Roscoe newspaper lamented on the same subject:

The forests of the Town of Rockland are disappearing into the acid factory retorts of that town like water into a rat hole. Each factory is a whirlpool around which the forests are eddying in a constantly diminishing circle finally to forever disappear in its ever hungry vortex . . . Surely the forests of Rockland cannot long service this careless demand.[256]

It was generally not profitable to haul wood long distances; acid factories harvested their wood from nearby areas. When their wood supplies were exhausted, some factories were dismantled and moved to a new location, where wood was again abundant.

Just prior to World War I and the peak period of the industry, the Arthur Leighton Company announced plans to revolutionize the wood alcohol business by cutting thousands of acres at the headwaters and floating the logs down the Beaverkill to its factory at Elk Brook. Until this time, deforestation had taken place only in the immediate areas of the acid factories, and the upper Beaverkill had been spared massive clear-cutting. The company owned more than eight thousand acres of timber along the headwaters of the Beaverkill and Willowemoc and intended to remove ten thousand cords of wood each year. The wood was to be cut and left to season in the woods; in the winter it would be hauled to the stream bank and piled, and in the spring it would be floated downstream to Elk Brook, where a giant boom placed across the Beaverkill would catch it.

In anticipation of its "inexhaustible supply" from the headwaters, the Leighton Company made a test run by floating a large quantity of logs from Roscoe downstream to Elk Brook. Even with a crew of men who followed along after the logs, freeing those that got washed on shore, the experiment met with only moderate success. This, however, did not alter the company's plans to cut and float timber from the headwaters of the Beaverkill. In fact, they were halted only when stream owners became alarmed over the effect

changed in character since that day many years ago, I rose my first fish to a floating fly.[277]

When he first began experimenting with dry flies, George La Branche, like others, believed they could only be used successfully on smooth, slow water. He used them only on water he believed Halford would approve, and he cast only to rising trout. Through experience, though, he learned dry flies could be fished on any part of swift-flowing streams. However, he remained uncomfortable doing so, being very much influenced by English writers, who insisted it was "practically impossible" to fish dry on mountain streams: "It seemed to me that by continuing to use the dry fly on them I was profaning the creed of authority and inviting the wrath of his gods upon my head."[278]

He continued to apply the dry fly to Catskill streams and, in addition, abandoned the idea of fishing only to rising trout. He was a true "presentationist," believing he could get by the whole season with just a few patterns. In fact, he became known for his ability to *make* a trout rise by creating an "artificial hatch." This he did by repeatedly casting a floating fly flawlessly, without drag, where he expected a good trout to be. After he had fished one of the more famous chalkstreams of England, the *Fishing Gazette* praised his casting skills:

His fishing is smooth and entirely effortless, line, cast and fly all under perfect control of brain, eye, muscle and sinew, in the air as well as in the water.

His flies go where he wishes them to go and act as he directs them when they get there. Briefly, Mr. La Branche is a very beautiful fisherman.[279]

La Branche fishing a dry fly on the Willowemoc Creek, most likely along a stretch of the present-day DeBruce Fly Fishing Club. *Recreation* magazine, July 1909

A dry-fly fisherman casts to a rising trout on the lower Beaverkill. Lee Van Put

While La Branche disagreed with his English mentors on where and when to use the dry fly, he did choose to abandon the wet fly altogether. In England, Halford and his followers had adopted the dry fly to the exclusion of all others, and Halford believed "that those who thought otherwise were either ignorant or incompetent."[280]

George La Branche knew Theodore Gordon; they corresponded and saw one another socially on occasion. Reviewing *The Dry Fly and Fast Water*, Gordon wrote:

> I know Mr. La Branche by reputation, and his ideals are high. He fishes the floating fly only, and kills a few of the largest trout. All the rest are returned to the water. His point of view is original, and there is not a dull page in this book. He has no great faith in the imitation of the natural insects and gives a very short list of artificial flies.[281]

La Branche was an excellent fly fisherman who saw little value in exact imitation. He proved to American anglers that they need not be locked to English traditions, especially about where and when to fish a dry fly and the theory that to be successful with dry flies one had to use an exact imitation of the natural.

In the *Dry Fly and Fast Water*, he stated, "I give the dressing of eight patterns, although I rarely use over six. If I were compelled to do so, I could get along very well with one—The Whirling Dun."[282] While Gordon, Gill, and La Branche were pioneers in the use of the dry fly, and while all three encouraged others, through their writings, to adopt the method, it was Theodore Gordon who was at the forefront of developing America's dry flies.

George W. Cooper, a blacksmith from DeBruce on the Willowe-moc. Cooper was known as a fine angler and fly tier and sold flies from a general store and post office. Jean Boyd

New York, including a few of the earliest American dry flies. Holden had met Theodore Gordon the summer before his death and considered him a "super angler." *Streamcraft* was the first book to praise Theodore Gordon and his contributions to American fly fishing.

Although Theodore Gordon tied and created flies along the banks of the Beaverkill, he was not the first professional tier to do so. The earliest professional fly tier of note to live in the Beaverkill watershed was a blacksmith from DeBruce by the name of George W. Cooper (1859–1932). Cooper was born in Napanoch, Ulster County, and when he was but six weeks old his parents, Mathias and Elizabeth Cooper, traveled the bridle paths through the forest and settled at what is now DeBruce. They were one of the first families to settle in that area, and it was truly a wilderness. Just three years earlier, in 1856, Cooper's grandfather had built the Hammond & Benedict tannery nearby, along Willowemoc Creek. The little settlement grew, and George Cooper became the village blacksmith. His shop was located along Mongaup Creek, a short distance from its famous junction with the Willowemoc.

As the tanning industry began fading out of existence in the late 1880s, the citizens of DeBruce focused on trout fishing and summer tourists. George Cooper enlarged his blacksmith operation to include a post office and general store, in which, for many years, he sold flies, baskets, boots, and fishing tackle. His two sisters, Ada Cooper and Elizabeth Royce, became pioneer summer boardinghouse keepers. They owned and operated two of the best-known trout-fishing resorts on the Willowemoc, the Homestead and the Hearthstone Inn. Old stocking records reveal that the sisters and Cooper were active in replenishing the Willowemoc and Mongaup with trout fry. Each season they would order fish from Caledonia and place them in nearby waters.

George Cooper was an avid outdoorsman; he was a fine angler and fly tier. Exactly when he began tying commercially is not known; however, some evidence suggests he was tying in the 1870s. The rugged physical demands placed on a blacksmith do not seem compatible with the patience and gentle hand needed to tie delicate trout flies; the occupations appear to be at odds with each other. Cooper, though, had a reputation for being a skillful tier who raised his own hackle, possessing prize Rhode Island Reds.

He was known to tie an excellent fly, and his reputation spread with his creation of the Female Beaverkill (another early American dry fly), developed in the Beaverkill watershed. The fly was a popular turn-of-the-century pattern. It is uncertain exactly when Cooper devised the Female Beaverkill, but it was being used as early as 1913.

Today's imitationists believe the fly George Cooper tied was created to imitate the female Hendrickson spinner (*Ephemerella invaria*), the most prolific hatch on the Beaverkill. Anyone who has fished the stream during this hatch can see the resemblance and, by noting the distinct

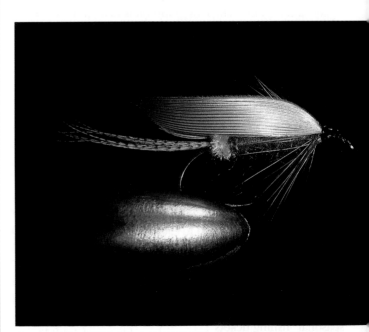

Female Beaverkill wet fly, created by George Cooper; imitationists believe he tied the fly to imitate the female Hendrickson spinner, which has a distinct yellow egg sac.

DeBruce post office and general store, a popular rendezvous of fly fishermen who purchased flies tied by George Cooper and Mahlon Davidson. Emerson Bouton

yellow egg sac of the natural, can understand why Cooper added this feature to his fly.

In 1923 George Cooper sold his store to Mahlon Davidson. Davidson was born in 1890 and grew up along the Beaverkill, in the Lew Beach area, where he hunted, fished, and trapped. Like Cooper, he was an avid fisherman and fly tier who raised his own roosters for hackle. He continued operating the post office and general store, which became a

regular stopping place for fly fishermen who visited the upper Willowemoc.

In addition to selling groceries, Davidson sold flies and other assorted fishing tackle, and he was one of the last to make solid wood fly rods out of bilberry or shadbush. Among the more popular patterns he sold was a fly he devised, similar to the Light Cahill, known as the Davidson Special, which he first tied in the 1920s.

"The Kettle That Washes Itself Clean"

The Indian name for the Beaverkill translates to "The Kettle That Washes Itself Clean." It is supposed that the name came about because of the river's spring freshets, which sweep away debris and scour the river bottom. Flooding can be devastating to trout habitat; it can erode stream banks, change watercourses, and scour streambeds. This scouring can destroy essential aquatic food supplies found in the bed of the stream and, if flooding takes place shortly after spawning, can eradicate redds or nests.

Trout populations on the Beaverkill have always been affected by natural disasters, particularly floods and droughts. The Beaverkill and its tributaries are steep-gradient, and runoff from rains and melting snow causes them to rise quickly and overflow their banks frequently. The stream's history is filled with incidents of droughts, floods, and the ravages of ice jams. These occurrences continue to be common and unpredictable. Their circumstances lead to rising water temperatures, scoured spawning beds, erosion, and, at times, degradation of trout habitat.

The climate of the Beaverkill region is one of long, cold, often snowy winters, with the mean annual snowfall in the Balsam Lake area being 100.3 inches. Temperatures below zero in winter are quite common, with a mean annual extreme being –18 degrees Fahrenheit. The coldest temperature ever recorded was –36 degrees, and was taken at a weather station in nearby Walton.

Each winter, the waters of the Beaverkill and Willowemoc freeze, with ice thickness of a foot or more. Following a mid-winter thaw, this ice usually breaks up and, depending on stream flow, temperatures, and weather, can accumulate in areas, forming ice jams.

Great amounts of broken ice can be backed up for a half mile or more; the severity of the ice jam varies with how long these stream blockages remain in position. Ice jams often divert stream flows into new channels, leaving the normal channel dry of water and causing havoc to aquatic insects and trout, which are left stranded. If the ice jam gives way suddenly, there can be great damage, as this mass of moving ice uproots trees, relocates boulders, scours the streambed, and rips and tears at stream banks.

Erosion is an ongoing process. Generally, it occurs slowly, almost without notice; but in times of freshets, or high flows, it can be dramatic. Banks formed of glacial till tend to erode easily. Although the root systems of trees along the banks hold the soils, they still become undermined, and sometimes the weight of mature trees alone is enough to collapse a stream bank. The gravel removed or eroded from one area deposits in another; some pools or riffles fill in, while others may deepen.

Perhaps one of the most memorable instances of stream erosion occurred on September 18, 1863. In less than twenty-four hours, Shin Creek went from being unusually low to a raging torrent. Early in the morning, the stream jumped its banks and swept away over an acre of adjoining lands, which happened to be the entire cemetery where early settlers of the Beaverkill Valley had buried their dead. The *Delaware Gazette*, on September 30, reported that as many as sixty bodies were taken downstream, "some of them with broken coffins lodged along the stream."

During times of drought, water temperatures often rise above those preferred by trout. Fish populations become concentrated, as great numbers gather at spring holes and off cooler tributary mouths. At these times, trout are in distress, become more vulnerable to predation by animals and birds, and are easily exploited by man. With insufficient flows, nursery streams (those containing young-of-the-year trout) that are not spring-fed may dry up entirely.

In summer, stream flows on the Beaverkill are dependent on rainfall; and while approximately fifty to fifty-two inches of rain falls annually near the headwaters, it is rarely distributed evenly. A dry summer can be followed by a year of devastating floods, as it was in 1894 and 1895. Reporting on stream conditions on the Beaverkill in July 1894, the *New York Times* stated:

> The stream is low now and the water is warm, and the trout, especially the Fontinalis, seek spring holes in the pools, and the mouths of brooks and the spring rills.
>
> Last week, taking an opera glass along, the writer saw between 4,000 and 5,000 trout, all beyond the catching limit, between the pool above the Suckerback and Shin Creek bridge, as he passed at least a dozen places where trout school at this season, without looking for them. At the Suckerback pool were between 300 and 400 trout luxuriating on the gravel bar at the mouth of the little mountain brook that aerates this large sweep of the water.

At the Second Docking, just above in a deep spring gully, was a school of 400 or 500 nice trout running from six inches in length to a pound and a half. At the head of Davidson's Pool were hundreds of smaller trout in a spring run, and there was school after school in the back waters at Sprague's. At the Rocks at Sprague's was a school of uniformly large fish not less than ten inches; some of them were fourteen-inch fish. At Hardie's Pool, just below the bridge, were several schools of nice trout off the mouth of the little spring brook which "keeps up" better than any other in this neighborhood.[294]

These warm-water conditions were found not on the lower river but far upstream, on a section of the upper Beaverkill just below Lew Beach. The following year, a major flood destroyed much of this critical habitat:

> The great rush of water that flows every few years in the Beaverkill causes many changes in the bed of the stream. One of these big "freshes," as they are called, occurred about the year 1895 and it made great havoc, especially between Shin Creek and Ellsworth's. Just below Shin Creek there was a large pool on Abel Sprague's land that we called

Old-timer Gus Bailey fishing the Beaverkill during the high flows of early spring, downstream of Shin Creek. *The American Fly Tier*, May 1941

Fanwing Royal Coachman dry fly tied by Rube Cross. The pattern was popular among fly fishers during the 1920s and '30s, with entire articles being devoted to its success; the fly was known to take difficult trout when all else failed.

A few of the better-known fishing writers during this time were Corey Ford; William J. Schaldach; the talented John Taintor Foote; Foote's fishing partner, Ray Holland, who edited *Field & Stream* from 1921 to 1941; Eugene V. Connett; and Sparse Grey Hackle (Alfred W. Miller). These men all knew one another and often fished together, sharing pools, flies, and the good fellowship that develops between stream mates. After the fading light of day gave way to the evening rise, and then darkness, the men retreated to the Antrim Lodge, Roscoe House, or Ferdon's River View Inn. On the verandas or at the bars, they gathered with others and reviewed the day's fishing experiences. There was tackle talk and discussion over which flies were hatching. Theories were exchanged, along with fly patterns and the good-natured ribbing that exists among close friends.

Frank Keener owned the Antrim Lodge, a fishermen's hotel that enjoyed a valued relationship with angling writers, who would visit the bar and mix with the colorful characters who fished the Beaverkill. The bar, with its mounted trout lining the adjoining walls, became known as Keener's Pool. This is understandable, as it was a famous watering hole for anglers, who often stood three and four deep, waiting for a drink to take away the river's chill. At the bar, stories were told of fish caught and lost, and big trout tended to increase in size in proportion to the number of drinks consumed. And it was part of local lore that some of the biggest trout ever taken from the Beaverkill came out of Keener's Pool!

The River View Inn was the favorite of Ted Townsend and Corey Ford, who for years wrote a *Field & Stream* column known as the "Lower Forty." Ford had a special fondness for the Beaverkill, having learned to fish dry flies in Barnhart's with Ted Townsend as his teacher. Years later he would

capture, warmly, the happy years he spent on the river in an article titled "The Best-Loved Trout Stream of Them All."[308]

William J. Schaldach (1896–1982) was a writer and artist well known to several generations of outdoorsmen; his fine artwork of fish and wildlife is still sought-after by those who appreciate his easily recognizable style. In the early 1920s, he wrote and illustrated for *Forest and Stream* and later became an associate editor at *Field & Stream*.

Bill Schaldach began fishing the Beaverkill in 1922. In the 1920s and '30s, he spent anywhere from two weeks to three months each season at the stream, making Roscoe his headquarters. During his many years on the river, he enjoyed the friendship and camaraderie of the regulars who fished the Beaverkill. He fished with the colorful Louis Rhead, who passed on to Schaldach his knowledge of the river and its trout and aquatic insect life. But it was the venerable "Pop" Robbins who was his mentor, and with whom he spent his happiest days. Pop's vast experience and wealth of Beaverkill lore were absorbed by Schaldach, who came to love the river, much in the manner of the older man. He would go on to write extensively of its charms, its trout, its anglers, and its natural beauty. His delightful *Currents & Eddies* included a chapter titled "The Bountiful Beaverkill."

Currents & Eddies was one of the first books to mention the famous pools on the lower river; Schaldach listed them in order, along with brief comments on their appearance, how they fish, their characteristics, and beauty. In his *The Wind on Your Cheek* is a drypoint drawing of Barnhart's Pool done in 1929, along with a drawing of the Conklin covered bridge pool on the upper Willowemoc.

John Taintor Foote (1881–1950) was a well-rounded fly fisherman, of a generation that generally fished wet flies in pairs, downstream, and then turned around and fished a dry fly back upstream. He purchased property along the Beaverkill in 1924, and while he was a member of the Fly Fishers Club of Brooklyn, he often fished the big water below Roscoe.

Though he was trained as an artist, John Taintor Foote made his living by writing, and by these means he also furthered the reputation of the Beaverkill. He was an author of popular sporting classics, and he wrote humorous stories and articles for such publications as *Colliers*, *The Saturday Evening Post*, and *Field & Stream*. In addition, he was a playwright and successful Hollywood screenwriter; he did particularly well with movies about horses, such as *Kentucky* and *Seabiscuit*. John Taintor Foote wrote seventeen books, including such favorites of fishermen as *A Wedding Gift* (1924), *Fatal Gesture* (1933), *Broadway Angler* (1937), and *Anglers All* (1947).

Eugene V. Connett III (1891–1969) is best remembered as the founder of Derrydale Press, which specialized in printing limited editions of sporting books. Derrydale flourished in the 1930s and '40s, and its books are still popular today with collectors, who regularly pay several hundred dollars or more for copies. The first book to carry the Derrydale imprint was written by Connett in 1927 and had the fanciful title of *Magic Hours Wherein We Cast a Fly Here and There*.

A well-traveled veteran fly fisherman, Connett contributed fishing articles to various magazines including *Forest and Stream* as early as 1916, and was one of the first to promote the use of the dry fly. He wrote several books on trout fishing—perhaps his most popular being *Any Luck?* (1933). The book contained practical information on equipment, casting, personal experiences, and flies and an introduction by his friend and angling companion George M. L. La Branche. Connett recalled memorable days spent on the Beaverkill and devoted an entire chapter to the Willowemoc, which he seemed to favor. His chapter on flies had high praise for the tying skills of Rube Cross, and Connett wrote glowingly of Catskill dry-fly patterns. *Any Luck?* was also the first book to extol the tying skills of Walt Dette, who was in the early years of his professional fly-tying career.

Alfred W. Miller (1892–1983) wrote under the pseudonym of Sparse Grey Hackle; and by that name, he was well known to fly fishermen who read his classic fishing stories. By profession he was a writer, beginning his career as a reporter for the *Wall Street Journal* and then running his own financial public relations business. For many years he contributed fishing articles to publications such as *Outdoor Life*, *Sports Illustrated*, and the *Anglers' Club Bulletin*, of which he was also the editor. He was friends with many of the syndicated outdoor columnists of his day, and it was common to find his work on the sports pages of New York's leading newspapers, where he served as guest contributor to Ray Camp, Don Stillman, and the great Red Smith.

An excellent writer, Sparse, as he was best known, was fascinated by the Catskills and spent many years fishing their storied streams, especially the Beaverkill and Willowemoc. While he wrote of his personal experiences along these streams, he also preserved Catskill history when he chronicled, in his popular *Fishless Days, Angling Nights*, the

John Taintor Foote, c. 1922. Trained as an artist, John Taintor Foote enjoyed a writing career. He was an author of popular sporting classics, wrote articles for magazines, and was a playwright and successful Hollywood screenwriter. Timothy Foote

after dark, with large wet flies or bucktails. Big browns decorated the walls of many of the bars, taverns, and hotels in and around Margaretville. This was trout country. The young McClane became an avid student of fly fishing and sought out local experts, eager to learn their fishing secrets.

His natural talent for the sport surfaced early. He was just fourteen years old when he stunned local veterans by taking a huge brown, weighing 7 pounds and 2 ounces, from the East Branch, on a nymph. Eager to learn more about fly tying, he traveled over to the Beaverkill Valley the following winter to visit the legendary Rube Cross. Rube had only recently set up shop in Lew Beach, yet he found the time to teach the youngster a few tricks of the trade. He must have seen the boy's keen interest and enthusiasm for learning everything about fly fishing; before Al left, Rube inscribed a copy of his *Tying American Trout Lures*. The two established a friendship that would last for life.

Al McClane had good teachers, and he thoroughly enjoyed his learning years in the Catskills:

> But these were truly wonderful years for me. I met and fished with many of the great Delaware anglers: Ray Neidig, Dan Todd, Mike Lorenz, John Alden Knight, Doc Faulkner and, sometimes, Pop Robbins and Reub Cross when they came over from the Beaverkill.[310]

His love for fishing and his talent for writing both surfaced early in his life, and it seemed inevitable that he would find a career as an angling journalist. In 1939 he entered Cornell University as a fisheries major. While in Ithaca, he worked in state fisheries programs, as a junior aquatic biologist, on lake and stream surveys, and on migration studies on Finger Lakes tributaries. And it was during his college years that he actually began freelancing, selling his first fishing article, at the age of nineteen, to *Outdoor Life*. One year later he sold another, to *Field & Stream*.

Just as his career looked promising, it was interrupted by World War II. In 1942 Al joined the U.S. Army. He saw combat in France and Germany, and by the time he was discharged, he had received the Bronze Star and the Purple Heart. Shortly after the war ended, *Field & Stream* began publishing his work regularly, and by June 1947 he was the fishing editor. His official byline was "A. J. McClane"; and in no time at all, he developed a large following of loyal readers, who discovered that he possessed unlimited angling knowledge, was unpretentious, and wrote honestly. His writing was precise, very descriptive—the best of modern journalism. For more than forty years, his was the most familiar and respected byline in angling literature.

A. J. McClane became a good teacher; he presented his knowledge and experiences clearly, often combining fisheries facts and science with angling techniques. Like Theodore Gordon, he had a style so original that if, by chance, his byline was ever absent, his work would still be easily recognized. Travel and writing assignments for *Field & Stream* kept him busy, yet Al managed to continue fishing the Catskills and the Beaverkill. He often wrote of the stream, its people, and even individual trout that challenged his angling skills. Though he wrote several books on angling, A. J. McClane is best known for *The Practical Fly Fisherman* (1953) and *McClane's Standard Fishing Encyclopedia* (1965; revised and expanded, 1974).

The Practical Fly Fisherman is considered a classic, comprehensive work on fly fishing. It contains many references to the Catskills and to experiences on the Beaverkill and Willowemoc. Also featured in the book are the tying skills of Walt Dette, whose fine examples of Catskill-style dry flies are depicted in color plates, along with wets, nymphs, streamers, and bucktails.

McClane's Standard Fishing Encyclopedia, a tremendously popular book, has sold nearly one million copies. It is a premier reference source for writers, editors, anglers, and fisheries professionals across the country. The book features decorative color plates of flies tied by Harry and Elsie Darbee, showing all of the Catskill classics as well as the standard patterns of the day. Also included are excellent illustrations of the Darbees' tying instructions, drawn by the noted Catskill wildlife artist Francis W. Davis.

Except for the period of time he spent in the military, Al McClane regularly found the time to fish the Beaverkill. He knew all of the famous pools on the lower river as well as anyone; and he learned how to fish the tricky currents and eddies of Junction Pool as intimately as he did the swirling waters of the deep plunge pool at Beaverkill Falls.

In 1954 Al McClane returned to the Catskills, seeking a place to write and relax and enjoy good fishing. He chose the upper Beaverkill, and for the next half-dozen years he leased the mile of water that flowed through the Arthur Marks estate, above Turnwood. (The land had originally been settled by Ransom Weaver in the 1870s. His farm was said to be the most beautiful on the Beaverkill and was a regular stopping place for fishermen, who found his boardinghouse accommodations and trout fishing to be among the best.)

On one side of the Beaverkill, the property was open fields or meadows and contained a large farmhouse, barn, and beautiful Norman-style chateau, which remained the residence of Margaret Marks following the death of her husband, Arthur. Hidden behind a knoll, among towering hemlocks on the opposite side, was a fishing lodge originally built by Jay Gould, who owned the property in 1912. Though rustic in appearance, the building was designed for comfort and solitude and was constructed right on the bank of the Beaverkill, in a very attractive setting. During the days of wagon roads and buckboards, it was visited by many famous men—heads of industry and politicians, including, it was said, President Grover Cleveland.

It was the Gould cottage in which Al and his wife, Patti, made their home each summer and where he wrote many of his articles. For a fishing writer, the surroundings were ideal. The stream was literally at his doorstep. Its sounds were a constant reminder that if he needed a break from his typewriter, or more inspiration, he had only to walk to the Beaverkill, tie on a fly, and test his skills against the craftiness of the trout that were his neighbors. When not at the typewriter, Al McClane mixed his interest in fisheries with his love of fly fishing by conducting his own fish-tagging experiments. He studied the trout on his water: how, where, and when they were caught, as well as the frequency of their capture and their movements. He caught a few of his tagged trout three miles downstream, at Beaverkill Falls; but his biggest surprise came when a couple of his trout turned up in the Delaware River, fifty to sixty miles downstream!

Over the years, Al and Patti frequently had fishing guests, and one of the earliest was Arnold Gingrich (1903–1975). Al and Arnold met in 1955, and they became instant friends. That the two took a liking to each other is not surprising; they shared a love of travel, fly fishing, and angling literature, and they had many friends in common. At the time, Arnold Gingrich was the well known publisher and vice president of *Esquire*. One of the founders, as well as the editor, of the literary publication, he is credited with making the magazine an instant success. He persuaded Ernest Hemingway to write for the first issue, and then he used Hemingway's name to lure other noted writers, including William Faulkner, F. Scott Fitzgerald, John Steinbeck, and Sinclair Lewis.

A warm, friendly man, Arnold was well spoken and gracious, and he had a passion for fly fishing. A year after they met, McClane invited him to share the Marks water with him, and for the next five seasons the two often fished the Beaverkill together, exchanging knowledge, experience, meals, and companionship. An excellent and widely respected writer, Arnold Gingrich wrote several books on fly fishing, including *The Well-Tempered Angler* (1965), in which he recalled their Beaverkill experiences in a chapter titled "The Turnwood Years."

These were wonderful years for Arnold. The fishing on the upper Beaverkill was superb; the stream, with its pristine waters flowing through the unspoiled wild forest, teemed with native trout. He became a short-rod enthusiast, his favorite a 6½-foot Midge, which, more often than not, was bent by the straining of one of the hefty brook, brown, or rainbow trout he caught with great regularity:

> The fishing on that stretch of the upper Beaverkill was so good, for all five of those seasons I fished it, that if I were condemned to go utterly fishless from here on out until I pass ninety, I would still figure that I was ahead on points. There were days when I would take and release better than forty fish, fishing from early morning until night . . .[311]

At the time, Arnold maintained a diary of his fishing experiences, recording the number of trout hooked, landed, and released, and which flies the fish had taken. While he was opposed to any competitive form of angling, he devised an updated version of the old practice of fishing for count. He urged anglers to throw away their creels and adopt bookkeeping methods instead of fish-keeping: "I did not begin to approach my present level of enjoyment of angling, however, until I began carrying a notebook instead of a creel, and started thinking of angling as an interesting game rather than as an uncertain meat-substitute."[312] Arnold's meticulously

Ellis Newman casting an entire fly line without a fly rod at the Roscoe High School athletic field. Ellis demonstrated his casting skills at National Sportsman's Shows in New York City. Joan Wulff, photo Francis W. Davis

While Ellis Newman paddles, A. J. McClane fishes in Forest Lake, a brook trout lake on the Marks estate. Francis W. Davis

kept records reveal that throughout the years he fished the upper Beaverkill, he averaged 21.6 trout per day!

Credit, in part, for the excellent fishing found on the mile of water Arnold Gingrich shared with Al McClane must go to Ellis Newman (1913–1965), who carefully managed the stream. Ellis came to the Beaverkill Valley in 1930, taking a position with the Marks family as their caretaker. As with most of the private water on the upper Beaverkill, the Marks water contained in-stream structures aimed at improving trout habitat. While the Beaverkill fishing clubs were engaged in habitat improvement as far back as the 1870s, structures along the Marks stretch were rather original. Ellis designed a unique type of pool digger: He drilled holes through a series of large boulders and then ran a steel cable through them, thus constructing a "necklace" rock dam.

While Ellis Newman was a proficient fly tier and skilled fly fisherman, he earned his reputation through his expertise

with a shotgun and his talent for casting a fly rod. Commenting on his abilities, Al McClane once called Ellis "the greatest wing shot and fly-caster who ever lived—bar none. Ellis regularly threw measured casts of over 200 feet, and his entire style of delivery—particularly the long, slow back cast—was breathtakingly beautiful."[313] A stocky man with enormous strength and extraordinary casting skill, he was famous for his ability to cast a standard HCH (DT-7) double-tapered fly line 90 feet—with his bare hands!

While he did not have the inclination to compete in fly-casting tournaments, Ellis demonstrated his casting skills many times before large audiences at National Sportsman's Shows in New York. For years, Al McClane hosted the *Field & Stream* fishing clinics; he would have Rube Cross demonstrate fly tying and Ellis Newman teach fly casting. Usually, when a crowd had gathered, Ellis would suddenly dispense with the rod entirely and astonish onlookers by casting with his right arm only!

Ellis Newman enjoyed teaching and helping others. In the 1950s he started a shooting and fishing school on the Marks estate, and while most of his students were able-bodied, he was a pioneer of the concept of providing hunting and fishing opportunities for the handicapped. At his own expense, he experimented with and designed wheelchairs and tractor-driven devices that enabled the physically challenged to fish and shoot. One such contraption was a bucket that hoisted a wheelchair-bound angler out over the stream, giving him the opportunity to place his fly in areas he would never be able to reach otherwise. While his innovations were not very refined—some would say even crude—they were, nonetheless, much appreciated by their users.

Unfortunately, Ellis Newman's life ended prematurely; in the summer of 1965, he met with a tragic accident. Though he had taught hundreds to cast and shoot and was an expert with rod and gun, he inexplicably shot himself. He apparently slipped on a log, discharging his rifle and shooting himself in the chest. A coroner's investigation ruled the death accidental.

Ellis Newman was also a good friend of Al McClane's; they fished the Beaverkill together often, at times "just for the pleasure of each other's company." One of the best articles Al ever wrote is titled "Song of the Angler." It is a philosophical, thought-provoking essay in which McClane explained why he enjoyed fishing. He made it clear that a large portion of his pleasure was derived from the company he kept on the stream. He fondly recalled several of his angling companions and reflected on their camaraderie, noting in particular their overall goodness and moral quality. One of his recollections was of the years spent on the Beaverkill, at the old Gould cottage, and of the kindness and sensitivity of Ellis Newman:

One day, when the mayflies were on the water, Ellis caught and released several good browns below the dam, one going about 3 pounds. At the top of the next run we met a young boy who proudly displayed a 9-inch brook trout. Ellis admired it so much that I thought we were looking at the biggest squaretail captured since Cook hit the jackpot on the Nipigon in 1914. When the lad asked Ellis if he had any luck, he looked very serious: "Oh, I caught a few, but none were as pretty as yours."[314]

A Siren Along the Beaverkill

There is a section of the Beaverkill, located midway between the hamlets of Beaverkill and Rockland, known as Craig-e-Clare. Today, it is not much more than a name on a map, at a bridge crossing. But there was a time when it was more populated, when it had its own post office and a stately castle—in which, it was rumored, lived a beautiful and seductive woman who enticed fishermen from the stream into her extravagant fortress. Known as Dundas Castle, the building with the mysterious past sat high on the bank overlooking the Beaverkill. It sits there still, though through neglect, mature trees and other forest vegetation now shield it from public view.

In 1891, Bradford L. Gilbert, a noted New York City architect, began acquiring land in the area. He amassed several hundred acres and constructed a beautiful summer home, known as Beaverkill Lodge. Gilbert's wife was a native of Ireland, and the steep hillsides and rapid-flowing stream so reminded her of home that in 1896, when the new post office at the tiny hamlet was to be named, she selected Craig-e-Clare. This was the name of her small Irish village, and translates to "Beautiful Mountainside."[315]

In 1915 Gilbert's estate was purchased by Ralph Wurts-Dundas, an eccentric millionaire who constructed a replica of a French Burgundian castle on the banks of the Beaverkill. Construction took more than eight years, with most of the building materials being imported from Europe. The roof and turrets were of slate brought in from England; the marble floors, stairs, and fireplaces for the nearly forty rooms came from Italy; and the huge iron gates were from an old French château. The Beaverkill provided the only native construction materials, as tons of gravel and stone were removed from the streambed and used for the outer facing of the beautiful building.

Dundas Castle entrance. Ralph Wurts-Dundas was an eccentric millionaire who constructed a replica of a French Burgundian castle on the banks of the Beaverkill. Ray Pomeroy

The Beaverkill, just upstream of Dundas Castle, where fishermen might hope to be lured.

Ralph Wurts-Dundas died just before the castle was completed. Shortly after his death in 1921, his wife was committed to a sanatorium and his estate, including the castle, was left to his daughter. Supposedly, the castle was never occupied—not by Dundas, his wife, or his daughter—yet the grounds were carefully guarded by police dogs. Visitors were never allowed access to the elegant estate.

In time, the daughter was also placed in an institution and declared by the courts to be mentally incompetent to manage her own affairs. This event, coupled with the excessive precautions taken to protect the privacy of the estate, caused local residents to ponder the unusual circumstances surrounding Dundas Castle. One rumor claimed that the young woman was confined to one of the castle's rooms.

In the 1930s those who fished the water at Craig-e-Clare heard various stories about the majestic castle overlooking the Beaverkill. Perhaps none were more bizarre than that reported by the sharp-witted Corey Ford:

Another favorite poaching preserve of mine, as I recall, was the deep run just below a forbidding stone mansion on the Little Beaverkill, known as Craigie Clair. There was always something of a mystery about Craigie Clair. Rumor had it that the sole occupant was a beautiful but demented young girl, who used to let down her golden hair from an upstairs window and lure unwary anglers into her granite castle, for what probably amounted to nothing worse than an afternoon's pleasant seduction. I fished past Craigie Clair, hopefully, a number of times, but I never got lured. Maybe I wasn't the type.[316]

Barnhart's Pool is a lengthy pool that parallels Route 17 at the base of a steep mountainside. The head of the pool is the beginning of the no-kill stretch. Richard Franklin

Hendrickson's Pool was named after Alfred E. Hendrickson, a regular on the Beaverkill who liked to stand on the large rock at the head of the pool. The Hendrickson dry fly is also named in his honor.

Falls, New York. Sandstrom, fishing a bucktail, hooked and landed a 25½-inch brown trout weighing 6 pounds.

Trout fishers today can all be thankful that, in 1939, Claude Barnhart conveyed a public fishing easement to the state, guaranteeing that future generations can walk the banks, wade the waters, and cast their flies in the same pool John Taintor Foote, Ted Townsend, and Corey Ford called their favorite.

Hendrickson's Pool

Hendrickson's Pool, like the famous dry fly, is named after Albert Everett Hendrickson. Hendrickson was a frequent Beaverkill angler, and the large, flat rock that lies in the middle of the pool was his favorite place to fish from.

Horse Brook Run

A long stretch of fast water that includes a collection of every type of cover or habitat a trout could desire describes Horse Brook Run. Large boulders are found throughout its length, and the river flowing against, over, and around them creates shelters and pocket water capable of harboring even the largest browns. The run takes its name from a small tributary named Horse Brook, which enters the river about halfway down the right bank.

Cairns Pool

Named after William Cairns (1844–1911), who lived in a neat hillside farmhouse overlooking the Beaverkill, Cairns Pool was also a docking area for rafts—and William Cairns was known as a hardy steersman on many a raft. He came from Scotland with his parents in 1851, and when his rafting days were over he became a successful newspaper columnist for the *Middletown Mercury*. Cairns wrote under the name of Rusticus and was widely read and respected. He wrote on a variety of subjects, but mostly about rural life, and many Catskill newspapers carried his column.

Cairns is a long, deep pool. Along its entire length, large rock covers the far bank, protecting a long-abandoned railroad bed from erosion. Over the years, rocks have slipped into the pool, providing shelter for some of the most fished-over trout on the Beaverkill. Cairns flows alongside the old highway running between Roscoe and Cooks Falls, and access is easy—too easy, some say. Even in the 1930s, "the biggest objection to Cairns Pool was its popularity."[319]

Horse Brook Run is a popular stretch of pocket water that holds large trout; boulders spread throughout its length form good trout habitat.
Lee Van Put

The bend in the river and the dangerous rocks were the reason raftsmen named this pool "Hell Hole" or "Whirling Eddy."

A rock ledge pool on the upper Beaverkill. Some of the best habitat on the river is created when the water flows up against rock ledges.

that the pool received its name back in rafting days, when a settler who lived along the Beaverkill raised more pork than he needed. His only outlet for selling it was the river, and he constructed a raft onto which he loaded three or four barrels of pork and started off to market. He had not traveled far before his raft was destroyed when it hit a large boulder, and his pork was deposited at the bottom of the Beaverkill; from then on the place was known as "Pork Eddy."[321]

● ● ●

The upper Beaverkill also contains "named" pools with historic backgrounds. Although most are located on private fishing club water, this has not always been the case; back in the early days before fishing clubs were established, pools such as Hardie's Pool, Big Bend, Beaverkill Falls, and Davidson's Eddy (possibly one of the most celebrated pools on the Beaverkill) were favorites of earlier generations. These pools were a part of angling literature when trout-fishing tourists stayed at boardinghouses such as Murdock's, Weaver's, Davidson's, Ed Sprague's, and dozens of others. A few of the more notable pools are described here.

Covered Bridge Pool

The covered bridge at the hamlet of Beaverkill is located on a bend in the river, where the water flows against a large rock formation on the right bank and creates a sizable deep pool. The scoured ledge rock provides excellent shelter for trout, and Covered Bridge Pool is known for holding some of the biggest found in the upper Beaverkill. Occasionally, during low flows, large trout can be seen resting under the overhanging ledges; because of the depth, they can be difficult to reach or to put a fly in front of. They are, at times, taken after dark on large wet flies, sizes 6 and 8, fished at the head of the pool. A favorite pool of Theodore Gordon's, this water is open to the public and is part of the Beaverkill Campgrounds, owned by the New York State Department of Environmental Conservation.

Beaverkill Falls Pool

Beaverkill Falls Pool is located upstream of the hamlet of Turnwood and is part of the Beaverkill Stream Club. The pool is the largest and deepest on the upper river and generally has a great population of brook, brown, and rainbow trout. Trout migrating upstream find that they cannot swim any farther, and because the pool provides such great habitat, they remain there. In addition, those trout moving downstream that come over the falls also find the pool inviting,

Beaverkill Covered Bridge Pool, c. 1900. One of the largest, deepest pools on the upper Beaverkill and a favorite of Theodore Gordon.

Beaverkill Falls at low flow. The great plunge pool formed by the falls is between 10 and 15 feet deep. Judy Van Put

Sylvia Willich, age seven, fishing on the right side of Willich Pool, c. 1936. The Willich family has owned this stretch of the river for more than one hundred years. Roger Lynker

and they stay; thus making Beaverkill Falls a favorite of trout fishermen.

Back in the 1880s Ned Buntline, "King of the Dime Novels," declared that Beaverkill Falls was his favorite place to fish. This statement is not surprising, as anyone who has ever fished at the falls would attest, and would give the same response. It is a special place; even on the warmest days of summer, trout will be seen rising to surface flies, and the fine, cool mist and pleasant sounds of the falls make for an extraordinary fishing experience.

Willich Pool

Sometimes the pools along the Beaverkill received their names from the families that have owned the lands and the river for an extended period of time. The Willich family has owned a stretch of the Beaverkill between Lew Beach and the hamlet of Beaverkill for more than a hundred years. William L. Willich and Theodore Willich were early members of the Beaverkill Trout Club, which was organized in 1910, and Willich Pool is part of the club's water.

He taught at the conservation camp, at Boy Scout meetings, in his home, or anywhere there was a vise handy. He loved young people and he loved to tie. He was still teaching kids even after his nails were splitting, his hands were arthritic, and his sight and hearing were bad.[323]

Harry believed, and stated so many times, that Roy Steenrod was the single person most responsible for passing along the distinct features of the Catskill style. Roy Steenrod was forced into retirement in 1952, when he reached the age of seventy; yet he continued teaching at DeBruce. Upon his retirement, his friends went out and found the largest place available for a dinner, since Roy had become one of Sullivan County's most beloved figures. Local lore has it that because he was such a widely respected individual, half of those in attendance were adversaries he had arrested for fish and game violations.

I met Roy Steenrod the year after I began employment with the Conservation Department. Burton Lindsley, the conservation officer who replaced Steenrod, took me to his home for a visit. Roy was eighty-seven at the time and had stopped fishing because of age and frailty. He graciously signed my copy of *The Complete Fly Fisherman* and gave me a Hairwing Royal Coachman he had tied.

We talked of the Big Beaverkill and what it was like to fish the river in the "old days." It had been years since he had fished there, and perhaps he had seen the best fishing. He asked wistfully, "Are there any more good fishermen on the Beaverkill?" A short time before his death, Roy wrote to Harry Darbee, requesting a copy of his book *Catskill Flytier*. Sadly, he concluded his letter:

> Since I gave up driving my car, have not been able to travel, and miss my visits with you. Go to see my daughter once in a while, at Geneva, N.Y., and as I ride along the Beaverkill in the bus, it is sad to see, in fact cry a little, when I think of all the happy days I enjoyed on the river.

Roy Steenrod lived a long and fruitful life; he was one of those individuals who readily shared with others those things that gave him pleasure. He died in 1977, at the age of ninety-four.

Rube Cross

No individual improved upon the Catskill style of dry fly (created by Theodore Gordon) more than Rube Cross. A native of Neversink, Reuben R. Cross was born on March 16, 1896. He grew up on the family farm on Mutton Hill, at a time when the beautiful Neversink valley and the river running through it were a fisherman's paradise. As a youngster, he developed a love of hunting, fishing, and trapping, and he possessed an eager curiosity about nature, spending much of his early years along trout streams and on forest trails.

Rube began tying trout flies in 1914, shortly after purchasing several dry flies at a local store and not having much success fishing with them. He claimed to have learned from Theodore Gordon, and he certainly could have, since he was in the right place at the right time. He was nineteen years old when Gordon died in 1915—old enough to have developed a friendship with him and to have been a student of his tying techniques.

Census records reveal that Rube Cross was living on Hollow Road, just outside the village of Neversink, in 1925, and that at twenty-nine years of age he was the "Head of the Household" and his occupation was "Maker (Trout flies)." At the time, he already had an established reputation; Cross flies were recognized as being the best, models of perfection, trout flies that set the standards his professional peers tried to meet.

In 1930, an informative little book devoted to tying dry flies was written by Dr. Edgar Burke. Titled *American Dry Flies and How to Tie Them*, the book was a guide to tying the more popular dry flies of the day, including instructions on Catskill patterns such as the Quill Gordon, Hendrickson, and Light Cahill. Burke used, as a model of a quality imitation, a dry fly tied by Rube Cross, and he stated that Rube was "one of the outstanding exponents of the Catskill 'school,' and one of the most expert fly tyers living."[324]

A Cross fly had perfectly matched wings; incredibly stiff, evenly wound hackle; a finely tapered body; and a tail of the stiffest hackle fibers available. The fly had a generally sparse appearance and was tied to "float and ride the rough water very much as does the natural insect."[325] Cross became known as a perfectionist, turning out dry flies with an exactness few could duplicate. He insisted on good, stiff hackle; and his flies had a distinct clean, trim appearance. During the 1930s and '40s, he was the premier fly tier in the country, annually demonstrating his skills across the land in the swankier tackle shops and before huge crowds at the National Sportsman's Show in New York, at the Grand Central Palace.

For several years he tied at Macy's, the renowned giant department store. Scores of shoppers watched, captivated, as this man with the massive hands of a lumberjack created delicate and elegant trout flies. His fingers magically used gossamer thread to bind dainty feathers and frail quills onto a hook—in a manner trout, too, found fascinating.

In 1936 Reuben R. Cross advanced the art of fly tying when Dodd, Mead & Company published his *Tying American Trout Lures*. At a time when most professionals guarded their skills, the gifted Cross revealed to all his methods and many of his secrets. He was the first professional fly tier in America to write a book devoted to the subject of fly tying. For years, *Tying American Trout Lures* had a greater circulation than any other book on fly tying. Experts and neophytes alike were influenced by his advanced techniques of successful fly making.

Reuben R. Cross. Rube Cross improved on the Catskill style of dry fly first created by Theodore Gordon. Throughout his life, he would spell his name both Rube and Reub, and fishing authors, in articles and books, used both spellings—sometimes in the same article! *The American Fly-Tyer*

Rube Cross–tied flies. Rube Cross was said to have had a pet rooster that would sit on his knee, and when he would pull out a feather the bird would crow, flap his wings, and then settle down again to wait for the next pull. Matt Vinceguerra

Following the breakup of their partnership with Harry Darbee, the Dettes produced a catalog, offering customers a choice of one hundred different dry-fly patterns; their business continued under the name of W. C. Dette. Their reputation as professional tiers was furthered, in 1937, when both Walt and Winnie demonstrated their skills at the National Sportsman's Show, at New York's Grand Central Palace. Each year, the show drew thousands of anglers, many of whom crowded around, standing three and four deep, as the Dettes tied their favorite patterns.

Walt became known as a perfectionist. He was precise, particularly about the length of hackle he selected. His

A Dette-tied Light Cahill. The Dettes tied all of the traditional Catskill patterns such as Quill Gordons, Hendricksons, and Light Cahills.

Winnie and Walt Dette, c. 1949. The Dettes tied flies in the Catskill tradition, using wood duck flank feathers and large amounts of natural dun hackle. Like other Catskill tiers, they raised their own roosters and kept a small flock of chickens at the rear of their home.
Mary Dette Clark

Catskill-style flies were tied as well as, if not better than, Rube Cross's. Walt tied to exact proportions, and so was able to produce one identical fly after another, with a consistency rarely seen from other tiers. A fine example of his work appears in A. J. McClane's *The Practical Fly Fisherman* (1953). The book features color plates of flies tied by Walt Dette, including dry flies, wet flies, nymphs, streamers, and bucktails.

For a few years the Dettes ran their fly shop in a portion of the Esso gas station on Route 17, just outside of Roscoe. They no longer sold fly-tying materials, but they carried tackle for all types of fishing. Business was good enough to hire two or three additional tiers and to stop tying wholesale for dealers. This was the only time that both Walt and Winnie were dependent on fly tying as their sole source of income.

In 1939 Winnie returned to the bank, and a couple of years later Walt found employment in a defense plant in Brooklyn. After the war he worked as a carpenter, and then for the New York City Board of Water Supply. While both pursued other careers, they never stopped tying flies professionally. The Dettes continued tying and selling their flies out of the Esso station until 1955, when they moved their equipment and materials into their home on Cottage Street in Roscoe. They sold retail from a room at the front of their home, and were busy filling mail orders from all over the country. Most of their walk-in customers were fly fishers who fished the Beaverkill and Willowemoc; and their most popular requests were for Hairwing and Fanwing Royal Coachmen, Hendricksons, Quill Gordons, and Light Cahills.

The Dettes tied in the Catskill tradition, using wood duck flank feathers and large amounts of dun hackle. In order to ensure a plentiful supply of quality hackle, especially blue dun, they raised their own roosters and kept a small flock of chickens behind their home. Over the years they created and re-created many patterns for their customers, the most popular being the Coffin Fly, which was developed by Walt and Ted Townsend in 1929. The fly was tied to imitate the large Green Drake spinner so common on the lower Beaverkill in early June.

While the Dettes' reputation as premier fly makers was established many years ago, they had a habit of downplaying their own importance and, at times, fly fishing and fly tying. "I never considered fly tying a great accomplishment," Walt stated in an interview. "It has been a way of making a little extra money."[331] In spite of such a negative opinion, the Dettes still received recognition in numerous articles and books, because their flies were of such outstanding quality.

E. B. and H. A. Darbee

When Harry Darbee decided to leave the Dettes and go into the business of fly tying with his new bride, he and Elsie did so under the name of E. B. & H. A. Darbee. A stipulation in his dissolved partnership agreement with the Dettes stated that if Harry went into the fly-tying business on his own, it could not be in Roscoe. So the Darbees moved to Livingston Manor and began tying along the banks of the Little Beaverkill, on Pearl Street.

Harry Darbee was born in Roscoe on April 7, 1906. That he would choose fly tying as a profession is not surprising, since he was a descendent of a family steeped in angling tradition. His ancestors were among the earliest to settle along the "Great Beaver Kill," in the 1790s, and were the first to cater to the needs of the earliest fishing tourists. Harry's great-uncle was Chester Darbee, a friend and angling companion of the renowned Thad Norris and the son of Mrs. Darbee, of the famous fishing resort that overlooked the junction of the Willowemoc and Beaverkill. The small stream that enters Junction Pool and once flowed through buckwheat fields belonging to Chester Darbee is known today as Darbee Brook.

In addition to fly fishing and fly tying, Harry also maintained a lifetime love of nature and the outdoors, having been influenced in childhood by John Burroughs. When he was a youngster, his family lived for a short time in West Park, not far from Burroughs's home. Harry became friendly with the naturalist and accompanied him on nature walks;

Harry Darbee was born in Roscoe on April 7, 1906; that his whole life would revolve around fly fishing is not surprising, as Harry was a descendent of Samuel and Hannah Darbee, who constructed the first fishing resort back in the early 1800s in what is now Roscoe. Agnes Van Put

he was fascinated with Burroughs's knowledge of the region's flora and fauna. Harry admired the man throughout his life, and one of his most cherished possessions was a book, titled *The American Boy's Book of Bugs, Butterflies and Beetles,* that John Burroughs had given him on his birthday.

While his family lived at West Park, Harry Darbee spent his summers at his grandfather's house in Lew Beach. He caught his first trout in Shin Creek, a stream he always maintained was home to the prettiest wild brown trout in the Catskills. When Harry was ten, the Darbees moved back to Roscoe, and Harry's interest in trout fishing intensified.

Elsie Bivins was born on September 13, 1912, in the Town of Neversink, alongside the headwaters of the Willowemoc. She, too, came from a family involved with trout fishing. In 1909 her parents acquired the famous fishing grounds previously owned by Matt Decker. This water was first leased by the old Willewemock Club, back in the 1870s, and was used as a fishing preserve by Matt Decker in the 1880s and '90s.[332] The Bivins family boarded trout fishermen, and their water was familiar to Theodore Gordon and all who took fly fishing seriously. Elsie was twenty-one years old when she learned the art of fly tying; little did she know, at the time, that it would become her life's work. At first, the vast majority of

Harry and Elsie's flies were sold wholesale, to dealers, at two-thirds the retail price; they were mostly wet flies and bucktails. The Darbees once filled a single order for eight hundred dozen wet flies, and they often tied a gross of a single fly pattern. This was hard and tedious work, but they gained experience and learned their craft well.

Harry had great hands for tying flies; they were small and fine and well suited to the delicate tasks associated with fly tying. Elsie possessed a sharp eye for color and quality hackle selection, and they both could wing a fly as quickly and expertly as anyone. The Darbees became accomplished professionals, experts with feathers, furs, and fly proportions. They continued improving their skills, becoming among the best of their trade.

As the demand for their flies increased during the 1930s, so did the price, which influenced the Darbees to specialize in floating flies. They tied in the traditional Catskill style, and said so in their first catalog, published in 1935:

> The dry flies in this catalog are the finest flies possible to produce and are dressed after the manner made famous by the late Theodore Gordon; who paid especial attention to tying the fly so it would balance on the water in the position of a natural insect.

Hendrickson dry flies tied by Elsie Darbee and Rube Cross. Note the great similarity between the two flies; Elsie's fly is on the left, and the only apparent difference is that Elsie's hackle is more in proportion to what it should be. Lee Van Put

Harry and Elsie Darbee. Harry had great hands for tying flies; they were small, fine, and well suited to the delicate tasks associated with fly tying. Elsie possessed a keen eye for color and quality hackle selection. They both could wing a fly as quickly and expertly as anyone.
Judie Darbee Vincequerra

During his learning years, Harry had "dissected" the flies of Theodore Gordon and was familiar with their construction. Throughout his life, he maintained a collection of Gordon's flies, which included thirty to forty original Quill Gordons. The Darbees began tying dry flies on odd-numbered hooks; instead of the traditional even-numbered sizes of 10, 12, and 14, they tied on sizes 11, 13, and 15. "People knew there was something different about my flies," Harry said, "but they couldn't quite figure it out. It was a good gimmick."[333]

In addition to the standard Catskill patterns, the Darbees became known for their superior deer-hair-bodied flies. They tied clipped-hair dry patterns, using deer hair, caribou, bighorn sheep, and antelope. Their flies were uniformly dense and evenly shaped; Harry tied on the tail and spun the bodies, Elsie trimmed them, and they both tied on the wings and hackle. They tied so much alike, it was impossible to tell their flies apart.

In 1936 they moved to the upper Beaverkill, becoming resident caretakers on the fishing estate of Henry G. Davis. Davis owned a mile of the stream, now known as Timber-doodle Farm, located immediately downstream of the present Beaverkill Valley Inn. Their main source of income continued to be professional tying, but Harry would also give casting instructions and do a little guiding. On one occasion, he had the distinction of having as one of his pupils the great American songwriter Irving Berlin. The Berlins were frequent guests of Henry Davis and his wife, the former Consuelo Vanderbilt.

In 1938 Irving Berlin purchased a beautiful streamside property along Shin Creek and desired to learn how to cast a fly rod. He was an eager student, but after several lessons he had not progressed—at least to his satisfaction. At the end of one particularly frustrating casting session, Berlin turned to Harry and asked, "How long is it going to take before I can

The beginning of a long, flat pool on the lower Beaverkill where a two-feather fly might be the answer for a successful day's fishing.
Lee Van Put

Beaverkill, it was a killing imitation. The two-feather fly was popularized in an article in *Field & Stream* by A. J. McClane in October 1960 and was also featured in an English book titled *Fly Tying Problems*, by noted British fly-tying authority John Veniard.

Surprisingly, the popularity of the fly was short-lived, perhaps because it ran against traditional tying methods. It may, however, resurface in the future, as it possesses many excellent qualities of a good imitation. The fly is lightweight, lifelike, easy to tie, and realistic in shape, and it catches trout in difficult conditions—flat, glassy water. Years later, the two-feather fly was illustrated in a book written by Harry Darbee and his friend Mac Francis. *Catskill Flytier* provided insight into the methods and techniques used by the Darbees throughout their professional career. The book told readers about their favorite patterns, their fly-tying experiences, and their acquaintances.

The Darbees' fly shop was always a social gathering place, for angling tales and trout talk. United by fly fishing, men and women with diverse backgrounds joined in conversation, sharing experiences and stream knowledge with one another.

There were clubmen and city firemen, men who drove trucks, and men who chaired the board at Exxon. Bob Boyle, a *Sports Illustrated* editor and writer, once described the scene as follows:

> It serves as a gathering point in or out of season, for anglers, local characters, fishery biologists, curious tourists and wandering oddballs who come to hear Darbee hold forth on all sorts of subjects, often until dawn. The atmosphere is Cannery Row, out of Abercrombie & Fitch.[336]

Their home and shop were busy year-round and, generally, the scene of a constant parade of visitors, most of whom traveled two hours or more to get there. They came to buy flies, materials, books, or tackle; whatever the pretext, they also came to see the Darbees. Harry and Elsie had a large following, and most of their customers were also their friends. E. B. & H. A. Darbee were to become the most famous husband-and-wife fly-tying team in the country. The Darbees and their flies have been featured in numerous magazine articles and newspaper stories, as well as more than seventy-five books on fishing and fly tying.

Fish Management and the Search for Public Fishing

During the 1930s the Beaverkill and its tributaries were still being stocked in the same manner they had been for more than half a century. Applications for trout were still being received from sportsmen, farmers, hunting and fishing clubs, and inn and boardinghouse owners. There was never a charge for these fish; applicants only had to agree to be on hand to receive them and to place the fry or fingerlings in the proper streams.

The system had numerous problems. Many thousands of trout were improperly planted in waters not fitted for their survival, waters that were badly polluted or too warm, or waters that dried up in summer. Many streams were known by more than one name, and there were times when the same stream was stocked repeatedly, resulting in overstocking. To complicate matters further, sportsmen's clubs often purchased trout from private hatcheries and, unknown to the Bureau of Fish Culture, placed them in streams already stocked. Printed instructions were usually furnished to each applicant, advising them not to plant brown trout in waters inhabited by brook trout and not to place brook trout in warm waters. For the safety of these fry and fingerlings, it was also recommended that they not be placed in large pools, where they could be preyed upon by larger fish.

During the 1920s the New York State Conservation Commission had increased its production of domestic trout by developing a number of new hatcheries throughout the state. The demand for more and more trout, to replenish streams, was being met; but it was growing more costly. The use of trucks aided the process somewhat, as men experienced in fisheries work, employees of the Conservation Commission, began hauling trout directly from the hatchery to the stream.

Beginning in 1926, comprehensive watershed surveys were conducted throughout New York State. The major objective was to develop an improved stocking policy for hatchery-reared fish, based upon field studies of each body of water. A further goal was to acquire essential information that would lead to better fisheries management. The surveys provided valuable data, a kind of blueprint for a long-term fisheries program. The unit responsible for scientific investigations of the state's watersheds was known as the Bureau of Biological Survey. The fieldwork included collecting various biological and physical data relative to fish production, such as fish distribution and abundance, water chemistry, pollution, temperature, volume of flow, habitat evaluation, quantitative food studies, and effects of disease. The science of fisheries management was in its infancy, and fortunately, the new Conservation Department was headed by Lithgow Osborne, under whose leadership fisheries programs in New York would make great progress.

Shortly after graduating Harvard in 1915, Osborne entered the diplomatic service and served in Germany until diplomatic relations were broken off in 1917. He was attached to the American Peace Commission in Paris in 1919 and served as assistant secretary general at the Disarmament Conference in 1922. Upon returning to his native Auburn, New York, he became the editor and owner of the *Auburn-Citizen Advertiser* and was active in promoting conservation and reforestation. On March 1, 1933, he was

While the Beaverkill and Willowemoc were not the first streams where these rights were purchased, they played a historic role in the development of the program. By the time automobile travel became popular, all of the best trout waters in the Catskills were closed to public fishing. Private clubs, inns, and boardinghouses posted the upper portions of the Beaverkill, Willowemoc, Neversink, and Rondout.

Following the introduction of brown trout, however, new waters became available, as browns thrived in the warmer, larger, lower river environments—stream sections that had escaped fishing clubs and posting. Brown trout created many additional miles of trout water and, importantly, made them available to all anglers. Because these lower river sections had never been posted, many fishermen believed they could not be. The tradition of fishing these waters, though, was never

Though considered a new field in the 1930s, stream improvement structures, such as this straight-log pool digger, were developed on the Beaverkill in the 1880s.

entirely legal, as landowners always had the right to exclude others from their property.

This fact became a reality on the Neversink when several miles of the best and most popular stretch of the river were closed. This was water that anglers had always taken for granted, water that was stocked for years by sportsmen, at public expense. The problem first surfaced in 1919, when the front page of the *Liberty Register* announced: "There have been parties around town the past week who are buying up the stream rights from Halls Mills bridge down to, or as near to our covered bridge as they can, says our Neversink correspondent."[342] A week later the newspaper's editorial declared:

> City residents blessed with money, and desirous of having something good all to themselves are buying up the Neversink River, it is said, with the intent to post it and keep it for themselves alone. People will not come here if there is no place to fish. Next year if all the streams are posted, the hundreds of fishermen who have been coming here will go elsewhere. Let's keep our streams open![343]

By the end of June, the secret was out. Edward R. Hewitt, an avid fly fisherman and wealthy New York City industrialist, had purchased large portions of the lower Neversink. When the season opened in 1922, anglers were excluded from fishing waters they had fished for generations. Hewitt announced, through local newspapers, that in the future his fishing grounds would be posted and no anglers would be allowed on his property without a permit. Hewitt's announcement that the Neversink would be closed touched off a flurry of angry letters and editorials, and his actions were pivotal in the search for public fishing.

Fearing the eventual closing of all lower river sections, members of twenty rod and gun clubs—representing five thousand area sportsmen from four counties—met to pursue a public fishing program. Sportsmen's concerns over posting were aired in Middletown, early in 1923, with the local effort being spearheaded by the ever-active Liberty Rod & Gun Club and its president, Roy Steenrod.

Reporting on the meeting, the *Sullivan County Democrat* stated, "Mr. Steenrod suggested that the four counties form an alliance, with the idea that sportsmen would be better represented." This was done, and bylaws were adopted:

> A bill was drawn up at the meeting, to be introduced at this session in Albany, asking that $1,000,000 be set aside for a purchase of streams, lakes and land in this section. If the bill passes, the streams of Sullivan County will be bought and opened up for fishing for all.[344]

The fact that such a request was made by a club from Liberty is not surprising, since some of its members lived along the Neversink and felt its loss through posting more personally. They were equally concerned over other area streams: Could this happen on the Beaverkill? The Willowemoc? Would there be a future for public fishing?

The purchase of public fishing easements along the Beaverkill has made it possible for fishermen to pursue their sport since the 1930s and on into the future. Richard Franklin

This particular group made the appeal to save its trout fishing as there was definitely more "rod" than "gun" in this club. Its membership included Roy Steenrod, William Chandler, George W. Cooper, and Herman Christian. Aside from their love of fly fishing, these men shared another common bond. They all knew Theodore Gordon and were influenced by his concern over the future of trout fishing.

The proposed bill was not successful; two years later, the Liberty Rod & Gun Club announced it would attempt to purchase, on its own, land along the Beaverkill, Willowemoc, and Neversink. Seeing the acquisition as a future necessity, the club proposed buying narrow strips of land along these streams, for the purpose of fishing. This idea never became a reality.

The first hint of a state public fishing program surfaced locally in a 1931 editorial of the *Liberty Register*. Citing a shortage of public trout streams near New York City, the editor stated that the Conservation Department was thinking of "leasing streams for public fishing, and two of those were nearby." In 1933 the subject was discussed in the Conservation Department's report to the legislature:

Anglers for trout slowly but with ever increasing numbers are being excluded from large sections of our finest streams. Good stream fishing will always be most difficult to maintain by reason of the limited number of suitable streams in each region, the seasonal changes in volume and temperature of water, and the comparative ease with which landowners can post them. Assuming the State had a far greater supply of funds to carry on. What then? . . . It could buy strips of land on either side and under large sections of our principal trout streams and develop them to carry greater numbers of larger fish.[345]

Finally, in 1935, a program of purchasing permanent fishing easements on the privately owned streams of the state became a reality when the legislature allocated $100,000 from the Conservation Fund for the acquisition of public fishing rights. The allocation was "for the acquisition of narrow strips of land including streams, and rights of way thereto, and the acquisition or lease of fishing rights in streams and rights of way thereto which are desirable to provide public fishing."[346] The aim was to preserve trout fishing for the public and ensure that future generations of anglers would have streams to fish in.

The acquisition from the landowner was for an easement, usually 33 or 66 feet wide. The easement allowed anglers the

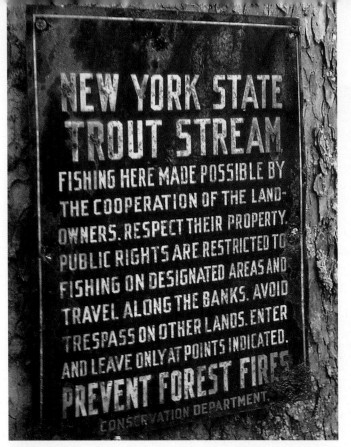

right to travel the stream and banks over those portions purchased, for the purpose of fishing only; swimming, camping, or any other activity except fishing was prohibited.

In a letter to the *Hancock Herald*, Commissioner Osborne revealed that the state had $100,000 to spend on fishing rights but that the purchase of fishing rights on the Beaverkill and Willowemoc would be too costly. The commissioner stated that acquisition had begun on streams in the western part of the state but not in the Catskills, claiming purchases there would be far more expensive than anywhere else.

Two years later, after he had secured additional funds from the legislature, Commissioner Osborne announced that negotiations were underway with landowners along the Beaverkill and Willowemoc. Speaking at the Lenape Hotel

An early Public Fishing Rights sign on the Beaverkill. After acquiring fishing rights along selected streams, the Conservation Deptartment would erect signs informing the public that they were welcome to fish there.

Hazel Bridge Pool, site of the first public fishing rights easement acquired in the watershed, signed by the Thomas Keery Company in December 1936 and closed in October 1937.

A stretch of the lower Beaverkill where public fishing rights were acquired in 1937. Lee Van Put

in Liberty, at the annual dinner of the Liberty Rod & Gun Club, he gave sportsmen the news they had waited so long to hear. The first public fishing rights easement acquired in the watershed was signed by the Thomas Keery Company in December 1936 and closed in October 1937. The Keery Company operated the acid factory at Hazel and owned a long stretch of the Willowemoc. Initially, easements were purchased on four miles of the Willowemoc and two miles of the Beaverkill.

Perhaps eager to sample the new fishing rights his department had recently secured, Commissioner Osborne returned in May for a speaking engagement and two days of trout fishing. Along on the trip was Duncan G. Rankin, supervising forester, who had successfully negotiated the fishing rights along the Willowemoc and Beaverkill.

With Game Protector Roy Steenrod acting as guide, the party fished the newly acquired waters at Hazel Bridge Pool, on the Willowemoc. Roy, a skilled fly caster and certainly one of the Catskills' most knowledgeable trout fishermen, saw to it that Commissioner Osborne caught some trout and received a few casting tips as well. The local press reported that the commissioner told his angling companions that he was greatly pleased with the state's purchase at Hazel and that he was "markedly impressed with the area as a trout fishing center."[347]

Persistent sportsmen and a Conservation Department that looked to the future worked together and developed a program that generations of trout fishers have enjoyed. The program's success along these streams was initially dependent on the cooperation of its landowners and their willingness to sell their fishing rights.

Another powerful club that lobbied against building a dam on the Beaverkill was the Beaverkill–Willowemoc Rod & Gun Club, a sportsmen's conservation organization with a membership of well over a thousand—the largest in Sullivan County. Harry Darbee was, at various times, president, conservation chairman, and editor of its informative newsletter, *Voice of the Beamoc.* His wife, Elsie, served as secretary and treasurer. The Beamoc, as the club became known, lobbied hard for legislation prohibiting any municipality from building a dam for water-supply purposes on the Beaverkill or Willowemoc. The bill was aimed at preventing New York City from completing its plan to use these waters for reservoirs.

The Beaverkill faithful rejoiced when later in the year it was learned that New York City had revised its plans, abandoning its interest in the Beaverkill and Willowemoc and turning its attention instead to the West Branch of the Delaware River. Hearings were held by the Water Power and Control Commission (of which Commissioner Duryea was a member) at Delhi, and many objections were filed against the proposal. It was at this hearing that trout fishermen first learned of the city's change in plans regarding the Beaverkill:

> Representatives of the City of New York officially stated that the City is no longer interested in the development of the Little Delaware, the Beaverkill or the Willowemoc as sources of water supply. In view of the above official statements, sportsmen are assured that if the proposed Cannonsville dam is eventually approved, the interests of fishermen will be protected. And they can rejoice, in the fact that the Little Delaware, the Beaverkill and the Willowemoc will be preserved for trout fishing.[353]

In November the Water Power and Control Commission granted approval for Cannonsville Reservoir, contingent upon the United States Supreme Court's modification of the 440-million-gallons-per-day restriction. (In June 1954, this

Present at a Beamoc field day at Roscoe in 1952 are Ellis Newman, Harry Darbee, Joan Salvato (Wulff), Bill Taylor, and Betty Bonavita.
Francis W. Davis

Garbage dump located at Elk Brook along the lower Beaverkill. There were more than fourteen sites along the lower river where household garbage was being dumped, along with tires, furniture, and appliances. Francis W. Davis

amount was increased to 800 million gallons per day.) Why the city turned its attention to the West Branch is uncertain. It may have been more practical to operate one large reservoir than three lesser ones; or, as reported, the city may have been discouraged by the failure to locate a suitable bedrock site for a dam on the Beaverkill. It is believed that growing opposition from organized sportsmen also played a part in this decision.

Perhaps it was all of these reasons, and more. But credit must be given to those angling conservationists who cared about the Beaverkill and became unified in their efforts to protect and preserve the stream. Their opposition to the construction of a dam and reservoir was the first major confrontation on the Beaverkill in which public interests were represented by organized sportsmen. Modern anglers were learning that there was strength in numbers, and that they had a voice when registering their concerns with politicians and government officials.

No one ever worked harder at protecting and preserving the Beaverkill than Harry and Elsie Darbee. They fought against anything that threatened stream habitat, water quality, or the Beaverkill's trout populations. They joined and helped form several conservation organizations, wrote numerous

letters, and lobbied state offices and politicians for stricter environmental legislation.

Harry Darbee had a special dislike for road builders. In the mountainous region of the Catskills, roads tend to parallel the stream courses, often too closely. They encroach on waterways, causing stream degradation, erosion, loss of shade trees, and a general destruction of trout habitat. In the 1950s, Harry campaigned against the abuses that highway departments inflicted on trout streams. At meetings of Rotary clubs, conservation groups, and hunting and fishing organizations he presented a slide program titled *What's Happening to our Streams?* The slides depicted specific abuses occurring along the Beaverkill and Willowemoc, such as gravel removal, bulldozing for flood control, and the dumping and filling of earth and rubble into watercourses. These activities were generally accepted by local people, who often saw them as reasonable and necessary, and who viewed Harry Darbee as something of a radical or extremist.

In 1955 Harry and Elsie Darbee tackled the problem of the open dumps and landfills found along the Beaverkill. At the time, there was an increasing use of stream banks for dumping; there were no fewer than fourteen sites along the lower river. Not only were local highway departments

Another garbage dump at Hazel Bridge, a popular pool for fly fishermen. This site was cleaned up during the late 1950s.
Francis W. Davis

An artistic fly fisher painted a fly on this Old Route 17 highway sign where the road first crossed the lower Beaverkill near Junction Pool.

depositing "thousands of tons of soil,"[354] but area residents, too, were dumping household garbage, unwanted tires, furniture, and appliances by the truckload.

Photographs were taken and sent to the Conservation Department. Harry used the power of the press, cajoling his outdoor friends to publicize the problem. Red Smith reported on the deplorable conditions in his weekly column in the *New York Herald Tribune*; and Alfred W. Miller (Sparse Grey Hackle) wrote an inflammatory article, titled "The Scandal of the Desecrated Shrine," for *Sports Illustrated*.

The Darbees traveled to Albany and visited lawmakers. Through their efforts and those of other Beamoc members, legislation was proposed; and in the spring of 1956, Governor Averell Harriman signed a bill making it unlawful to dump "earth, soil, refuse or other solid substances except snow and ice in any stream or tributaries therein which is inhabited by trout." Dumping practices were halted; trash was removed in some areas of the Beaverkill and covered in others.

One year later, the Darbees engaged in a campaign to halt the spraying of DDT in the Catskills. Airplanes, spraying for gypsy moths, had a habit of not shutting off the valves that dispensed their lethal poisons when flying over rivers and streams. The Darbees wrote letters of opposition to newspapers and organized volunteer scientists and specialists to monitor operations along the Neversink, where the spraying was then taking place. The spraying caused the death of massive numbers of aquatic insects, which, as they fell back onto the water, were eaten; in turn, the trout that had eaten the insects turned belly-up. Through the Darbees' efforts, including the documentations of the fish kills resulting from the environmental effects of DDT, spraying practices were altered and eventually curtailed in the Catskills.

When automobile travel came to the Beaverkill, in the early 1900s, the lower river was paralleled by a narrow, two-lane roadway with twists and turns and steep gradients. The road was located on only one side of the Beaverkill and contained no bridges. Its impact on the river was minimal, though it did encroach along the river's banks and make the Beaverkill more easily accessible to increased fishing pressure and environmental abuses.

The need for a new highway became inevitable as automobile and truck traffic steadily increased, especially after the region was no longer serviced by the railroad. In the late 1950s, the state's Department of Public Works unveiled plans to construct a major four-lane expressway (Route 17) along the lower Willowemoc and Beaverkill, all the way to East Branch and beyond, to Binghamton. Fishermen from across the state found it inconceivable that a modern, high-speed highway was charted to run through, and along, New York's most historic trout stream, within sight and sound of the Beaverkill's most famous pools.

The expressway would closely follow the rivers, crossing them no fewer than nine times and destroying the aesthetics that generations of trout fishers had come to revere. Those anglers seeking the peacefulness and tranquility often associated with the riffling waters of a trout stream would now find their solitude destroyed by the deafening din of speeding traffic and the echoing of diesels racing through the valley floor.

Members of the Beamoc saw the construction of the expressway as the ruination of the Beaverkill. A storm of protest began to build in opposition to the plan; and Harry Darbee, as chairman of the conservation committee, became the leading spokesman, spearheading a massive campaign. Fishermen from across the country were angered that the Beaverkill would be despoiled by channelization, bridge piers, and concrete retaining walls.

The Darbees had many other concerns about the impact that the highway would have on the Beaverkill's future. Harry believed that the river would be polluted by highway runoff, such as the salt, chemicals, and sand spread on the roadway in winter. He felt that rainwater runoff from the asphalt pavement and paved drainage sluices would be speeded to the river, raising water temperatures, and that major construction could ruin important springs entering the lower Beaverkill, which were vital to trout survival in times when low flows led to warm water temperatures.

Harry thought that contractors would be insensitive to the stream, and one of his greatest concerns was for the aquatic insect population, a mainstay of the lower river. The Beaverkill was famous for its abundant mayfly hatches, and aquatic insects contributed enormously to the food supply of the river's brown trout population.

In the past, automobiles traveling the old road had destroyed countless numbers of mayflies and other aquatic insects, plastering them against windshields, hoods, and radiators. This problem intensified whenever it rained, as many mating mayflies mistook the wet roadway for the river and deposited their eggs on the pavement. One passing vehicle would drive over thousands of flies. With construction of four high-speed lanes and the additional traffic crisscrossing and paralleling both sides of the Beaverkill, Harry's concern seemed valid.

The fight between highway proponents and conservationist-anglers lasted several years. Following initial meetings with members of the Beamoc, the Department of Public Works consented to alter their plans and not divert or rechannel sections of the Beaverkill and Willowemoc. They also agreed not to construct concrete retaining walls along the stream banks. It was announced that these changes were made to

Dual highway bridges frequently crisscross the lower Beaverkill. While the Beamoc and other organized sportsmen's groups lost their battle to move Route 17 to a different location, construction of the highway would have been much worse had they not fought the New York State Deptartment of Transportation.

Lee Wulff abandoned the business world and decided to become a freelance outdoor writer; he began fishing with a camera around his neck. Joan Wulff

tied the White Wulff. Lee tied thicker-bodied flies and used bucktail for wings and tails, developing a high-floating, durable dry fly. He first tried these flies on the Esopus, then on the Beaverkill—and they were successful right from the start. He also created the Royal Wulff "to give utility to the Fanwing Royal Coachman," changing the pattern to white bucktail wings and a brown bucktail tail. Today, Wulff-style dry flies are known and used all over the world, not only for trout but for salmon as well.

During the 1930s Lee Wulff decided to abandon the business world and become a freelance outdoor writer and filmmaker. He began fishing with a camera around his neck and quickly became a talented writer, photographer, and illustrator.

Soon he was contributing articles to many magazines, including *Field & Stream*, *Outdoor Life*, *Esquire*, and *Sports*

Afield. He published the first of several books in 1937; by 1950 Lee Wulff had become one of America's foremost outdoor writers. In 1938 he produced his first film, and during the 1960s and '70s he produced and was featured in a great many fishing films for television, including the first network angling films on CBS's *Sports Spectacular* and ABC's *American Sportsman*.

In 1977, at the time of the Wulffs' visit to the Beaverkill, they were searching for a location to start a fly-fishing school. They had traveled the country and seen many of the best fishing locations. While there were many aspects to consider, one that was important was the mileage of no-kill water along the Beaverkill. As a longtime proponent of catch and release, Lee was greatly impressed with the Beaverkill's successful regulation promoting this philosophy. The Wulffs moved to the area in 1978 and established their now-famous fly-fishing school on the upper Beaverkill the following year. Both Lee and Joan participated in every phase of their school, demonstrating, lecturing, teaching, and passing on their knowledge of fly fishing to their students; the school became an immediate success.

● ● ●

In 1988 the Beaverkill played a somewhat notable role in bringing about important changes between two of the world's "super powers." Americans who lived through the lengthy Cold War era can recall the constant tension between the United States and the communist Union of Soviet Socialist Republics (USSR). The two "super power" nations spread propaganda throughout the world, each claiming their form of government was better. Spying and distrust ruled the day; the possibility of a nuclear war was real and was a constant threat to world peace.

By the late 1980s, however, the Soviet Union began to change, and a more open policy was introduced by then–Soviet President Mikhail Gorbachev. New freedoms were given to the Russian people and there was increasing criticism of communist ideology. This lessening of restrictions encouraged greater communication between Russians and Americans in business as well as in culture.

It was announced during the summer of 1986 that the American organization Trout Unlimited and Rosohotrybolovsoyuz, the All Russian Union of Hunters and Anglers, were meeting in Moscow to work on a cooperative agreement that would allow American anglers to travel to Russia and fish the vast cold-water fishery resources of the Soviet Union. The Russian government believed that by providing fishing opportunities to Americans it would receive an economic boost to tourism; and it was hoped that Russians would in turn learn about U.S. fisheries management, tackle, and techniques. The TU delegates planned to share technical information, and were eager to introduce fly fishing to the Soviets. There were very few fly fishers in Russia, and there was hardly any fly-fishing equipment available to them. For the next year and a half, articles citing an agreement between the All Russian Union of Hunters and Anglers and Trout Unlimited appeared in newspaper columns of the *Chicago Sun-Times*, the *Washington Post*, and the *New York Times*.

Delegation member Stephen Lundy, of Colorado, had visited Russia several times to set up the program and helped draft the Trout Unlimited agreement. During a dinner with his Soviet hosts, Lundy was quoted as saying, "It is my fondest

The Anglers Exchange patch was prepared by Trout Unlimited and shared between Soviet and American anglers to celebrate the Russians' historic visit.

Front row, left to right: Dave Pabst (tan jacket), Andre Velikanov, Lev Stroguin, the author. Second row, left to right: Ed Sharbonneau (translator), Lee and Joan Wulff, Earl Worsham (TU International), and Nelson Bryant (sportswriter). Standing, left to right: Sevelo Gnevashov, Leonid Prodanova, Larica Gubanova, Dot and Budge Loeckle, Luda Sharbonneau (translator), Richard Talleur, Ella (translator), Dale Hardeman (NYCTU president), Aleksandr Klushin, and Gardner Grant. Shelly Rusten

Mary Dette Clark continued in the fly-tying tradition of her parents, though her favorite patterns were the Quill Gordon and Coffin Fly.
Barbara Jaffe

Today the Dette fly shop is operated by Mary's grandson, Joe Fox. As a youngster, Joe visited the Dette shop and learned to tie by watching his grandmother. Lee Van Put

In the late 1990s, Jane Timken, a New York City publisher and fly fisher, was interested in stream-related projects in the Beaverkill watershed, and while we spoke of several different ideas, she particularly liked the concept of preserving and commemorating the famous pools. Jane provided the funding for the project and, as a member of Theodore Gordon Flyfishers, she contacted the various state agencies, seeking approval and permission to install the markers.

It was decided to erect historical markers at nine different locations, including Hazel Bridge, Beaverkill Covered Bridge, Ferdon's Eddy, Wagon Tracks, Hendrickson's, Painter's Bend, Barnhart's, Horse Brook Run, and Cairns Pool. In my eagerness to see the project come to fruition I not only provided the text, but ordered the signs, picked them up upon completion, dug the holes, mixed the cement, and erected the markers.

The last historical marker was placed at the Beaverkill Covered Bridge and was dedicated to Theodore Gordon, who fished there often. Theodore Gordon Flyfishers sent out a message proclaiming that on May 29, 1998, a celebration would be held, complete with refreshments and fishing at the site. Since these historical markers first appeared along the stream, a couple of other organizations have also chosen a noted pool and have followed the lead of Theodore Gordon Flyfishers and contributed to the commemoration of these special sites.

● ● ●

While working on a list of trout flies with a connection to the Beaverkill, I researched a number of patterns to learn where they originated, who tied them, and which dressings were correct. At times my research led me down an entirely new path, discovering information from sources or directions I was not accustomed to.

The Complete Fly Fisherman: The Notes and Letters of Theodore Gordon is one of my favorite books, and I've read it several times. In a letter dated February 9, 1915, Gordon writes to Roy Steenrod: "The priest at Livingston Manor is a great fisher. Mr. Ward said he told him that he killed 800 trout last season. He has a small automobile." (The term "killed" was commonly used at the time, instead of "caught"; "Mr. Ward" was Charles B. Ward, who acquired 2½ to 3 miles of the Willowemoc at DeBruce and owned a popular fishing resort known as the DeBruce Club Inn.)

For many years I have wondered about the identity of the priest that Theodore Gordon thought was a "great fisher"; and considering it was Gordon himself making the comment only added interest to discovering who this mysterious fly fisher was. The church in Livingston Manor is named St. Aloysius Church, and over the years I have mentioned Gordon's remarks to a couple of parish priests in the hope of learning whom Gordon was referring to, but had no success.

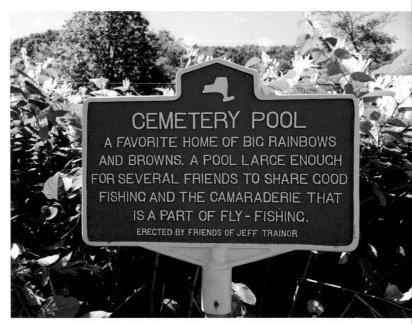

In the late 1990s, Jane Timken, a New York City publisher and fly fisher, provided funding to erect historical markers at many of the famous pools along the Beaverkill. This encouraged others, and at Cemetery Pool, the Friends of Jeff Trainor erected this marker.
Anisha Arouza

Recently, however, while looking at some of the fly patterns mentioned by Rube Cross in *Fur, Feathers and Steel* (1940), I found a fly named Monsignor, created by Claude Norton, of Newburgh, New York. Norton named the fly in honor of Monsignor Henry O'Carroll, whom Cross called "one of the most ardent anglers in the East." This led me to more research, and I discovered that Monsignor O'Carroll had been born in County Kerry, Ireland, and was ordained a priest in 1893. He was then sent to America to assist at St. Patrick's in Newburgh, where he served for fourteen years; and then was appointed pastor of St. Aloysius Church in Livingston Manor, in the heart of the Sullivan County troutfishing region that included the Beaverkill and Willowemoc.

Once, in an interview with a reporter, Father O'Carroll stated that he had learned to fish in Ireland as soon as he learned to walk; throughout his life he fished for trout and salmon, developing a reputation of being an "ardent and famous fisherman." While at Livingston Manor he regularly fished the nearby Willowemoc and Beaverkill and at some point became a member of the Beaverkill Trout Club. Father O'Carroll served at St. Aloysius for seven years (1907–1914), and so the mystery of the priest whom Theodore Gordon referred to as a "great fisher" is solved.

In December of 1914, Father O'Carroll was called back to St. Patrick's in Newburgh where, in 1929, he became a Monsignor and continued serving for forty-three years. When he left Livingston Manor he had informed his many friends and parishioners that he was leaving behind his hunting and fishing gear, but would frequently return to make

Notes

1. Ruttenber, *The Indian Tribes of Hudson's River*, p. 45.
2. Hodge, *Handbook of American Indians North of Mexico*, p. 385.
3. Ruttenber, *The Indian Tribes of Hudson's River*, p. 45.
4. Brinton, *The Lenape and Their Legends*, p. 36.
5. Murray, *Centennial History of Delaware County, N.Y., 1797–1897*, p. 310.
6. Irwin, *Hunters of the Eastern Forest*, p. 48.
7. Evers, *The Catskills: From Wilderness to Woodstock*, p. 10.
8. Fried, *The Early History of Kingston and Ulster County, New York*, p. xxiv.
9. Brink, *Olde Ulster*, Vol. IV, p. 116.
10. Ibid., Vol. I, p. 98.
11. Ibid., Vol. IV, p. 131.
12. Liber EE, Ulster County Clerk's Office, p. 61.
13. Brink, *Olde Ulster*, Vol. III, p. 323.
14. Ritchie, *Conservationist*, Dec.–Jan. 1955–56, p. 23–27.
15. Quinlen, *History of Sullivan County*, p. 493.
16. Wood, *Holt! T'Other Way*, p. 243–244.
17. Murray, *Centennial History of Delaware County, N.Y., 1797–1880*, p. 212.
18. George W. Van Siclen, *Forest and Stream*, May 6, 1880, p. 175.
19. Willis, *The Pioneer*, p. 18.
20. *Walton Reporter*, October 29, 1904, p. 1.
21. Ibid., November 20, 1926, p. 2.
22. *Bloomville Mirror*, May 25, 1858, p. 2.
23. *Liberty Register*, April 6, 1923, p. 2.
24. Ibid.
25. *American Turf Register and Sporting Magazine*, August 1838, p. 369.
26. Lossing, *Our Countrymen, or Brief Memoirs of Eminent Americans*, p. 386.
27. Henry Inman, "The Fisher Boy," *The Atlantic Souvenir*, 1830, p. 251.
28. Thomas Picton, "Reminiscences of a Sporting Journalist," *Spirit of the Times*, April 23, 1881, p. 282–283.
29. T. B. Thorpe, "A Visit to John Brown's Tract," *Harper's New Monthly Magazine*, July 1859, p. 162.
30. The son of Hannah Darbee.
31. Thomas Picton, "Old Time Disciples of Rod and Gun," *The Rod and Gun*, February 12, 1876, p. 313.
32. Ibid.
33. Ibid.
34. Bulletin of the American Art-Union, "Henry Inman," August 1850, p. 71.
35. *Spirit of the Times*, April 6, 1844, p. 61.
36. Huntington, *A General View of the Fine Arts, Critical and Historical*, p. 284.
37. *Spirit of the Times*, January 24, 1846, p. 561.
38. *Forest and Stream*, December 12, 1896, p. 471.
39. J. S. Van Cleef, *Forest and Stream*, March 16, 1901, p. 209.
40. Fitz-James Fitch, *The American Angler*, July 24, 1886, p. 1.
41. Sturgis, *Fly Tying*, p. 104.
42. Smedley, *Fly Patterns and Their Origins*, p. 5.
43. Fitz-James Fitch, *Shooting and Fishing*, August 22, 1889, p. 326.
44. *Kingston Weekly Freeman & Journal*, May 2, 1879, p. 1.
45. *The People's Press* (Kingston), August 29, 1861, p. 1.
46. *The American Angler*, April 22, 1882, p. 259.
47. J. S. Van Cleef, "Trout Waters and Trout Weights," *Forest and Stream*, May 21, 1898, p. 413.
48. *Delaware Gazette*, May 16, 1860, p. 4
49. *Ulster Republican*, June 6, 1860, p. 3.
50. C. M. McDougall, *Forest and Stream*, February 21, 1914, p. 245.
51. Fitz-James Fitch, "Fishing—A Healthful Pastime," *American Agriculturist*, June 1886, p. 259.
52. *Republican Watchman*, June 15, 1859, p. 2.
53. Norris, *American Fish Culture*, p. 29.
54. *Roscoe-Rockland Review*, April 30, 1903, p. 3.
55. *Forest and Stream*, December 28, 1901, p. 1.
56. *Wildwood's Magazine*, May 1888, p. 47.
57. J. S. Van Cleef, *Forest and Stream*, September 11, 1897, p. 210.
58. Ibid., "The Sabbath Day on the Beaverkill," *Forest and Stream*, May 18, 1901, p. 387.
59. *Rondout Courier*, February 26, 1869, p. 2.
60. N. L. Britton, "Cornelius Van Brunt," Bulletin of the Torrey Botanical Club, December 1903.
61. New York Natural Heritage Program, 2013, Online Conservation Guide for *Polemonium vanbruntiae*.
62. *Forest and Stream*, April 23, 1874, p. 173.
63. *Ellenville Journal*, July 20, 1877, p. 1.
64. Berner, *Treatyse of Fysshynge Wyth an Angle*, An American edition, Van Siclen, 1875, p. 14–15.
65. *Kingston Weekly Leader*, June 7, 1889, p. 7.
66. *Rondout Courier*, February 11, 1853, p. 2.
67. Ibid.
68. *The Spirit of the Times*, September 18, 1847, p. 352.
69. *Bloomville Mirror*, July 27, 1858, p. 2.
70. Wetzel, *American Fishing Books*, p. 38.

Bibliography

Public Records

Delaware, Greene, Sullivan, and Ulster County Clerk's Offices: deed and mortgage books; miscellaneous books (Sullivan County); maps placed on record, often bound in books, but earliest found in deed books.

New York State Census Records, Delaware and Sullivan Counties.

Delaware, Greene, Sullivan, and Ulster County surrogates' records, wills, and probate records.

Field Books: Hardenbergh Patent Great Lot 6—1809; Delaware County Clerk's Office, Delhi, New York.

Public Libraries

Albany Institute of History & Art, Albany, NY

Archives of American Art, Smithsonian Institution, Washington, D.C.

Cannon Free Library, Delhi, NY

Ellenville Public Library, Ellenville, NY

Fairview Library, Margaretville, NY

Kingston Area Library, Kingston, NY

Liberty Public Library, Liberty, NY

Library of Congress

Livingston Manor Free Public Library, Livingston Manor, NY

Louise Adelia Read Memorial Library, Hancock, NY

Macdonald De Witt Library, Ulster County Community College, Stone Ridge, NY

Mann Library, Cornell University, Ithaca, NY

Mudd Library, Yale University, New Haven, CT

Munson-Williams-Proctor Arts Institute, Utica, NY

Newark Public Library, Newark, NJ

Newburgh Free Library, Newburgh, NY

New York Historical Society, New York, NY

New York Public Library, New York, NY

New York State Historical Association, Cooperstown, NY

New York State Library, Albany, NY

Orange County Community College, Middletown, NY

Phoenicia Library Association, Jerry Bartlett Memorial Angling Collection, Phoenicia, NY

Roscoe Library, Roscoe, NY

Sojourner Truth Library, SUNY at New Paltz, NY

Stamford Village Library, Stamford, NY

William B. Ogden Free Library, Walton, NY

Newspapers

The years indicate the period researched. The location is where the research was done.

Andes Recorder (1867–92), Delaware County Historical Society, Delhi, NY

Bloomville Mirror (1853–74), Stamford Village Library, Stamford, NY

Catskill Mountain News (1902–55), Offices of the *Catskill Mountain News*, Margaretville, NY

Delaware Gazette (1819–1903), Cannon Free Library, Delhi, NY

Delaware Republican (Jan. 2, 1886–Mar. 29, 1890), New York State Library, Albany, NY

Downsville Herald (Nov. 27, 1947–Feb. 27, 1953), New York State Library, Albany, NY

Downsville News (Mar. 31, 1938–Apr. 25, 1946), New York State Library, Albany, NY

Ellenville Journal (1849–1916), Ellenville Public Library, Ellenville, NY

Hancock Herald (1874–97), Louise Adelia Read Memorial Library, Hancock, NY

Kingston Argus (1873–1905), Kingston Area Library, Kingston, NY

Kingston Craftsman (1820–22), Kingston Area Library, Kingston, NY

Kingston Democratic Journal (1849–64), Kingston Area Library, Kingston, NY

Kingston Press (1863–74), Kingston Area Library, Kingston, NY

Kingston Weekly Freeman & Journal (1868–99), Kingston Area Library, Kingston, NY

Kingston Weekly Reader (1887–1904), Kingston Area Library, Kingston, NY

Liberty Register (1878–1967), Liberty Public Library, Liberty, NY

Livingston Manor Times (1922–60), Dr. Paul D'Amico, Livingston Manor, NY

Narrowsburg Democrat (1914), Offices of the *Sullivan County Democrat*, Callicoon, NY

New York Times (1851–1950), Orange Community College, Middletown, NY

The People's Press (1857–63), Kingston Area Library, Kingston, NY

Pine Hill Sentinel (1885–1908) Ulster Community College, Stone Ridge, NY

Political Reformer (1839–40), Kingston Area Library, Kingston, NY